Slow Growth and the Service Economy

Slow Growth and the Service Economy

Pascal Petit

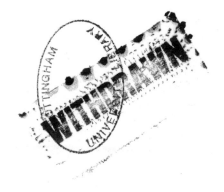

Frances Pinter (Publishers), London

© Pascal Petit, 1986

First published in Great Britain in 1986 by
Frances Pinter (Publishers) Limited
25 Floral Street, London WC2E 9DS

British Library Cataloguing in Publication Data
Slow growth and the service economy.
　1.　Economic development　2.　Service industries
　I.　　Petit, Pascal
　339.5　HD82
　ISBN 0-86187-291-6

Typeset by Joshua Associates Limited, Oxford
Printed by SRP Ltd, Exeter

Contents

1
Services: problem or solution?

The slow-down in economic growth and the rise in unemployment in the 1970s have revived some of the uncertainties experienced by the industrialized economies during the inter-war period. After more than a decade of stagnation, the period of sustained growth in the thirty years following the Second World War now seems increasingly to have been an exceptional phase in an overall development process still dominated by wide fluctuations in economic growth rates. In this new climate, the issues have changed. The future is no longer thought of in terms of an affluent society. The main area of concern is employment. The relatively full employment of the late 1950s was evidence of the successful transformation of social and economic systems which had exhibited such dangerous weaknesses during the inter-war period. There is concern in all countries about the future prospects for employment: for each country, the primary objective of a society based on services is its capacity to create an adequate number of jobs. The transformation of tasks and the related proliferation of white-collar jobs, which attracted such attention in the 1960s, is now a widely acknowledged fact. However, there are good and bad jobs in the white-collar sector, just as there are in the manual sector. While the number of jobs in manufacturing industry is declining, jobs are being created in the service sector, sometimes in insufficient numbers and sometimes poorly paid.

The aim of this book is to clarify what can be expected in terms of growth and employment from the development of service activities. This question deals in essence with the possibilities of balancing an extension in markets with favourable developments in the division of labour in different sectors, i.e. with a system of work organization capable of preserving the quality of jobs and of bringing about a subsequent increase in demand. It was in fact just such a synchronization between the development of demand (i.e. mass consumption) and the organization of production (based on productivity gains and high wages) that underlay the growth of the industrialized economies in the past. Analysis of the relationship between economic growth and the development of tertiary activities must precede any analysis of employment. Moreover, with regard to employment, the experience of each country is defined by differences in patterns of growth of the working population (i.e. wage employment and self-employment), as well as by the movement of labour from rural to urban areas.

I The spectre of unemployment

There are enormous differences in terms of employment between countries such as the United States and Japan, where the working population has almost doubled since the 1930s, and countries such as the Federal Republic of Germany, France and the United Kingdom, where the working population today is barely 25 per cent higher. For this reason, full employment does not have the same meaning for all countries, nor does unemployment refer to the same historical experience.

Since 1973, the number of unemployed in the OECD countries has tripled, from 11.2 million to 31.5 million in 1985 (33 million in 1983). The percentage of unemployed in the working population has exceeded 11 per cent in the European countries. The level of unemployment is particularly high in the smaller European countries (with an average unemployment rate of 13.5 per cent in 1985). In the United States, after rising above 10 per cent in 1983, the unemployment rate has declined in 1985 to 7.5 per cent, a rate not much higher than that of the 'full employment' period of the 1950s.

We shall examine in some detail the experience of seven industrialized countries: the United States, four medium-sized countries (the Federal Republic of Germany, France, the United Kingdom and Italy) and two small countries (Belgium and the Netherlands). Depending on the country, current employment is either higher or lower than during the 1930s. For a country such as France, the present lack of jobs is an entirely new phenomenon. In Belgium and the Netherlands, current rates exceed even the 10 to 11 per cent of the 1930s. On the other hand, in the United Kingdom and, above all, in Germany and the United States, the rates today are still far below the record rates of the Great Depression (when they stood at 15.3 per cent, 17.2 per cent and 22.3 per cent respectively) (see Table 1.1.).

Comparison with the unemployment of the 1930s is therefore misleading. It is also true that, besides differences in nature between the depression of the inter-war years and the stagnation of economies during the 1970s and 1980s, individual workers' experience of unemployment has changed. With the development of social insurance

Table 1.1 Employment and unemployment from the 1930s to the 1980s

	USA	FRG	France	UK	Italy	NL	Belgium
Working population (in millions)							
1938	57.2	21.5	19.7	22.9	18.8	3.5	3.6
1982	111.8	27.5	23.4	26.7	23.2	5.7	4.2
Unemployment (as % of working population)							
1930s (max.)	22.3	17.2	4.5	15.3	5.9	11.9	11.9
1980s (max.)	9.5	8.0	8.0	13.1	9.7	13.7	14.5

Sources: A. Maddison (1982); OECD (1984d).
Note: The estimate of the maximum rate for the 1980s only takes account of standardized rates observed until 1983.

programmes during the post-war period, unemployment compensation has clearly improved, as have other systems of income maintenance for households. The principle of insuring households generally against risks of income loss has replaced the principle of giving relief only in the most extreme cases of hardship. Again, the situation remains very unequal, not only between one country and another, but also between different job categories and different households.

Many of the unemployed do not receive any unemployment compensation (e.g. the long-term unemployed and new entrants to the labour force), and the average level of allowances represents only a fraction of the average national wage. A rough measurement of average compensation levels estimated by the OECD (ratio of average compensation to average income, OECD 1985) reveals wide discrepancies between countries: in 1981, this ratio was 0.18 in Italy, 0.22 in the United States, 0.32 in the United Kingdom, 0.65 in the Federal Republic of Germany, 0.82 in France and 0.87 in Belgium.

These inequalities tend to accumulate at the level of the individual household. Low earnings and the risk of unemployment often go hand in hand. Furthermore, although national incomes are still growing, albeit very slowly, the number of poor people is increasing. In this respect, the most striking example is that of the United States, especially in view of its apparently smaller increases in unemployment. In 1983, 7.6 million families—equal to 12.3 per cent of all families and representing 35.5 million people—were living below the official poverty line. Not since 1963 have there been similar levels of poverty.

Unemployment and stagnation therefore have serious social consequences. Their effects undermine the sources of growth just as surely,
if not as rapidly, as was the case during the 1930s.

II Industrial crisis and the development of the service economy

The relative decline of manufacturing industry as a whole during this
period is one of the phenomena common to the advanced industrialized countries. Because of the large productivity gains originating
from this sector and the potential for diffusion through its large
markets, manufacturing industry has been the driving force behind
economic growth. An increasing part of that driving force was directed
in the 1960s and 1970s towards the extension of markets on a world
scale. But this externalization undermines the conditions for the
continued growth of demand. These disequilibria, emphasized by
Keynes in his time, were increasingly able to reappear, to the extent that
the national policies of demand management which he himself recommended have become less and less applicable in the absence of any
coordination between trading partners. The difficulties encountered by
the developed economies to the new situation caused firstly by the
collapse of the international monetary system (the 'gold exchange'
standard established immediately after the Second World War at
Bretton Woods with the active participation of Keynes) and then by the
oil price increases in 1973 show the vulnerability created by the internationalization of trade. The forms that this industrial slow-down—or
deindustrialization—has taken in different countries in the face of a
more or less pressing need to balance the current account over the
medium term will be analysed in greater detail in Chapter 3.

It is principally in this context that the opportunities for growth and
employment created by the development of the service economy
should be discussed. This trend was already evident in the 1930s, when
the notion of the 'service economy' appeared (as will be shown in
greater detail in Chapter 2). Given this perspective, the crucial aspect in
the development of tertiary activities is their 'local' character and their
dependence on local demand. This reduces their susceptibility to falling
aggregate demand and provides a certain degree of freedom for
traditional Keynesian policies. A major aim of this book is to show the
limits of such propositions by analysing both the dynamics of the
different components of the demand for services and those conditions
of production that are more or less favourable to the medium and long-

Table 1.2 Long-term trends in employment, in services: shares of total employment during years 1920, 1950, 1970 and 1980

	United States				France				FRG				UK				Italy			
	1920	1950	1970	1982	1920	1950	1970	1982	1920	1950	1970	1982	1920	1950	1970	1982†	1920	1950	1970	1982
Distributive Services (transportation, trade, communications)	18.7	22.4	22.1	21.2	14.4	14.4	15.5	20.0	11.9	15.7	16.9	18.8	19.3	19.2	17.9	22.4	8.6	10.6	13.1*	21.5
Productive Services (including banking and insurance)	2.8	4.8	9.3	9.1	1.6	2.7	5.5	7.4	2.1	2.5	5.1	6.4	2.6	3.2	5.6	8.2	1.3	1.9	2.0*	3.1
Social Services (health, education, government)	8.7	12.4	21.5	} 37.7	5.3	9.4	14.8	} 29.8	6.0	11.5	17.4	20.2	8.9	12.1	19.4	23.3	4.1	7.9	9.4*	} 26.0
Personal Services	8.2	12.1	8.6		5.6	7.4	7.9		7.7	6.8	6.5	6.4	12.9	11.3	9.0	8.8	4.6	4.7	5.9*	
Services total in %	38.4	51.7	61.5	68.0	26.9	33.9	43.7	57.2	27.7	36.5	45.9	51.8	43.7	45.8	51.9	62.6	18.6	25.1	30.4	50.6
in thousands	17,280	31,873	51,153	67,708	5,515	6,515	8,912	11,952	4,986	7,725	12,196	12,984	8,172	10,259	12,836	14,744	3,162	4,653	6,240	10,400
Total employment in thousands	45,000	61,651	83,176	99,571	20,500	19,218	20,393	20,895	18,000	21,164	26,570	25,065	18,700	22,400	24,732	23,553	17,000	18,536	20,528	20,553

Sources: Singelmann (1978) for years 1920, 1950, 1970, OCED 1984d, p. 45.
* 1960
† 1981

term expansion of tertiary activities. The main characteristic of the development of the tertiary economy is the removal of borderlines within production and consumption activities. Thus our main concern is with the development of products and markets, while the evolution of tertiary-type jobs is of secondary importance.

The basic facts of the development of the service economy are simple and can be summarized thus:

(1) the historic expansion of employment in services: from 24 per cent of total employment in 1870 to 58 per cent in 1979 on average in sixteen OECD countries (see Maddison, 1982);

(2) the relative increase in the production of services in the *volume* of the domestic product which only manifested itself after 1973. Taken as an average for the six largest OECD countries, industrial production grew between 1950 and 1973 at an annual rate of 6.7 per cent, compared to 4.9 per cent p.a. for services. Between 1973 and 1983, however, these rates were 1.2 per cent and 2.8 per cent respectively.

Appendix I and Table 1.2 indicate the great periods of growth in tertiary employment, and also emphasize how a global approach conceals the disappearance of old services (e.g. various personal services) and the appearance of new activities (e.g. some producer and social services).

The evolution of the relative shares in the volume of domestic production of the manufacturing and service sectors is less clearly established. In particular, it is more recent and may change in the longer term (if, for example, the slow-down in the growth of tertiary activities is delayed). Moreover, this raises the question of the conventions used in the measurement of the volume of services, which is an issue that will be discussed later in this chapter. The only conclusion that emerges clearly at this point from the evolution of the volume of production is the extent of the slow-down in industrial growth. Whether or not the dynamics of growth in the service sector will be able to compensate for this decline in manufacturing industry remains to be seen. The conditions for such a substitution are the subject of Chapters 4, 5 and 6.

The United States, where the development of the service economy is much more advanced, nevertheless plays a special role in this analysis.

III The United States: an example of a tertiary economy

As early as 1973, tertiary employment in the United States accounted for 63 per cent of total employment, compared to 45 per cent in the OECD countries of Europe. Moreover, in the period 1950–73, the growth in the volume of services (4.1 per cent p.a.) exceeded that of manufacturing industry (3.8 per cent). In 1983, employment in the service sector reached 69 per cent of total employment. Given that service employment grew at an average annual rate of 2.6 per cent, 20 million (!) new jobs were created in this manner between 1973 and 1983. This abundance of service jobs was accompanied by an even greater expansion of the working population (91.2 million in 1973, 113.2 million in 1983). In comparison with such large movements in the labour force, the growth of the American economy seems weak: 2.0 per cent p.a. between 1973 and 1983. With this pattern of extensive growth, in which output per worker has actually fallen, the development of tertiary activities (3.1 per cent p.a.) has clearly been more sustained than that of manufacturing industry (0.1 per cent p.a.). These features are sufficient to enable us to characterize a specific pattern of economic growth:

(a) *slow*: even in comparison with the experience of the preceding twenty years, GNP grew between 1953 and 1973 by an annual average of 3.6 per cent;

(b) *extensive*: with the working population growing at least as rapidly as GNP, the number of people aged 16 and over increased by 27 million.

This growth pattern gives rise to speculation about the quality of the massive numbers of newly created jobs. The percentage of part-time jobs is significant (14.5 per cent of the total in 1981). But the most striking characteristic of this development seems to be the trend towards a growing bipolarization of income distribution. Only in 1983 did the average family income of $24,580 reach a level comparable to that of 1968 ($24,720). But during that period, the number of households below the poverty line increased from 5 million (i.e. 10 per cent of all families) to 7.6 million (equal to 12.3 per cent of all households).

The growing importance of services, where the coexistence of good and bad jobs is more striking than elsewhere, has played a major role in the decline of the middle-income classes implied by the figures above (see Steinberg, 1985). It remains to be seen whether this slow, extensive and unequal ('dual') pattern of growth is generally typical of a tertiary economy or whether it is specific to the American economy. We shall specify in this book precisely those aspects which are due to the development of the service economy.

In order to make this distinction, it is necessary to understand the extraordinarily extensive nature of economic growth in the United States. This is best indicated by the extent to which America's working population has grown; it has increased by a factor of five over a century (from 20 million in 1880 to 109 million in 1980), whereas it has only doubled in most European countries (and increased by only 17 per cent in France).

The wide fluctuations in production are another sign of the extensive nature of American development. For a century now, the United States has experienced in each cyclical sub-period the strongest variations between peaks and troughs of growth: −12.9 per cent between 1950 and 1973, compared to an average variation of −5.1 per cent in the other countries (see Maddison, 1982, p. 84). It is with this instability in mind that the burst of growth in 1984 must be viewed; in that year, GNP increased by 5.6 per cent, one of the highest annual rates since the Korean War. This burst of growth combined the effects of record unemployment levels for men (11 per cent) and machines (69 per cent of production capacity utilized) with an economic recovery triggered by an unprecedented budget deficit of $200 million, or 5 per cent of GNP.

On the other hand, the diversity of services and the threat of a declining middle class in the wake of their expansion is not simply a characteristic of the American economy, but quite possibly the lot of service economies in general. It is maybe time, therefore, to define what is meant by the concept of services.

IV   Service and services

Until now we have been satisfied with using the term 'services' in its usual sense. If we want to understand the diversity of services, however, we have first to specify what it is that distinguishes, for example, tertiary activities from manufacturing activities. This question has been widely and cogently discussed in those books on services to which we shall be referring. To judge from the length of the debates, which seem incapable of being settled, there is not yet any universal definition of the term 'services'. Depending on the objectives to be achieved, different aspects can be stressed. Given our preoccupation here with the problems of growth in an open economy, we shall focus in particular on what determines the mode of social validation of so-called tertiary activities: social perception of product characteristics, nature of market relationships, the role of competition, etc. To begin with, this approach ignores all aspects of the nature of tasks. The practice and content of service occupations are not part of our study, except to the extent that the internal division of labour may turn into a reorganization of the division of labour between firms.

That said, it may still be useful to recall certain classic characterizations of service products which specify the nature of their market relationships. One of the oldest and best-established, which dates back to Adam Smith, emphasizes that services can neither be stockpiled nor incorporated into any other production: 'they perish in the very instant of their performance'. This lack of material existence, which implies a simultaneity between the production and consumption of services, has had, for classical and Marxist scholars investigating the 'circuit of value', the major consequence of laying the foundations for a theoretical distinction between productive and unproductive labour.[1] In the world of prices, as opposed to the world of value (see Lipietz, 1983), this 'immateriality' of tertiary services establishes their character as a *local monopoly* to the extent that it implies a direct relationship between producers and consumers.

Another consequence relates to the difficulty of identifying the product, especially since the quality of a service involves not only how it is delivered but also the conditions of its accessibility, its duration and the possibility of its being repeated. This implies in a number of cases a more extensive producer–consumer relationship, both currently and in the future. The usefulness of a service thus depends on the manner in which it is performed in terms of both space (proximity) and time (duration, availability, frequency). However, these properties are not usually sufficiently marked to establish a clear distinction between services and other activities. A number of services only display the above characteristics in a very rudimentary way. Firstly, the constraint of localization does not fundamentally imply a monopoly, but rather a restriction of competition among local producers. On the other hand, several other characteristics, such as low set-up costs (compared to manufacturing industry), actually imply (local) conditions of particularly intense competition. Secondly, the constraint of localization does not hold for all activities. A striking example of this is the existence of international trade in services, such as transport and tourism, financial activities, insurance and business services (e.g. engineering, legal services, research and development and advertising). Besides, wherever such a constraint does exist, such as when having to provide access to dispersed clients of small firms and individuals, it tends to be minimized by the technological developments in telecommunications and data processing.

As far as these points are concerned, we shall try to specify in Chapter 4 the nature of and prospects for international trade in services. And in Chapter 6 we shall try to illustrate the new areas being opened up for tertiary activities by the emerging information technologies. The aforementioned characteristics of services remain useful for understanding the market dynamics of services, for example. But it is clear that they do not provide a simple, universal and workable definition of tertiary activity. In the context, it is tempting to use a negative definition of services, including in it everything that is not part of agriculture or manufacturing industry.

Nevertheless, current practice seems to determine well enough what is a service and what is not. Economics tends to see the world as a system which produces and distributes a fixed basket of merchandise, goods or services, useful or rare, while everyday experience consists rather of a variety of relationships between people: to serve here has a precise meaning for individuals which extends to relationships between two *separate* economic units.

It is by re-evaluating the traditional, rigid economic approach that Hill (1977, 1979) recovers the precision of current practice. According to Hill, the production of a service is a process which, in essence, aims at modifying in some way the recipient or his/her belongings. It is no longer a matter of knowing whether the services are perishable, as was emphasized by Adam Smith, but of distinguishing the production of a service from the service itself and of investigating the duration of the change that it represents. Different categories of service can thus be distinguished: durable or non-durable services, services related to objects or people, services for oneself or for others, for free or paid, etc. Hill notes quite correctly that a service can only be carried out by a person other than the one/ones requesting it (one cannot eat or sleep for someone else).

This definition of services underlines how the activities concerned can be located at the interface between the social and the domestic, between the internal and external activities of firms, between the old and the new/renewed. Unfortunately, this rather enlightening definition is scarcely workable. First of all, it would involve a reformulation of the standard conceptual framework of economic analysis, in which goods are strictly defined, produced and exchanged but do not interact, and in which there are given economic agents who are not transformed in the process of exchange. In addition, the extension of this definition to services exchanged between firms introduces some problems: any subcontracting relationship would now be categorized as a producer service. This problem can be resolved by a more restrictive definition of what a firm is and what its 'belongings' are.[2] Even if it is difficult to draw from this approach any workable definitions, those put forward by traditional economics do remain valuable. Hill's definition has the double advantage of emphasizing both a unifying characteristic in the field of tertiary activities and the limits set by current frameworks of economic analysis which do not really take into account physical changes (innovations, transformations, etc). In such a situation, where frameworks of economic analysis are not likely to overcome this particular limitation, the previous assessment supports those who wish to establish stronger distinctions within service activities (cf. de Bandt, 1985). The above discussion also confirms the validity of most empirical classifications of service activities used in national accounts and proposed by various applied studies.

The classification of services

Thus there is a certain consensus on what is generally understood to be a service, but none on how to subdivide this large, empirically defined set of activities.[3] Most approaches consider as services those products defined in the four major divisions 6, 7, 8 and 9 of the ISIC (International Standard Industrial Classification) outlined as follows:

(6) wholesale and retail trades, hotels and restaurants;
(7) transport, storage and communications;
(8) finance, insurance, real estate and business services;
(9) community, social and personal services.

There is sometimes a certain degree of haziness with regard to the classification of transport and communications, which certain authors compare rather with the production of goods. Much more exceptional is the position of those who, like Colin Clark, also regard construction as a service activity.

However, within this large group of activities, the subdivisions made by national accounting systems and by studies on services are very heterogeneous. This makes comparisons between countries rather difficult.

All the classifications attempt to group together different tertiary activities according to their principal function. Among the varied headings there are usually four distinct services: business services, household services, collective services (public or private) and distribution or intermediation services, which link the activities of the previous three categories (businesses, households and institutions). Within this very general structure, however, there are many shifts of activities, according to differences in the distribution of users of the service in question. These shifts concern in particular financial activities, which are divided between the functions of servicing businesses and the (more symmetrical) function of intermediation, and collective activities, where the scope for intervention by public or private institutions differs a great deal from one country to another. The following provides an example of such classifications of service activity by function similar to those proposed by Browning and Singlemann (1978) and by Leveson (1983).

(1) *Business services*: accounting, research and development, engineering, advertising, employment agencies.
(2) *Household services*: hotels, restaurants, personal care, leisure, repairs.
(3) *Collective services*: (under public or private supervision): health, education, government, defence, non-profit organizations.
(4) *Integration and intermediation services*: trade, transport, communications, insurance and finance.

Certainly, these classifications only take account of 'officially productive' activities and therefore tend to exclude domestic, undeclared and illegal activities. The articulation between the official and the non-official economies is, nevertheless, at the core of the dynamics of market extension for services. The example of domestic labour is particularly striking. The growing participation of women in the labour force, for example, is made possible in part by the consumption of goods and services to substitute for domestic labour. These points are analysed in greater detail in Chapter 5, in the discussion of the dynamics of demand for household services.

Generally speaking, it seems that statistical knowledge (both official and unofficial) improved in most countries during the 1970s. The increase in international trade in services should in turn facilitate, during the 1980s, the harmonization of statistics between countries, e.g. in the area of business services.[4] One of the questions still outstanding is that of the measurement of the volume of activities.

V Measuring the volume of services

The measurement of the volume of goods and services is necessarily imprecise because of the constant changes in the number and type of products available. The use of volume indicators, obtained by comparing production outputs at constant prices, is only a partial solution to the problem, since it requires product stability and an identification of unit prices which are largely illusory; as a result, it is necessary to formulate numerous ad-hoc hypotheses. This arbitrary component affects the measurement of the volume of goods just as much as that of services, as the following telling examples will indicate.

The manufacture of computers provides a striking example of such difficulties in the area of material productions. Baily (1982) points out that technological progress in this industry has been so rapid that the price deflators could lead to a considerable underestimation of the volume of production. He quotes, as an extreme, but none the less plausible, case, a study according to which the production volume had been underestimated in 1980 by more than 300 per cent ($15.8 billion in 1972 dollars instead of 57 billion 1972 dollars). This is a large discrepancy, especially with regard to the problem posed by the slow-down in industrial productivity gains. In nominal terms, however, this production does not represent more than 1.4 per cent of manufacturing. In the area of services, the findings may be less spectacular, in the absence of a similarly far-reaching revolution in the nature of tertiary products, but their impact on, for example, the measurement of the national product, is very much greater. The most striking example is provided here by the measurement of the production of commercial activities. The most widespread hypothesis, used in the United States in particular, assumes that the ratio of the volume of commercial activity to the volume of products sold is the same as that of the commercial margin (given in value terms) to the value of products sold.[5] But this arbitrariness (without direct link to the specification of price indices or physical indicators) represented in 1981, in nominal value, 16 per cent of the American national product. There are problems of this nature (i.e. fictitious volume of activity derived from normative assumptions on profits) with the volume measurement of rental services, while other measures only refer, on the other hand, specifically to the volumes of employment necessary for production.

The importance of these hypotheses can be assessed by looking at estimation methods for volumes in comparison to weights of activities in tertiary production as a whole. Kendrick (1982) has summarized, in the case of the United States, the principal hypotheses used by the Bureau of Economic Analysis for estimating the volume of service activities. We have drawn up these data in Table 1.3 by grouping in Category C both commercial activities and renting services (classified in Category A by Kendrick, 1982) where the hypotheses concerning

Table 1.3 Estimation of real gross product origination (GPO) in service industries, USA, 1981

Industries by method of measurement (Bureau of economic analysis (USA)	GPO billions $ 1981	%	Ranked by industries' capital intensity, 1973	Ranked by labour intensity (1981)
			(by decile in descending order)	
(A) *Independent output estimates*	260.6	15.8		
Personal services	16.7			
Automotive repairs, garage	19.0		2	2
Amusements	13.5		2	3
Health	118.3			
Insurance carriers	36.8			
Hotels	20.6			1
Insurance agents	15.1			6
Federal government enterprises	20.6			
(B) *Estimates using labour indicators*	587.6	35.7		
General government				
Federal	92.3			
State–local	207.4			
State–local government enterprises	16.4			
Business services	71.3		4*	2*
Miscellaneous repair services	8.7		2	3
Banking	57.0			
Credit agencies other than banks				
Security, commodity brokers	3.2		4	4
	12.7			
Holding companies, investment offices	0.6			
Educational services	17.4		3	1
Motion pictures	6.4			
Legal services	24.1			
Social services and non-profit making	27.9		3	1
Private households	7.0			
Miscellaneous professional services	35.8		3	3
(C) *Estimates using profit-margin indicators*	796.7	48.4		
Wholesale trade	312.2		7	2
Real estate	324.0		1	10
Retail trade	260.5		7	1
Total services, 1981 GPO (billions of dollars)	1,645.5			

Sources: columns 2 and 3, Kendrick (1982); columns 4 and 5, Kutscher and Mark (1983).

Note: * Miscellaneous business services

the rate of margin are used with the arbitrariness indicated above. Thus, for more than 80 per cent of tertiary production, the volume measures seem directly questionable because of the weakness of the hypotheses on labour productivity (as in Category B) or the relationship between income from commerce or real estate property and the volume of activities (as in Category C).

A relative homogeneity of productive combinations of labour and capital in service activities can alleviate the arbitrariness of the hypotheses, by facilitating their interpretation. If, for example, there were in these hypotheses a clear distinction between capital intensive and labour intensive services, the usefulness as well as the limits of volume measures focusing on the creation of profits or on the evolution of employment alone could be better understood. But this dichotomy does not exist, and there is instead a great diversity of productive combinations within tertiary activities fulfilling similar functions. This diversity of tertiary activities has been illustrated in Table 1.3, which refers to different estimates of capital intensities or labour contents made by Kutscher and Mark (1983) for the United States. It must be concluded that the significance of the measures in question is not very clear.

Smith (1972) has shown that these hypotheses on the measurement of services could lead to estimations directly reversing the actual relative growth of secondary and tertiary production: the growth rates for manufacturing industry and services of 2.8 per cent and 1.9 per cent p.a. between 1951 and 1966 would become, respectively, 1.9 per cent and 2.8 per cent if other hypotheses were used.

At the same time, Hill (1971) has emphasized the diversity of hypotheses used from one country to another to measure the volume of services. Consequently, the usefulness of such measures in comparing the evolution of services between countries is considerably reduced.

Of dubious value with regards to evolutions in any given country, and heterogeneous when it comes to international comparisons, volume measures seem to incorporate too many *ad hoc* hypotheses to be really useful. This criticism is a leitmotiv in all analyses of the sectoral dimensions of growth.[6] We shall try in this book to take note of this and to use estimates of movements in the volume of tertiary activities as little as possible.

VI Services in the crisis: a macroeconomic perspective

Has the emergence of an economy more orientated towards services contributed to the slow-down of growth? Or does this development, as reflected in the evolution of employment and production, pave the way for a new type of growth? These are the principal questions underlying the sequence of arguments in this book.

Chapter 3 attempts to specify the industrial dimensions at the core of the stagnation in developed economies during the last ten years. The analysis of constraints on the expansion of demand brings out the importance in the medium term of equilibrating current account balances. This calls into question the prospects for autonomous growth in the demand for services protected from external competition. Chapter 4 is an attempt to assess the sphere and the determinants of international trade in services. Chapter 5 extends this analysis to internal demand for services. This is a matter of evaluating the prospects for a cumulative development of demand from both businesses and households. Chapter 6 investigates the long-term effects of production conditions in tertiary sectors on demand, before emphasizing in conclusion the opportunities for the development of tertiary activities and the broad policy options which they require.

It is, however, in Chapter 2 that we attempt to specify the macroeconomic framework for the analysis of the sectoral dimensions of growth put forward in this book. The division of labour between sectors evolves: new activities appear for the benefit not only of businesses but also of households, whose life styles change. This division of labour may pass through different phases, but the conditions of transition from one phase to another are still frequently unexplained. This is the lesson to be drawn from the theories of stages of growth (Chapter 2, Section 1). Account should also be taken of the ways in which productivity gains are generated in each sector and spread through the economy as a whole (Chapter 2, Section 2).

The proposition by Adam Smith, for whom the extension of markets is the primary condition for an increase in the division of labour, is a good starting point. This leads to an analysis of demand-led growth, where effectively industrial and tertiary products are clearly differentiated by the dynamic of their productivity gains. The specific nature of services reduces the opportunities for economies of scale and the division of tasks (except for job splitting).

However, an economy is more than the simple juxtaposition of production processes. A range of institutions and social practices maintain the structure of demand and the functioning of the labour market. This social fabric gives a certain unity to the social division of labour in an economy.

Durkheim's analysis specifies the foundations of that division of labour and its consequences for the pattern of economic growth. There is here a reciprocal to Adam Smith's Law. Theorists of the French 'régulation' school offer a framework for the synthesis of the two preceding propositions: that of the dynamic of productivity gains based on the extension of markets and that of the social relations of production (Chapter 2, section 3).

The nature of this articulation at the national level between the mode of demand formation and social relations of production largely determines and conditions the ability of each country to integrate itself into a world economy undergoing radical change.

Notes

1. This theoretical position has often led Marxists to a confusion between the productive and unproductive character of labour and the definitions of social classes. Certainly, the works of Adam Smith lend themselves to this erroneous interpretation: 'The Value of some of the most respectable orders in society is like that of menial servants, unproductive of any value, and does not fix or realize itself in any permanent subject or vendible commodity which endures after the labour is past. . . . In the same class we must rank . . . churchmen, lawyers, players, buffoons, musicians, Opera singers' (*The Wealth of Nations*, Book 2).
2. A service, by definition, represents a modification of the person requesting it or of his/her own belongings. Therefore, a definition of the goods belonging to a person or business must exclude products in the process of being made (i.e. work in progress), but include design functions, in order to distinguish, as in the case of a car manufacturer, the subcontracting of bodywork painting (a good) from the design of the bodywork itself (a service).
3. In 1956 Stigler even disputed whether there was any consensus at all on the overall definition of service activities. Thirty years later, the use of national accounts seems to have lessened this initial uncertainty.
4. An initial indication of this is that GATT was, at the beginning of 1985, given the task of putting together studies on these questions.
5. Brender *et al.* (1980, p. 111) have noted that this hypothesis includes in the volume measures of commercial activities both wages and productivity in industry and commerce.
6. W. Mitchell (quoted by Leveson, 1983) warned of this problem fifty years ago: 'The best of our production indices give inadequate representation to new industries, to services as compared to commodities, to 'secondary' production', to the utilization of by-products, and to improvements in the quality of products'.

2

Growth and the division of labour by sector

I Theories of the stages of growth: the problems of transitional phases

The origin and basis of the division into primary, secondary and tertiary sectors (1930–1960)

Any discussion of the service or tertiary economy must take into account the analyses of the economy in terms of stages of growth. The general approach of these analyses is to assume that all societies take the same road to economic development, passing through various stages on the way. However, although these stages of economic growth are for the most part clearly identified, the same is certainly not true of the transitional phases between stages.

The current division of economic activity into primary, secondary and tertiary activities is due to the work of Fisher (1935, 1939). He considered that the primary sector comprised agriculture, mining, forestry and fishing, that the secondary sector was made up of manufacturing industry and that all other activities could be grouped together in the tertiary sector. In making this division, Fisher emphasized the relationship between the distribution of employment among these three sectors and the level of development of an economy. The national income per capita gradually increased as the economy moved from the stage in which activities such as agriculture predominated through the stage in which manufacturing industry prevailed to the stage in which services formed the bulk of economic activity. Clark (1940) collected data in support of Fisher's arguments. In a sense, there is a link between these analyses and those of the physiocrats (Montchrestien, Quesnay) and of the classical economists (Smith, Petty, Ricardo, Malthus), since both these latter groups put their arguments in terms of social classes. However, while the physiocrats and the classical economists were concerned with the questions of income distribution and social reproduction, Fisher was concerned with economic growth; in this, he was

following Marx (himself heir to the classical economists), who identified several stages of economic development (feudalism, capitalism
and socialism).[1]

The theory of the stages of growth is directly inspired by the apparent
link, in a comparison of a series of countries, between per capita income
and the distribution of activities. As early as the seventeenth century, Sir
William Petty used the relatively high standard of living of the Dutch in
comparison with that of the French and the English to argue that:
'There is much more profit to be made from industry than from agriculture, and much more to be made from commerce than from
industry'.

The analysis of the process of economic growth, by which, according
to Fisher, economies move from the primary stage through the
secondary stage to the tertiary stage, is thus based on two 'observations'.
On the production side, on the one hand, there is a constant increase in
yields. On the demand side, on the other hand, there are growing
preferences, as income increases, for secondary and then tertiary
products.

Thus, the dynamism of production is ensured through innovations
and technical progress, although this increase in yields is much quicker
in industry than in the service sector. This surplus created in the whole
of the economy is channelled by the structure of demand mainly into
the secondary and then into the tertiary sectors, in accordance with the
observations made as early as the nineteenth century by the Prussian
statistician Engel, who pointed out that, beyond a certain level of
income, proportionally less of any increase in income was spent on
staple foods. These studies of consumption were concerned basically
with the utilization of income (cf. Stigler 1965) and not with the
development of the volume of consumption. Nevertheless, the model of
the stages of growth implicitly assumed that the consumption of
services increased by at least as much as the consumption of other
products. On this basis, the dynamism of the supply side, which created
an increasing surplus, and the law of demand contributed to a process
of rapid development, in which service activities and the consumption
of services had an increasing share.

This was therefore the explanation given for the process by which
societies would develop to the stage in which the tertiary sector would
provide most jobs and in which household income would be spent
mainly on the purchase of services.

This growth model has three major limitations:

(1) analysis of the value of final demand (in terms of income shares) is used to draw conclusions about developments in the volume of demand;
(2) there is no mention of the demand from firms for intermediate services for their production needs;
(3) there is no explicit mention of a growth mechanism which would explain the change from one stage to another.

The first two criticisms are direct ones. Clark, who as early as 1940 attempted to clarify in his book *The Conditions of Economic Progress* (and in the new editions of 1951 and 1957) the statistical foundations of Fisher's model, pointed out the uncertainties and diversity of the relationships used to express the consumption patterns of households. Moreover, the classification of products into basic and luxury goods does not match up with the classification into primary, secondary and tertiary sectors. If products are classified according to their income elasticity, there are basic services and luxury agricultural products. Also, the absence of intermediate services appears especially important (even if transport, communications and commerce are excluded) in view of the development in the last twenty years of services to firms. These questions will be taken up again in Chapter 5 in the analysis of the demand for services. Appendix III contains a formalization of the growth model which brings out the bases of the simple model mentioned above.

We shall now focus on the third criticism of the simple model: the absence of any real dynamic of growth. The critical debate on the theory of the stages of growth that developed during the 1950s and 1960s centred on the static nature of the analysis. Furthermore, it is of central importance in understanding the inability of such analyses to take account of the conditions of the present economic crisis, in which stagnation and high unemployment are accompanied by the growth of the tertiary sector.

The problem of the transition from one stage to another is central to all the analyses and to the work of authors such as Fourastie (1952) and Baumol (1967), who have subsequently put particular emphasis on the great disparity in the opportunities for increasing yields in industry and in the service sector. The paradoxes that they bring to light by comparing the productivity gains in a manufacturing industry with the very limited opportunities for such gains in hairdressing or opera production are influenced by deliberately simplified presentations of the growth process. We shall return to these paradoxes in order to explain the importance of inter-sectoral relationships in the growth process.

The revival of analyses in terms of stages of growth (1950–1960)

In the 1950s and 1960s, when the developed economies were experiencing rapid growth rates after the post-war reconstruction, these analyses in terms of stages of growth were developed further by Rostow, Kuznets and Chenery, who were concerned to describe more precisely the models and stages of growth in order to gain a better understanding of the dynamics of the growth process. It was Rostow (1953, 1956, 1960) who made the greatest contribution to reviving and popularizing the theme. In his work published in 1960, he distinguished five stages: (1) traditional society; (2) the preconditions for take-off; (3) take-off; (4) the phase of maturation; (5) the age of mass consumption, which described the process of industrialization from its beginning to its end. His analysis of the growth process itself (cf. Rostow 1953) is based to a large extent on characteristics inherent in each society that explain its propensity to innovate, to carry out basic and applied research, to seek material well-being, to consume and to increase its population. Thus, the growth of each economy depends to a large extent on the desire for development in each society, taking into account certain basic facts, such as size of country and natural resources. These propensities are assumed to evolve only slowly. As they develop, and as growth continues, they help to strengthen the impetus of the expanding economy. This cumulative process led Rostow to believe that after the take-off stage was completed, growth became self-sustaining. Thus, in his analysis, the problems of transition from one stage to another are basically limited to the initial take-off phase. As a result, much of the literature of economic development has been concerned with characterizing the conditions under which an economy starts to grow (cf. Rostow 1963). Part of the debate polarized around the importance and the nature of particular leading sectors: those in favour of investment in particular industries (taking the example of the textiles industry in England and of the railways in the United States) (Rostow, 1956; Streeten, 1961; Hirschman, 1958) opposed those who supported the need for balanced industrial development (Rosenstein–Rodan, 1961).[2] All, however, were agreed that the question of leading sectors did not arise in the same way in the mature phase, when the interdependence between industries took on a more natural role. For developed economies, therefore, Rostow's arguments can be reduced to the principle of self-sustaining growth. The characteristics of the final phase, the age of mass consumption, remain vague.[3] Rostow stresses that in this final phase the consumer durables and the service sector act as the leading sectors; this stage is an age of abundance in which the major problems are concerned with establishing priorities in the competition for resources between military expenditure, the Welfare State and the expansion of private consumption. The description of post-industrial society is somewhat brief and the problem of transition from one stage to another is avoided by assuming that growth is self-sustained.

From the start, Kuznets criticized these approaches which claimed to have identified a stage of economic take-off and which assumed that subsequent economic growth would be quite automatic in nature.[4] In the 1950s and 1960s, Kuznets was concerned in a series of books on the quantitative aspects of growth to assemble data from a period of a century in order to assess the empiricial bases of these growth theories. These studies certainly bring out a correlation between levels of development as measured by the national income per capita (in dollars) and the distribution of employment and production among the primary, secondary and tertiary sectors, but it is a very long-term phenomenon and the path taken and the rate of growth vary significantly from country to country. The very general correlation between levels of development and distribution by sector is not very useful in predicting the rate and form of growth in a given country over a period of two or three decades, contrary to the implications contained in the theories that assume that growth in developed countries is self-sustaining. Close study of the available data thus led Kuznets to be extremely sceptical about the relevance of these theories.

The imprecise nature of the transitional phases

Studies by Chenery (1960) and Chenery and Taylor (1968) were an attempt not so much to establish the validity of Rostow's theories as to clarify the paths taken towards economic growth, taking into account certain specific characteristics of individual countries such as size and natural resources. Their analysis of changes in the distribution of national income among the primary, secondary and tertiary sectors as a function of the growth of income per capita is revealing on several points. The experience of fifty-four countries for the period 1950–63 highlights[5] the development of the industrial sector. The share of the industrial sector in production grows more quickly than the national income per capita when the latter is very low, which confirms the rapidity of the first phase of industrialization. This share continues to grow (but less quickly than income per capita) until income per capita reaches a level of $1,200 (US, 1960). Beyond this level, the share of the industrial sector tends to fall as income increases. Moreover, with same income per capita, the larger the country the larger the industrial sector. This echoes the broad outline of industrial development predicted by those who advanced the theories of the stages of growth.

Although this characterization of the share of the industrial sector is fairly precise, these analyses reveal very little of the development of the respective share of the other two sectors. No significant link is established between the relative size of the service sector and national income per capita.[6]

This has important consequences. Those who advanced the theories of the stages of growth highlighted a process of industrial development with an initial take-off stage and stages of maturity. Chenery and Taylor carried out more detailed analyses of separate industrial sectors and succeeded in identifying, as a function of the increase in income per capita, industries that characterize the initial period (low quality consumer goods industries), the intermediate period (certain consumer goods and intermediate products) and the final period (capital goods and consumer durables).[7] But this description of industrial development does not explain the development of the other sectors. There are large service sectors in countries with a low income per capita. This is the case in poor countries in Africa (Zaïre, Mali) and Latin America (Bolivia). There are also countries with a high level of income per capita where the share of the service sector is relatively low, as it is in Germany. This is simply indirect confirmation of the existence of a traditional and a modern tertiary sector. The theory of the stages of growth assumed that a modern tertiary sector would emerge. However, there is no guarantee of this transition. Reduced growth in the manufacturing sectors may be accompanied by very different patterns of development in the tertiary sector.

The ambiguous concept of the service society

Two important and complementary conclusions can be drawn from this long-established fact, both of which shed further light on the ins and outs of the debate on the stages of growth, a debate which has had a great influence on the concepts of the post-industrial or service society.

The first of these conclusions is that the analysis of the stages of growth can be reduced, in view of the historical data, to a description solely of the industrial sector until its stage of maturity. What happens subsequently? Industrial decline is conceived of only in relative terms, as a consequence of the higher growth rate in the tertiary sector. However, in the past decade, it has been real stagnation in industrial production that has caused the annual growth rates between 1973 and 1982 of +1.5 per cent in the United States, +1.9 per cent in France, +1.5 per cent in West Germany and −2 per cent in the United Kingdom; the comparative figures for the period 1960–73 are: +4.7 per cent in the United States, +6.6 per cent for France, +5.2 per cent for West Germany and +3 per cent for the United Kingdom.

The second conclusion is that the link between the development of the primary, secondary and tertiary sectors is conceived as a purely mechanical one, without any account being taken of the growth rate in the economy. However, on the one hand, changes in the distribution of national income do not seem to follow a single pattern and, on the other, the general slowing down of the economy that has accompanied the decline of manufacturing industry underlines the key role of the growth rate. In particular, the kind of tertiary sector that is likely to develop in a period of low growth is able to incorporate a high proportion of traditional services.

At the end of the 1960s, the debate on the theory of the stages of growth brought out very clearly the shaky foundations of a linear interpretation of economic growth linking growth and the emergence of a post-industrial society. Although real changes in the organization of industrial work were taking place from the 1960s onwards, when increased productivity gains and technical progress seemed to be leading towards the disappearance of manual work in its traditional form, there was in fact no evidence to link these changes with the dawning of an age of abundance. There was nothing to guarantee that economic growth would continue.

However, it is precisely because they are based on false premises (i.e. that a small, hyper-productive industrial sector would guarantee an abundance of material goods) that theories of post-industrial society (cf. Bell, 1973 and Touraine, 1969) have contributed to the present confusion of the present debate on the policies needed to escape the present crisis. Gershuny (1978) has carried out a critical analysis of the illusions developed in four studies of post-industrial societies, all of which are based on the same false premises despite their very different approaches to the subject.[8] It is as well to remember that Fisher introduced the distinction between primary, secondary and tertiary sectors in 1935 with the avowed intent of pointing out to his contemporaries that a 'return to the land' was a simplistic and irrational idea born of a backward-looking ideology. It is ironical that in the present crisis the idea of the service society should play the same role of providing an irrational escape from the difficult realities of our times. The idea of a fourth stage (the so-called quaternary stage) linked to the growth of the information sector (see Chapter 1 for the activities listed under this heading), although obviously dating from later than the debate on the theories of the stages of growth, presents similar problems of vagueness and lack of precision. The best way of preventing the concept of post-industrial society becoming really 'vague and dangerous'[9] as a result of the confusion about the future of our societies that it fosters is to return to an examination of the nature of the industrial crisis. It seems that the studies made in the 1960s that concentrated on the causes of the disparities in growth rates between developed economies highlighted two or three components that are essential to economic growth in the modern world.

II The division of labour and the role of manufacturing industry as a leading sector

Technical progress, the division of labour and the expansion of markets

One of the major criticisms that can be directed at the theories outlined above is that they assumed that growth was automatic and self-sustaining. The main justification for this assumption was in fact a belief in the spontaneous nature of technical progress, innovation and the spirit of free enterprise. In Rostow's view, each country had its own propensities for enterprise, research and innovation. Fisher and Clark had similar views. In fact the concept of technical progress shared by these authors is the one defined by Schumpeter as the combination of a spirit of free enterprise and an exogenous flow of innovations.

This is virtually to ignore Adam Smith's fundamental law, according to which the division of labour depends on the extent of the markets. It is precisely this possibility of extending markets that determines the emergence and development of new forms and new means of organizing the work process, what is very generally known as technical progress. The spirits of enterprise and innovation are not empty concepts. The spirit of enterprise is above all the quest for markets, and innovations are derived largely from this momentum. It fell to Young in 1928 to rediscover the full amplitude of this first fundamental law laid down by Adam Smith.

This law implied that increasing returns to scale might exist for the industry as a whole. Generally speaking, increasing returns to scale imply that an increase in the means of production in terms of manpower and equipment is reflected in an even greater increase in the volume of production. The originality of Young's argument was that he stressed that this characteristic was not simply the result of the existence of firms with increasing returns to scale (a very real possibility for all that), nor even simply of the effects of intermediate innovations, but was due very largely to the appearance of new products and new modes of production made possible by the extension of the markets. A market certainly implies purchasing power, but it is also a series of productive activities linked by a network of exchange. The extension of a market starts a chain reaction. In the first instance, it makes possible an increased division of labour in the production process concerned, which opens the way for the introduction of new machines, which in turn develop new markets and cut the number of obsolete production processes. This momentum is disseminated within all the activities participating in the market. In this context of evolution, increasing returns to scale become extremely *possible*. This momentum may lead to the establishment of monopolies, although this is not necessarily the case. The entrepreneurial spirit, that is the drive to create, to extend and to conquer markets, remains central. But the dynamics of increasing returns to scale can only be understood at the level of the industry as a whole.

From this point of view, increasing returns to scale could in no way be reduced to externalities as formalized by Marshall in his attempt to synthesize Adam Smith's classical idea of increasing returns to scale and the neo-classical synthesis of the 'marginalist school', which based its theory of general equilibrium on diminishing returns to scale (cf. Blitch, 1983). The widespread acceptance of Adam Smith's law suggested by A. A. Young made it possible to examine the emergence of new markets, new products and new methods of production. However simple it might have been, it was a conceptual tool that could be used in the examination of the phenomena of economic growth. Young's 're-discovery', just before the depression of the 1930s and the upheavals that followed, was not taken up.[10] In fact he was only highlighting the potential of Adam Smith's law; its actual character and the conditions for its implementation still had to be clarified.

Increasing returns to scale in manufacturing industry

Kaldor's analysis of the causes of the slow growth rate in Great Britain (Kaldor, 1966) had the merit of establishing a link between A. A.

Young's analysis and the increasing returns to scale at industry level in European countries that emerged from Verdoorn's study (1949).[11] In his attempt to find a simple criterion by which European planners of the 1950s could estimate the manpower requirements of industrial growth, Verdoorn pointed out the stability of the relationship between productivity gains and growth in production. The productivity gains in question here are simply variations in the volume of production measured in terms of value added per person employed. Verdoorn's estimates showed that an increase of 1 per cent in production was accompanied by an increase of approximately 0.5 per cent in production per capita. These estimates were made by country and by industry and made it possible for future employment needs to be assessed. By highlighting increasing returns to scale at the level of manufacturing industry as a whole, this empirical law could also be used in support of the arguments put foward by Young. This relationship established by Verdoorn continues even in periods of slow growth to account for the medium-term relationship between productivity gains and increased demand for manufacturing industries in developed countries (cf. Appendix II).

However, Young's analysis suggesting the potential existence of increasing returns to scale was located explicitly at the level of manufacturing industry as a whole. Analysis of the growth process at the level of the economy as a whole makes it necessary firstly to clarify the nature of the links between the other sectors of the economy, and secondly to examine the conditions under which effective demand for industrial products increases.

Manufacturing industry as an engine of growth

In order to characterize the links with the other sectors of the economy, and in particular with the service sector, supporters of Young's argument speak of the role of manufacturing industry as an engine of growth. According to Lewis (1978), the term was introduced by Prebisch in 1950. It applied then to manufacturing industry as a whole in the most developed countries; the latter were considered to be the centre of a growth process that spreads outwards to encompass other activities or other economies. Various authors (Kaldor, 1966; Beckerman *et al.*, 1965; Kindleberger, 1967; Lamfalussy, 1963; Cornwall, 1977) later used the term to describe the role of the manufacturing sector in the growth of a developed economy. This description of manufacturing industry as a driving force exerting influence on other sectors is often very general, as it is in Young's argument. It is true that Hirschman (1958) suggested criteria, based on an estimate of exchanges between industries, for identifying the leading sectors of an economy, but this proposition inspired comparative studies of industrial structures (cf. Cella, 1984) rather than research on the general process of growth, which is what concerns us here. Young's supporters compared the nature of manufacturing industry, with its ability to extend its markets and to bring about productivity gains, with that of the service sector, where opportunities for extending markets and thus the division of labour are much smaller. This difference in the opportunities for productivity gains between activities operating within the same labour market and directed at the same consumer market gives rise to tensions. According to those who see manufacturing industry as an engine of growth, these forces have a dynamic effect on the conditions of production and on demand in the other sectors. Some of the elements of this effect will now be examined in more detail.

The role of manufacturing industry as a driving force acting on the service sector is very often understood only in a very general way in terms of the differences in productivity on the one hand and, on the other, the correlation between increased production in the manufacturing and in the service sector. This correlation is a material representation of the forces acting on the production of services, despite the fewer opportunities in the tertiary sector for productivity gains and increased division of labour. There are several stages missing in the presentation of this argument.

Let us take the initial hypothesis, in which manufacturing industry increases its productivity by extending its markets and increasing the division of labour. Markets may be extended by opening up a foreign market, which leads in turn to an increase in imports, or by developing new product markets. This extension of the market for goods stimulates the demand for services from households and firms in two ways. Firstly, the demand for services is stimulated directly by the growth in the activity of firms and by the increase in the income of households. To these short-term effects on the demand for services should be added the more long-term effects of the transformation of the conditions under which services are produced, brought about by the rapid rise in productivity gains in manufacturing industry. Let us examine these effects in more detail.

In order to illustrate the dynamic effect of increasing returns to scale induced by the extension of an industrial market, we shall firstly examine the development of demand when productivity is constant, and then consider the main effects of productivity gains as they increase with the level of industrial production.

It is easy to imagine the effects of an exogneous increase in industrial production that occurs without any increase in production techniques. This new demand increases the demand for services to firms by the same amount.[12] The increase in the demand for industrial products and for services to firms gives rise to a surplus of income which, according to Engel's law, is used to purchase so-called luxury products, into which category most services fall.

Let us now assume that productivity increases in manufacturing industry, while productivity in the service sector remains constant over time. We shall not concern ourselves any further here with the effects of direct demand described above, but with the implications of the growth in productivity in manufacturing industry. As Young suggested, it will be assumed that these productivity gains are the result of an extension of industrial markets. The role that might be played by services to firms in bringing about these productivity gains is a priori important. The historical role played by the development of transportation in the growth of the industrial countries is well known. Little is known of the effect of new services to firms, such as accountancy and research. An attempt will be made in Chapter 5 to assess its extent. It will be assumed for the present that services to firms are still activities complementary to industrial development. The productivity gains created in manufacturing industry can be of use in three ways: wages can be increased, profits can be increased, or prices can be allowed to fall behind the average for production prices. It is possible to combine these three methods of using productivity gains. If wages or profits in manufacturing industry rise more rapidly than in the service sector, pressure begins to build up on the formation of wages and profits in the tertiary sector. The actual nature of this upward pressure on wages and profits in the service sector depends on the characteristics of the capital and labour market in each country. If wages and profits in the service sector are able to maintain their relative positions in comparison with wages and profits in manufacturing industry, then the increase in costs will be reflected in an increase in prices, or by a growth in productivity in the service sector.

Thus, the extension of industrial markets has the effect of either increasing the relative price of services or of transforming their mode of production in order to reduce costs. The elasticity of the demand for services to variations in price indicates the conditions in which the market for services can be extended, despite rising production costs. If the income elasticity of the consumption of services is high enough to counteract the price effect, an increase in the price of services and a simultaneous rise in the consumption of services by volume will be observed as a result of the extension of industrial markets. A model presented in Appendix III specifies the values of the different parameters that come into play: income elasticity, the elasticity of productivity relative to demand in manufacturing industry and the service sector and input–output coefficients. A set of simple hypotheses can be used to specify the conditions in which the momentum of industrial expansion is able to play to the full its role as a driving force. One important result of this formalization is to clarify the initial conditions in terms of price and consumer expenditure ratios in the two sectors that are necessary for the schema presented above to be valid. If, for example, too high a proportion of consumer expenditure is already channelled towards the service sector, or if the price ratio in the initial situation is excessively favourable to the service sector, then an extension of the market for goods will be accompanied by a reduction in the consumption of services and a reduction in price differences. Appendix II therefore specifies the conditions under which manufacturing industry can act as an engine of growth for the rest of the economy.

The transformation of services and the origin of goods

These conditions contrast with the exponential development of the share of income or employment in the service sector, which is the end result of the situations examined by Fourastie (1949) and Baumol (1967), in which in particular there is no intermediate consumption nor any endogenous momentum in the increases in productivity. According to these hypotheses, in a world with rigid modes of production, consumption and distribution, a disparity in productivity gains between the two sectors leads eventually to the greater part of income and labour being given over to the less dynamic production process. These paradoxes obviously stem from over-rigid hypotheses. If those that conflict most obviously with the dynamics of growth are relaxed, it is possible to specify the bases and limits of the dynamics of the extension of industrial markets. This, however, leads only to a partial understanding of the dynamics of the division of labour, since it ignores the emergence of new products and of new production processes. The endogenization of productivity gains in manufacturing industry might be expected to take account of these innovations within the manufacturing sector. The main omissions as far as innovation is concerned are those that occur at the interface between industrial and service activities. Mention has already been made of some of the sources of new services to firms, made possible by the transformation of modes of production in manufacturing industry or by the introduction of new capital goods such as the present generation of electronic goods. But the pressure exerted on services by increased costs also leads to interesting tendencies to substitution, resulting in the extension of the market for durable goods. Thus the very significant relative price increase for certain services with particularly low productivity gains, such as Fourastie's example of hairdressing or Baumol's example of an opera performance, is reflected in a reduction or stagnation of their market shares and the development of the market for goods offering the user a partial substitute and a new product. In this sense, it is more accurate to speak of a change in consumption patterns than of a straight substitution of goods for services.

The 'classic' examples of hairdressing and opera require further clarification. The limits to any extension of productivity gains in these areas are obvious: the very nature of the services is altered if hair is cut more quickly or the opera performed more rapidly. Moreover, there are differences of quality from one performance to another and from one haircut to another. These differences may very well be reflected in considerable price differences. In the absence of a standardized production process, it is very difficult to quantify any change in the volume of production. Nevertheless, over and above these difficulties, it is easy to understand that, if twice as many haircuts are to be provided or twice as many opera performances to be put on, then twice as many hairdressers and singers will be required unless the quality of the services provided is to be radically altered. In this way the price paid by the customer for a haircut or an opera ticket will continue to increase in relation to the price of an industrial product, unless the hairdresser and singer are paid at increasingly low rates. In this case, the distortion of relative prices may well become so great that, despite the increase in household incomes, their demand for these services will stagnate or even fall. In fact, the existence of products that make it possible to look after one's own hair and to play one's own choice of music on a stereo system makes it easier for the potential demand for these services to be transferred.

The limited opportunities for extending the markets for certain services thus contributes to the extension of the markets for industrial products. These substitution effects have been examined by Gershuny (1978, 1983), who speaks of the emergence of a 'self-service society'.

This description is somewhat exaggerated, since the phenomenon of substitution between commercial services and domestic activities is not a new one. Indeed, it could be said that this tendency is the basis of the division of labour and the origin of most goods. In other words, the social utility of a product is based mainly on its ability to reduce the labour cost of a service activity, whether the activity be commercial or domestic. However, the 'utilitarian' aspect of each product stressed in this argument must of course be offset against the leisure and relational investment that may be represented by the products.

The most important elements in the dynamic process brought about by the division of labour in manufacturing industry have thus been specified. However, this view of the division of labour is still too schematic and abstract to accommodate the interactions between sectors that lie at the heart of the growth process. Two essential steps must be taken before the sectoral analysis of growth in an economy can be used to explain the causes and consequences of an increase in service activities, although care must be taken to avoid the pitfalls of a mechanistic analysis for which the theories of the stages of growth were criticized above. The first step is to examine what until now has been called the interrelationships between production conditions in each sector. This question in fact determines the very nature of the division of labour, that has until now been little more than an abstract entity. It is known that the organization of work is closely linked to the nature of the social relationships that determine the characteristics of the labour market in each national economy. In this respect, Lewis (1954) pointed out that a sector with a relatively low level of productivity could act as a reservoir of manpower in the growth process for a sector in which productivity was higher. The second, equally important step refers back to the conditions under which the market for manufacturing industry as a whole can be extended. In order that manufacturing industry can act as an engine of growth and make full use of its particular potential for increasing returns to scale, it must possess both the opportunities for creating new markets and the ability to exploit them. This implies examination of the way in which mature industries are integrated into the world economy of today. The nature of the division of labour in each country and the characteristics of industrial organization within the system of world trade are discussed in the following paragraphs.

III   The forms of the division of labour and productive systems

The division of labour and social cohesion

In comparison with the very descriptive nature of the theory of the stages of growth, the second section of this chapter puts forward an analysis on two levels of the links between sectors in the process of economic growth. Firstly, the interrelationship between the extension of markets and the division of labour, in accordance with the elaboration of Adam Smith's argument put foward by Young, was presented as the main engine of economic growth. Secondly, the characteristics of the production of services in comparison with the production of goods was seen to place limitations on the application of this principle to the service sector, thus providing indirect evidence for considering manufacturing industry as an engine of growth.

It remains to be discovered how markets are actually extended, and what factors prevent them from being so. This section is an attempt to demonstrate the importance in this dynamic process of the forms of the division of labour. Durkheim's analysis will help to lay the initial foundations of this converse of Adam Smith's law.

The concept of solidarity

The establishment of a commercial relationship presupposes the existence of a customary or statute law of commerce and property and of a monetary institution, as well as institutions for arbitration, regulation and control. Similarly, the division of labour presupposes a customary or statute labour law which lays down the conditions under which human labour can be bought or sold. The diversity of social roles means that the members of a society fall into homogeneous groups, divided according to the community of interest conferred on the groups by their social roles. This is the foundation of a relationship based on social class. But it is equally true that the cohesion of a society depends on the complementary relationships established between classes with different functions. This duality between the division of activities and social solidarity that lies at the heart of the social organization is central to Durkheim's analysis (1898). In Durkheim's view, the development of the division of labour is the basis for the development of a more complete form of social solidarity. Durkheim thus made a distinction between the mechanical solidarity embodied in respect of the series of prohibitions considered by society to be crimes and the organic solidarity that manifests itself in a series of juridicial rules which, if violated, give rise to 'compensation without expiation'.

This analysis of the division of labour in industrial societies contrasts with that put foward by Spencer, which is based on an atomized multitude of individual, unrelated contracts (contractual solidarity in Durkheim's terminology). Durkheim, on the other hand, stressed the institutional nature of the relationships within the division of labour in a society:

> Consequently, even where society relies most completely upon the division of labour, it does not become a jumble of juxtaposed atoms, between which it can establish only external, transient contacts. Rather, the members are united by ties which extend deeper and far beyond the short moments during which the exchange is made. Each of the functions that they exercise is, in a fixed way, dependent upon others, and with them forms a solidary system. Accordingly, from the nature of the chosen task permanent duties arise. Because we fulfil a certain domestic or social function, we are involved in a complex of obligations from which we have no right to free ourselves. There is, above all, an organ upon which we are tending to depend more and more; this is the State. The points at which we are in contact with it multiply, as do the occasions when it is entrusted with the duty of reminding us of the sentiment of common solidarity. [Durkheim, 1898].

Conflicts and tendencies

Durkheim hardly touches upon the conflicts that lie at the heart of the development of the division of labour. In his view, conflicts in the world of work are the result of 'abnormal' forms of the division of labour, which occur either because relationships are not codified or because the codification in use has been imposed on the weaker of the parties to the contract. He considers this 'anomy' to be a disease of the social structure, for which Durkheim's suggested remedy is more dialogue and consultation. He rejects the notion that conflicts about distribution and the organization of work may be a driving force in the social division of labour.[13]

A number of authors, such as Gorz (1973), Marglin (1973) and Braverman (1974), have since gained widespread acceptance for the notion that the precise form of the division of labour has often had the purpose of creating or perpetuating the inequality between those who hire and those who sell labour. In contrast, the institutionalization of a genuine 'organic solidarity' has often been brought about by social conflicts.

However, although Durkheim does not acknowledge that conflicts within the world of work act as a driving force in the division of labour, his analysis nevertheless leads him to two very general conclusions that still appear relevant.

Firstly, he states that the persistence of unjust or unequal situations damages the economic and social efficiency of the extension of the division of labour. Secondly, in order to overcome this limitation, society will tend to institutionalize and codify those social relationships in which unequal situations have arisen.

The ideal of our societies 'is to make our social relationships increasingly more equal, in order that all socially useful forces may be more freely deployed'. (Durkheim, 1898).

The state and its institutions are thus presented as organizations for the prevention and regulation of conflicts, thus enabling all socially useful forces to be freely deployed. 'Reducing the inequalities in the external conditions of the struggle' between the parties to the work contract is presented as a major challenge for all societies. This challenge is a permanent one. Kalecki (1943), sixty years later, was to make the point even more forcibly:

> Full employment capitalism will have, of course, to develop new social and political institutions which will reflect the increased power of the working class. If capitalism can adjust itself to full employment a fundamental reform will have been incorporated in it. If not, it will show itself an outmoded system which must be scrapped. [Kalecki, 1943].[14]

This constant necessity for a society to reduce its inequalities in order to fully exploit its productive forces is thus only a general tendency. Paradoxically, it does not mean that inequalities will be reduced but rather that there will be an increase in the contractualization of relationships.

The injustices and conflicts inherent in the forms of the division of labour have not disappeared. The persistence of insecure, badly paid jobs with poor working conditions highlighted by analyses of the segmentation of the labour market (e.g. Piore, 1979) suggests that the continued existence of such jobs is necessary to the functioning of the labour market.

Causalities

How are these tendencies and counter-tendencies brought into play by the dynamics of the markets? According to Adam Smith, the extension of the markets encourages the extension of the division of labour. Durkheim's analysis and the theories of labour market segmentation suggest that this extension may take forms that are more or less beneficial from a social point of view. In order to examine this backlash effect more closely, the following paragraphs will analyse those approaches in which the growth of the markets is indissociable from a change in the organization of society which makes it possible to extend the division of labour. This extension enables productivity gains to be diffused, thus ensuring that internal demand is increased. The process of diffusion is carried out not only by means of direct wage increase but also through the development of social security systems. Moreover, the spread of paid work (of which the growing number of women entering the labour market is particular evidence) and the concentration of employment in urban areas creates needs that can be satisfied by the newly distributed purchasing power. These new markets encourage producers to invest.

These analyses stress the link between the growth of supply and the growth of demand created by a particular type of labour relations in a given period. Thus, the institutionalization of labour relations and the development of wage guarantee systems since 1945 play an important role in explaining the sustained economic growth in European countries during the period from 1945 to 1975.

The present crisis, which is characterized by high levels of unemployment and cutbacks in social security systems, is reflected in the questioning of the *rapport salarial*[15] that underpinned the period of growth. The evolution of the conditions of production is largely responsible for these changes.

The growth of international trade means that very different systems of labour relations come into competition with each other. This competition exerts downward pressures on the *rapport salarial* in each country, the aim of which is to reduce costs and to increase the mobility of labour. The resultant weakening of 'organic solidarity' leads to diverging patterns of development for labour relations in the manufacturing industry and the service sector. The characteristics of these divergent tendencies, which result in different product and market characteristics for each sector, are less constrained by a common institutional framework as regards working hours, the division of labour, employment conditions and wages.

The outcome of the crisis would appear to depend on this transformation of the *rapport salarial*: the economy will either alternate between growth and slump as it did in the 1920s, or a new kind of growth will emerge, combining the needs of competitiveness with those of the social security system in order to encourage the stable expansion of the internal and external components of demand.

Global approaches to productive systems: the arguments of the French 'régulation' school

Young and Kaldor put foward the following cumulative sequence:

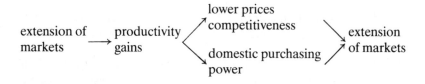

to which, following on from Durkheim's propositions, a second sequence might be linked, in which the development of the social division of labour plays a central role:

division of labour → organic solidarity → development of production → division of labour

There are obvious similarities and differences between these two sequences. Although they both bring into play the same cumulative causality, the first refers only to adjustments in supply and demand, whereas the second takes account of the institutionalism of social relationships.

Those analyses which attempt to link these two aspects might be called the *global approach to the productive system*. This is what characterizes the analyses of the French '*régulation*' school.[16]

The notion of 'cumulative causation' locates the analysis of the interrelationships between supply and demand in the medium to long term. This long-term relationship between production and consumption underlies the concept of 'accumulation regime' that is central to the theories of the French '*régulation*' school. In fact, this concept is used to describe the various ways in which the methods and organization of production develop by responding to and at the same time creating needs.

The accumulation regime is commonly described as either intensive or extensive in character, according to whether or not the growth of capital disrupts the methods of production. This phenomenon can be seen mainly in changes in the productivity of labour. But this distinction between intensive and extensive regimes still leaves undefined many characteristics of the growth of capital. What, for example, are the roles of finance capital and foreign trade, and what is the share of the traditional sectors in the process?

In order to analyse the structural characteristics of growth, which in turn define the accumulation regimes, three types of characteristics can be distinguished:

— those relating to the production process (the relative and absolute amounts of capital and labour), otherwise known as *production norms*;
— those relating to patterns of consumption (standardization of life styles, consumption of industrial, craft or domestic products), otherwise known as *consumption norms*;
— those that explain the link between the dynamics of the modes of production and consumption (the link between mass production and mass consumption), otherwise known as the *mode of 'régulation'*.

The mode of *régulation* describes the respective roles of market mechanisms, of institutions and of power relationships in linking the dynamics of production and consumption. If the effects of competition in the markets predominate, then the *régulation* is described as competitive; if the influence of monopolistic structures prevails, then the *régulation* is described as monopolistic.

The wage relationship, that is the set of laws, institutions and customs that control the use of wage labour, and the system of monetary management are essential elements of the mode of *régulation*.

It is at the level of the mode of *régulation* that the obvious signs of crisis will emerge. It is possible to base a periodization of capitalist development on the existence of relatively permanent phases in the development of the institutions and practices governing work and employment. These old mechanisms tend to become frozen in periods of crisis, as a result of the pressures exerted by the development of the accumulation regimes on the systems of manpower and monetary management and on the forms of state intervention.

Economic crises take different forms. The structural evolution characteristic of any accumulation regime may lead to conjunctural mismatches between supply and demand, which the mode of *régulation* may offset, even at the cost of marginal changes. This was the pattern of cyclical evolution in the inter-war period. Strictly speaking, it is only appropriate to give the label 'crisis' to those situations in which the resolution of such mismatches leads to a complete change in the mode of *régulation* itself. However, it should not be assumed that the emergence of a new type of *régulation* will in itself bring about an end to the crisis. The only remaining possibility is to call into question the dynamics of the accumulation regime itself.

The link between these concepts can be illustrated by taking as an example the archetype of the 'Fordist' accumulation regime. On the production side, large batch or process production gives rise to large and rapidly increasing productivity gains, while on the consumption side there is an equally rapid acceptance of a mass standard. Traditional production and consumption patterns continue alongside this process, but decrease in importance with the expansion of mass production. This 'Fordist' type of growth is regulated by the continuous growth of purchasing power (and the gradual reduction of the traditional sector) brought about by rapidly increasing wages, a monetary policy favouring the expansion of credit and the development of the social security system.

The size of the domestic market is the main limit to the development of this accumulation regime on a purely national level. As a result, the opportunities for extending markets offered by the world market and the advantages of importing products that are either not available or too costly locally leads to growing involvement in the system of world trade. Thus, the 'Fordist' model of the national economy must also be described in terms of the conditions of its involvement with the world economy.

The internationalization of production may influence to a greater or lesser extent the *rapport salarial* (if there is a significant degree of competition—in volume terms—with countries where wages are very low) or the system of monetary management (according to the exigencies of the international monetary system that prevails as trade is developed).

Generally speaking, a characterization of the development of accumulation regimes will bring out the constraints on the mode of *régulation*. This leads in turn to a periodization of the growth of developed economies based on the changes in the mode of *régulation* and in the accumulation regimes (see Appendix IV).

This historical perspective makes it possible to conceptualize the notion of crisis. The origin of the tensions and the crisis in the institutions are thus placed in the double context of the current mode of *régulation* and the trends in the accumulation regime.

The link between the accumulation regime and the mode of *régulation* thus provides a conceptual framework for analysing the conjunction, in the medium to long term, between the expansion of markets and changes in the institutional foundations of economic activity.

These arguments are an extension on these two levels of the long-term questions posed for Marxist (cf. Weinstein, 1983) or Keynesian economists (cf. Eatwell, 1983) by structural crises.

Growth and 'régulation' in a tertiary economy

The theories of the French school of *régulation* can be used to characterize on several levels the role of tertiary activities. Our only concern here is to bring out the main questions posed within the framework of these theories by the growth observed in tertiary activities.

Firstly, the importance of the service sector is characteristic of the accumulation regimes in two ways. It reflects both the particular dynamics of productivity gains and the existence of a market largely protected from outside competition. Thus, the dynamics of both production and consumption are involved.

On the production side, the importance of the tertiary sector tends a priori to moderate the rate of growth of productivity as a whole. In the same way as Kaldor's analysis of cumulative causation stresses it, the French school stresses the endogenous nature of productivity gains and the way in which high productivity gains stimulate growth. If we start from the hypothesis that it is in the manufacturing sector that significant productivity gains are made, these two analyses regard the development of the tertiary sector, in which productivity gains are lower, as a factor in the slowing down of growth. The term tertiary economy thus implies a low rate of accumulation, as is illustrated by the experience of the United States in the 1970s.[17] Two points arise out of this characterization. On the one hand, the reduction in productivity gains in the crisis has a particular effect on manufacturing industry itself. It will be shown in Chapter 3 that the growth of the tertiary sector has had only a slight influence, because of a composition effect, on the reduction in productivity gains in the economy as a whole since 1973. On the other hand, the growth in productivity gains in the industrial sectors may very well be dependent on the development of a certain number of services to firms. In this case, the growth of the service sector would be due in part to an over-rigid division into sectors of activity. It will be shown in Chapter 5 that this is not the case.

On the consumption side, the growth of the tertiary sector may, on the other hand, have the effect of reserving a large proportion of domestic demand for nationally-based activities sheltered from foreign competition. A distinction was made above between activities with high and those with low productivity gains; another distinction must now be made between sectors exposed to foreign competition and those sheltered from such competition. From this point of view, the growth of the service economy reflects in part the way in which an accumulation regime is involved in the world economy. Again, this statement gives rise to two reservations. On the one hand, it must be established that service activities actually are sheltered from foreign competition (cf. Chapter 4). On the other hand, it is necessary to make sure that the growth of the service economy, as manifested in the increasing share of this sector in national production and employment, is actually reflected in real terms by a growth in the volume of the share of demand reserved for services. This again raises the problem of how to measure prices and volumes for service activities. Moreover, an increase in the known volume of demand for services does not imply that this demand is not to a large extent complementary to that for goods (cf. Chapter 5).

Finally, it would not be possible to speak of the growth of a service economy without further qualification unless the data for the various countries studied all pointed towards the same conclusions. The term would thus be used to describe a general type of slow growth in mature economies, a return to sustained growth unaffected by foreign competition, or a period of restructuring of the industrial base of the economy. Analysis of the various foreign, intermediate and final components of the demand for services (Chapters 4, 5 and 6) and of the factors that put a brake on the driving force of industrial growth (Chapter 3) tends to reveal a 'tertiary' type of growth without, however, any universal validity, since the initial situations of the countries concerned in the world economy differ so widely.

But it is at the level of the mode of *régulation* in economies that the disruption caused by the size of the service sector in a period of economic crisis may make itself particularly felt. This brings us to the social aspect of a slow growth rate. The nature of the wage relationship, that is the general conditions of employment and pay, is one of the components of the mode of *régulation* in an economy. However, in the service sector this *rapport salarial* takes a specific form, which is different from that in the manufacturing sectors.

It is possible to summarize very schematically the main differences between the *rapport salarial* in the two sectors as follows:

(1) The nature of the tertiary products favours the development of a local monopoly (the specificity of the tertiary product).
(2) The value of the tertiary product is still linked to the methods of production (specificity of price determination).
(3) Job structures remain flexible (tasks can be divided and extended).

In contrast, industrial production remains open to a vast field of foreign competition. The value of production lies essentially in the product, regardless of the greater or lesser efficiency of production methods. Job structures are constrained by a standard of technical efficiency. In the exaggeratedly contrasting situations taken as reference points, tertiary activities can be profitable in all the situations that exist in local labour markets. Where there is a labour shortage, these activities can pay a high price for labour and then without constraint pass the cost on in prices. If there is an excess supply of labour, these same activities can redefine their jobs in order to take advantage of an abundant supply of cheap labour. Moreover, this process can be reversed if conditions in the local labour market change. This outline of the functioning of local labour markets, in which tertiary activities act as a sponge, even inspired the tax on tertiary employment (the Selective Employment Tax) introduced on the advice of Kaldor (1980) during the 1960s. This approach polarizes to an excessive degree the differences in the *rapport salarial* at the level of the firm between the manufacturing and the tertiary sectors. In fact, it is the distinction between so-called 'modern' and 'traditional' activities which is commonly used to explain these disparities in the general organization and payment of labour. This dualism between modern and traditional is a major aspect of the mode of *régulation* within tertiary activities, as it is within the industrial sectors. However, economic crisis tends to have different effects on traditional manufacturing activities from those that it has on traditional service activities. In the one case, it intensifies competition and thus exerts strong pressure either to adapt or go under; in the other case, it is uncertain whether the crisis will result in the consolidation of the previous system of labour relations or in a relative worsening of employment conditions. Under the circumstances, the quality of jobs seems to be as important as their quantity. Rising unemployment in Europe and the worsening of employment conditions and wages in the

United States raise the question of long-term changes in the *rapport salarial*. These developments may be temporary or permanent. The question is whether the types of growth in the tertiary sector alter the course of these developments.

IV Relaxing the constraints on growth

The analysis of the theories of the stages of growth (Section I) had the dual aim of reviewing the arguments about the emergence of a post-industrial age and of underlining their limitations in explaining the present slowing down of economic growth. This highlighted the need for a concept of growth that would explicitly take into account the division of labour by sector. Sections II and III were an attempt to provide such a concept. The aim of this section is to take stock of these arguments.

Economic crisis and lack of demand

The first point to be made in Section II was the dynamic process triggered off by the extension of markets. The increase in sales outlets gives rise to opportunities for economies of scale and the reorganization of the work process that lead in turn to increased productivity gains in accordance with the principle put foward by Adam Smith.

This dynamic process comes into full play in the case of manufacturing industries. According to this analysis of the growth process, the relative economic stagnation of the industrial economies in the past ten years can basically be explained by a lack of demand.

In more precise terms, this analysis assumes that the mechanisms that created previous extensions of markets have become jammed. This applies both to domestic demand and to that originating abroad. This restriction of demand may arise out of the disruption of markets, that is of the formation and distribution of purchasing powers. Relaxing credit restrictions, distributing new purchasing powers or protecting markets from foreign disruptions all seem to be possible ways of relaunching the process of economic growth.

The economic crisis of the 1930s revealed the deflationary dangers of a lack of domestic demand in a period of under-utilization of manpower and machinery. The economic policies of the post-war period were thus concerned with sustaining the growth of domestic demand. But the high growth rates achieved during this period were accompanied in most industrial economies by increased openness to foreign trade, and those analyses of the crisis that are concerned solely with the demand side regard the blocking of the dynamics of foreign demand as the cause of the slowing down of economic growth. The need to balance foreign trade may become a constraint on growth as soon as it is no longer possible to use export markets to compensate for imports.

This inability to balance the import needs that correspond to high levels of growth implies long-term structural changes, the acuteness of which became evident at different times in different countries during the 1970s. The break-up of the Bretton Woods international monetary system and the rise in the prices of raw materials, particularly of oil, in the early 1970s played a particularly active role in revealing the structural problems of growth in the developed countries.

In all cases, the distinction between a manufacturing sector exposed to foreign competition and a tertiary sector largely sheltered from such competition appears to play a decisive role in these analyses of the constraints on growth exerted by a chronic balance of payments deficit.

A shift in demand towards services may thus seem to be a means of relaxing the external constraint and relaunching economic growth. In other words, these analyses suggest that the development of the tertiary sector would lead to a return to sustained growth. However, such a shift in demand towards service activities ought to meet very precise conditions as to exchanges between industries (see Appendix III) in order to reduce the structural imbalance in foreign trade.

More fundamentally, the means by which such a shift in the structure of demand could actually be made remain to be specified. The classic Keynesian measures of stimulating demand by increasing household income or through public expenditure are a priori inappropriate. In order for new economic policies to be drawn up, the conditions under which demand is formed need to be re-examined. Both on the side of intermediate demand for services from firms and on the side of the final demand from households, this implies investigation of the ways in which work is organized and paid for, that is examination of the 'supply' side of the growth process.

The crisis and changes in the supply side

The main aim of Section III was to stress the importance of the 'supply' side in the formation of demand.

There are two reasons for not limiting an outline of the growth process to factors on the demand side. Firstly, the restriction of demand, and in particular of its external component, differs according to country in its importance as an explanation of the present economic stagnation, making it necessary to look to other factors for an explanation. Secondly, the need to act at the national level in order to relax this external constraint implies taking measures at the level of industrial structures that would affect both the organization and payment of work.

From this point of view, it is possible to propose a circular pattern of causation in which Adam Smith's law is linked to its converse, according to which the forms of the division of labour (in Durkheim's sense of the term) determine the extension of markets. Taking into account this effect of the conditions of production on the development of markets can be justified on two levels. On the level of the economy as a whole (as is stressed by the French school of *régulation*), the actual forms of work organization that enable significant productivity gains to be made are directly linked to consumption patterns. Thus it might be said that the so-called Fordist regime of growth links mass production, high productivity gains and rising wages with mass consumption. At a more sectoral level, it is a particular characteristic of tertiary activities that there is a close link between conditions of production and consumption. This interaction appears particularly strong when the factors determining employment in tertiary activities are considered. The level of employment is not closely linked to the volume of production, which is in any case difficult to measure. It implies the conditions in the local labour market, which may in themselves be an index of the quality of production. The unstable employment situations that may develop in certain services to households and firms contrast with the high levels of job security observed in adjacent tertiary activities. The strong link between the type of production and the quality of the product explains why it is so difficult to apply to this type of production the notions of productivity currently used for manufacturing production.

A similar duality arises when the conditions under which capital is used are considered. There are as many different levels of capital intensity in service industries as there are in other activities (cf. Chapter 6), but there are two very different types of basic situation, according to whether capital is a complement to or substitute for human labour. A relatively large share of fixed assets in service industries increases the complementary nature of the relationships between capital and labour in the tertiary sector. The relative share of machinery has certainly tended to increase with the development of computerization. The experience of the banking and insurance sectors, however, shows that, according to the system of work organization and the type of competition, this equipment substitutes for labour or extends job content.

Some analyses see the primary causes of the crisis as a change in the conditions of production. This position is frequently used to explain, for example, the reduction in productivity gains in the United States, where the smaller share of foreign trade in the economy and the autonomy of the dollar limit the extent of any external constraint. In this case, the explanations put forward include a lower level of motivation on the part of both workers and entrepreneurs, the absolute limits of economies of scale, the exhaustion of technical progress, variations in the price of raw materials and the development of the service economy.

The development of the service economy as a condition for increasing demand and adapting production systems?

The analyses in Sections II and III provide a conceptual framework for investigating the causes of the crisis and its relationship with the division of labour by sector. The framework links demand and supply by means of Adam Smith's law and its converse. The demand side is concerned with the causes of the stagnation in the markets, whereas the supply side is concerned with the obstacles encountered at the level of production. The expansion of the service sector is sometimes presented as the structural cause of these problems, when, for example, it is blamed for the reduction in productivity gains, and sometimes as the consequence, if the growth in employment in the service sector is stimulated by difficulties in local labour markets.

If manufacturing industry is regarded as the engine of growth, it is then logical to associate slow growth with a trend towards deindustrialization. The analysis of the trend towards the service economy will thus be prefaced by an investigation of the nature and causes of relative industrial decline.

Although the debate on deindustrialization is common to most of the developed industrial economies, it nevertheless covers a wide diversity of theories for explaining the weakness of manufacturing industry. The main arguments, which differ according to country, will be outlined in Chapter 3; this will be followed by an examination of the ability of the service sector to solve these problems or to initiate new forms of development.

Notes

1. A huge list of modes of production and their historical sequence can be found in Fossaert (1977). German sociologists and economists share the same preoccupations. List, for example, distinguishes between pastoral life, agriculture, agriculture + manufacturing and agriculture + manufacturing + foreign trade. Hildebrand identifies barter, cash and credit economies, while Bucker emphasizes the movement from the domestic economy through the city economy to the national economy (cf. Kindleberger, 1958).
2. Many authors have accepted the notion of balanced growth, starting with Harrod and Domar, for whom production and consumption balance out in a situation of full employment. However, a large part of the literature on balanced growth refers to this debate on industrial take-off in the years from 1950 to 1960. See Nurkse (1953), D. S. Swamy (1967), C. Ohlin (1959), T. Scitovsky (1959), Lipton (1962) and C. Haberler (1961).
3. However, the stages of growth are not the same in Rostow (1953) and Rostow (1960). In 1953 the last stage was located after the age of mass consumption. For a recent assessment of Rostow's arguments see Kindleberger and Tella (eds) (1982).
4. These studies have been published under the general title of 'Quantitative Aspects of the Economic Growth of Nations' in various volumes of the periodical *Economic Development and Cultural Change* between October 1956 and January 1967.
5. Cf. the results of the B-type regressions in Chenery and Taylor (1968) for countries with more than 15 million inhabitants. They relate the development of the logarithm of the share of each sector in national income to the logarithm of income per capita in dollars in 1960, to the square of the previous logarithm and to the logarithm of the size of the population in millions.
6. In underdeveloped countries with a large population, the agricultural sector retains a fundamental importance which may influence the results. In the developed countries, a large population may accelerate industrial development; conversely, in these same countries, the service sector may act as a reservoir of manpower.
7. This classification of industrial sectors gives some structure to the debate on the leading sectors at various stages of the industrialization process. The important role of the transport sector, and of telecommunications, whose role as engines of growth in the United States is often noted, remains to be clarified. In Chenery (1960), the share of these activities in national income has an income elasticity of 1.3, which is very close to that for the manufacturing sector.
8. Dahrendorf (1975), Bell (1973), Schumacher (1973), Galbraith (1974).
9. To quote Julien, Lamonde and Latouche (1976).
10. Young died in 1929.

11. Young was Kaldor's professor at the London School of Economics in the 1920s. It should also be noted that Clark, who was Young's assistant in London, pointed out the importance of the phenomena highlighted by Young (cf. Clark, 1960, pp. 353–74) and the limits imposed by the way in which a national industry is integrated into the world economy (cf. Chapters 2 and 3).

12. For the purposes of simplification, it will be assumed that these services to firms do not themselves have any intermediate consumption of intermediate products, in order that the multiplier effect that that would imply can be ignored.

13. Durkheim points out the intensity of social conflicts in heavy industry during the period, but refuses to see the workers' claims as anything other than a symptom of social unrest. He was also very critical of Marxist analyses (cf. Tosel, 1985). The notion of immanent social progress, of the establishment of 'organic solidarity' that would transcend political choices, be they liberal or Marxist, was to give rise in France to the doctrine of 'Solidarism', to use Charles Gide's term. This doctrine was used at the beginning of the twentieth century as the foundation of the reformist arguments on which the Third Republic based the initial stages of its social policy (cf. Donzelot, 1984).

14. Robinson and Wilkinson (1977) asked the same question just as clearly at the beginning of the present crisis.

15. *Rapport salarial* is a term coined by economists of the French *régulation* school to refer to the multiple dimensions of the relationship between wage-earners and the economy. The main point of the concept is that it includes the parallel, if not necessarily simultaneous, transformation of working conditions on the one hand and of life styles on the other. It is a synthetic notion, which relates both to work organization, qualifications and employment as well as to wages and social benefits.

16. Recent studies by the French *régulation* school include: Aglietta (1979), Boyer (1979a, 1979b), Boyer and Mistral (1983), Coriat (1979), Granou, Baron and Billaudot (1983), Lipietz (1979), Lorenzi, Pastre and Toledano (1980).

17. See the studies published by CEPII (Paris), in particular Aglietta *et al.* (1982).

3
Stagnation and de-industrialization the developed economies

The arguments that see the cause of the present crisis in the relative weakening of the industrial sector remain very controversial in most countries. It is also true that the diversity of situations and of definitions of the notion of deindustrialization does not contribute to the clarity of the debate. The first purpose of this chapter is therefore to specify the main criteria used to show the relative decline of industry and the halting of its role as an engine of growth.

I Clear signs of a slowing down of industrial growth

The first point to be made is that the slowing down of economic growth in the 1970s coincided with a slowing down in the growth of national industrial sectors. Table 3.1 compares the average annual growth rates of total output and of manufacturing industry respectively for the periods 1960–73 and 1974–84 for eight countries. These two growth rates seem to be correlated for all countries and for both periods. This is made clearer by a figure like Figure A.1 in Appendix II. The same is true of productivity gains in manufacturing industry and in the economy as a whole: the slowing down of the growth of productivity in the economy as a whole is associated with falling productivity gains in manufacturing industry (cf. Table 3.1). Moreover, in most of the countries concerned, the deceleration of production and productivity is greater in manufacturing industry than in the economy as a whole.

These correlations between growth rates can be explained in many ways. The only explanations ruled out are those that attribute the present economic stagnation solely to changes in the sectoral structure of the economies. According to these arguments, the growth of the tertiary sector, in which productivity gains are lower, would explain a large part of the fall in productivity gains in the economy as a whole. However, as shown in Appendix V most estimates show that the impact of a sectoral redistribution of labour on the development of average

Table 3.1 The reduction of growth in manufacturing industry after 1973 is even more marked than in the economy as a whole (figures given are average annual growth rates)

	Reduction of growth in production						Reduction in productivity gains					
	Economy as a whole			Manufacturing sectors			Economy as a whole			Manufacturing sectors		
	1960–73	1973–84			1960–73	1973–84	1960–73	1973–84			1960–73	1973–84
	(1)	(2)	(2)–(1)	(4)–(3)	(3)	(4)	(5)	(6)	(6)–(5)	(8)–(7)	(7)	(8)
West Germany	4.5	1.8	−2.7	−3.8	4.9	1.1	4.2	2.4	−1.8	−1.7	4.8	3.1
France	5.6	2.1	−3.5	−5.7	7.3	1.6	4.9	2.2	−2.7	−3.2	6.5	3.4
Italy	5.3	1.8	−3.5	−5.1	7.3	2.2	5.7	1.3	−4.4	−3.5	6.4	2.9
Netherlands	5.0	1.4	−3.6	−3.8	5.3	1.5	4.1	2.1	−2.0	−1.2	5.4	4.2
Belgium	7.0	1.8	−5.2	−4.3	4.9	0.6	4.3	2.3	−2.0	−1.5	6.6	5.1
UK	3.1	1.1	−2.0	−4.4	3.0	−1.4	2.9	1.9	−1.0	−1.8	3.6	1.8
USA	4.2	2.4	−1.8	−3.6	5.0	1.4	2.3	0.8	−1.5	−1.7	3.6	1.9
Japan	10.0	3.8	−6.2	−8.5	12.8	4.3	8.5	3.1	−5.4	−4.8	9.5	4.7

productivity is very slight. There are two reasons for this result; on the one hand, productivity levels in some service sectors such as banking, insurance, advertising and research are higher than in manufacturing industry (and in this case the composition effect exerts upward pressure), on the other, there are high productivity gains in sectors such as transport and telecommunications that are assimilated into the tertiary sector.

The similarity in the changes in industrial growth rates since 1973 hides a diversity of rates of structural change according to country. The main characteristics of this change can be seen in the changes in the share of industrial employment and valued added in the economy as a whole (cf. Table 3.2).

The fall in the share of employment in manufacturing industry in total employment is a generally long-established trend. It began in the United States, West Germany, Belgium and the Netherlands in the 1960s, and somewhat earlier in the United Kingdom. Industrial employment in France, Italy and Japan did not begin to fall until the mid-1970s. More directly indicative of the change in manufacturing industry is the actual fall in employment in manufacturing industry. Generally speaking, this fall is more recent. Although it began in the United Kingdom and the Netherlands as early as 1965 and in West Germany in 1970, it did not become obvious in France and Belgium until after 1974 and in Italy until after 1980. Moreover, in the United States after 1969 and in Japan after 1973, employment in manufacturing industry has stagnated and fluctuated rather than fallen consistently.

An examination of the changing share of industrial production in total output (measured in 1975 prices) underlines the diversity of the changes over time, but confirms that deindustrialization is a widespread phenomenon. In all the countries, with the exception of Japan and, to a lesser extent, Italy, the share of industrial production in total output was falling by the beginning of the 1980s. Despite the wide fluctuations that characterize the American economy, this trend was noticeable in the United States from the mid-1960s onwards. In Belgium, the United Kingdom and in France, this decline did not become obvious until after 1975 (or even 1978 in the case of France), while it began as early as 1970 in West Germany and the Netherlands. Table 3.2 summarizes the development of these various structural criteria for manufacturing industry in the eight countries in question. On this general level, it is difficult to formulate a typology of the various form of deindustrialization.

Table 3.2 Indicators of the weakening of the relative importance of the manufacturing sector

	Share of manufacturing employment (%)			Share of manufacturing production —volume (%)			Changes in manufacturing employment (index with base 1960 = 100)			Slowdown in manufacturing production growth over the last two cycles (average annual growth rates)		
	1960	Max	1984	1960	Max	1984	1960	Max	1984	1960	peak years	1984
West Germany	35.5	(1970) 36.6	30	30.6	(1969) 33.6	30	100	(1970) 105	82	(1974) 4.2	(1979) 2.8	0.1
France	26.5	(1974) 27.2	22.6	21.5	(1974) 26.7	25.2	100	(1974) 112	91	(1974) 7.0	(1980) 2.8	0.1
Italy	23.9	(1962) 28.1	24.2	24.4	(1980) 32.6	32.2	100	(1980) 114	102	(1974) 7.2	(1980) 3.1	−1.4
Netherlands	27.7	(1964) 27.9	19.5	20.8	(1973) 21.6	20.7	100	(1965) 107	74	(1974) 5.2	(1980) 1.0	0.6
Belgium	30.3	(1960) 31.3	21.7	20.3	(1973) 26.3	25	100	(1965) 108	73	(1973) 6.8	(1979) 1.8	1.4
UK	33.1	(1966) 33.1	22.8	29.7	(1969) 30.5	22.2	100	(1961) 101	65	(1973) 3.0	(1979) −0.7	−2.3
USA	25.5	(1966) 26.1	19.7	23.3	(1966) 25.9	24	100	(1979) 127	118	(1973) 5.0	(1979) 2.1	1.3
Japan	21.3	(1973) 27.3	24.3	22.9	(1980) 35.4	34	100	(1973) 153	146	(1973) 12.8	(1981) 5.4	4.5

Source: SOEC Structural Data Bank

There is, nevertheless, some similarity in the patterns of development, some more delayed than others, in the European countries under consideration (an exception should perhaps be made in the case of Italy, where the effects are so delayed that they cannot be considered established; the same is true of the relative share of the volume of industrial production, which has not begun to fall). There is no doubt that the United Kingdom was the first of the countries to experience the effects of deindustrialization (cf. Blackaby, 1978). It is similarly clear that a relative decline in manufacturing industry began to appear in the Netherlands and West Germany at the end of the 1960s, whereas the trend did not become noticeable in Belgium and France until after 1974 and 1977 respectively.

The case of the United States is very different, since there has been both a long-term decline in the relative share of manufacturing industry in total employment or in total output as well as maintenance of the level of employment in manufacturing industry, despite flucutations such as the recent 6 per cent increase in numbers employed in manufacturing industry between 1983 and 1984. It is easy to understand in these circumstances why there is doubt as to whether the United States is actually experiencing a process of deindustrialization at all (cf. in particular Lawrence, 1984). It is true that the slowing down in the American economy in the period 1974–84 has been less marked than in Europe (cf. Table 3.1), but this can perhaps be explained by the favourable conditions under which the American economy is integrated into the world economy. These favourable conditions include greater resistance in the domestic markets to foreign goods and the privileged role of the dollar, which limits the effects of any external constraint, together with the technological supremacy of some of the new industries.

Japan is obviously a special case; this is due to structural reasons, in particular the importance that certain pre-capitalist economic activities retained until well into the 1970s (in 1973, non-wage earners represented a third of all employment, compared with only 20 per cent in France and 10 per cent in the United States at the same period). These internal characteristics made it possible for the Japanese economy to absorb in a quite unique way the fluctuations caused by the redistribution of world markets in the 1970s (cf. Sautter, 1979). Thus, despite a considerable reduction in growth rates (cf. Table 3.1), employment in manufacturing industry began to rise again after the sharp falls of the years between 1974 and 1978, while the share of manufacturing industry in total output maintained its upward tendency. It is thus not possible to speak of deindustrialization in the case of Japan, where growth rates after 1973 are comparable to those experienced by the other countries between 1960 and 1973. Only two forms of deindustrialization can therefore be distinguished, corresponding respectively to the experience of the United States and that of the European countries.

II Two general approaches to an explanation of de-industrialization

There are two types of explanation for the failure of manufacturing industry to maintain its role as an engine of growth; one is based on the conditions of the formation of demand, while the other relates to the conditions of the production process. This duality would seem a priori to make it possible to distinguish the main factors in the structural changes in the European economies, in which balance of payments constraints lead to a reduction in domestic demand, from those that underlie developments in the United States, which are mainly the result of a change in the conditions of production. However, the situation is not so clear-cut, and the debates on deindustrialization in Europe and the United States cite both types of argument.

The arguments which see reduced demand as the cause of the crisis identify deindustrialization with the inability of the manufacturing sector to relax the external constraint by balancing trade at a level that would permit sustained economic growth (cf. Singh, 1977). In other words, over and above the structural changes discussed above, the notion of deindustrialization underlines 'the progressive failure to achieve a sufficient surplus of exports over imports to keep the economy in external balance at full employment' (Blackaby, 1978, p. 263).This approach is directly inspired by the studies that link the dynamism of exports and growth differentials (Beckermann *et al.*, 1965; Kaldor, 1975; Lamfalussy, 1963).[1] Following in the tradition of Keynes (the importance of the autonomous component of demand), and particularly of Harrod (cf. Appendix VI), the supporters of these arguments attribute the poor performance of manufacturing industry and thus of the economy as a whole to the excessively high level of imports compared to exports.[2]

According to these approaches, the failure to balance increased imports with a corresponding extension of foreign markets is the cause of the reduction in demand for the products of domestic manufacturing industry. They thus stress the role of income elasticities.

On the other hand, those who see the cause of the present stagnation in a change in the conditions of production stress the effects of changes in the price of raw materials or production factors, or even developments in labour relations and opportunities for the use of capital. These analyses focus on the development of production functions, in which they attempt to find the cause of the reduction in productivity gains. In these approaches, this fall in productivity gains is considered to be the main indication of deindustrialization. This approach contains a great diversity of studies, from analyses of the effects of the rapid rise in oil prices (Bruno and Sachs, 1982), through examinations of the rates and orientations of investment (Baily, 1982; Bacon and Eltis, 1976), to discussions of workers' motivation (Weisskopf, Bowles, and Gordon, 1983).

This debate, in which the reduction in productivity gains is held to originate on the production side, flourishes, particularly in the United States, where the effect of an external constraint on growth appears less immediate. But the studies of the impact of changes in oil prices or of the reduction in investment in manufacturing industry caused by high interest rates concern all the developed industries. All these analyses attach great importance to prices in market adjustment mechanisms. In accordance with the principles of the international division of labour put forward by Ricardo, it is price elasticities that are stressed in the analysis and not income elasticities as emphasized by Kaldor (1978).

These two sets of arguments which use income effects on the one hand and price effects on the other to explain the trend towards deindustrialization are not of equal importance to all the countries. External constraints and changes in the conditions of production differ in significance according to the opportunities in each country for balancing its foreign trade and according to the general conditions of capital profitability and wages.

III The balance of payments and the balance of trade in manufactures

The need to made good a foreign trade deficit in order to bring the balance of payments into equilibrium is a function of the international credit available to each country and of the level of foreign indebtedness that it permits. Furthermore, the opportunities for adjusting the foreign trade balance through fluctuations in the exchange rate depend, among other things, on commitment to monetary agreements (e.g. the EMS or the gold exchange standard). In these two areas, the United States has an obvious advantage over the European countries.

The privileged role of the dollar in the world trade system means that the American economy is not forced to reduce its trade deficit through deflationary measures in order to bring its balance of payments into equilibrium. The United States thus benefited from the abolition of the gold standard at the beginning of the 1970s, which had been established at Bretton Woods immediately after the Second World War. In order to limit the destabilizing effects of currency speculation, the European countries, in the absence of any international monetary system, set up the European Monetary System at the end of the 1970s, in an attempt to stabilize exchange rates. The need to balance foreign trade in the medium term is a more direct constraint on growth for these European economies. The United Kingdom, which does not belong to the EMS, finds itself subject to other obligations in order to preserve the credit of the sterling zone in the face of the dollar, as the experience of the years between 1960 and 1970 showed.

Over and above the international power and status of each currency, the importance of the balance of trade in manufactures in the balance of payments as a whole depends on the balance of trade in services or primary products. Table 3.3 summarizes the share of the main headings in current balances of payments. It underlines the high levels of manufacturing surpluses in West Germany and Japan and the low levels of such surpluses in the United States and the United Kingdom. It is thus necessary to distinguish between those countries with plentiful natural resources (fossil energy reserves, agricultural potential) or income from their position in the international finance system or from tourism, which can make a large contribution to the balance of payments, and those which have to finance their imports of goods and services from a surplus in their balance of trade in manufactures. West Germany and Japan are classic examples of this latter category.[3]

This structuring of trade balances is not immutable. The contribution of non-manufacturing sectors such as agriculture or services to foreign trade may alter in the long term as a consequence of the reorganization of markets, such as the establishment of the Common Market. Nevertheless, it will be shown in Chapter 4 that this initial structure is relatively rigid in the case of the service sector. Only the discovery of natural resources, as in the Netherlands and the United Kingdom, can alter this trade structure in the short to medium term. The balances of trade in manufactures are thus very low for both the Netherlands and the United Kingdom (cf. Table 3.3). Indeed, the term 'Dutch disease' was

Table 3.3 Structure of the current balance of payments*

Balances in millions of ECUs	FRG 1973	FRG 1979	France 1973	France 1979	Italy 1973	Italy 1979	Netherlands 1973	Netherlands 1979	Belgium 1973	Belgium 1979	UK 1973	UK 1979	USA 1973	USA 1979	Japan 1973	Japan 1979
A. Trade balance	12,170	11,719	409	-1,525	-3,222	-683	813	-1,026	1,010	-3,473	-5,111	-5,275	707	-19,922	2,973	1,377
— balance in manufactured goods	35,276	76,470	2,680	17,840	6,033	32,550	-1,770	-7,120	3,570	4,300	4,920	3,060	-3,060	1,320	25,530	95,600
B. Services	-3,605	-7,697	2,204	8,250	951	4,336	1,210	123	184	1,954	4,048	7,850	8,319	23,967	-2,799	-6,911
C. Unrequited transfers	-4,757	-8,465	-1,408	-2,938	201	337	-50	-593	-253	-708	-881	-3,500	-3,332	-4,403	-242	-801
D. (A+B+C) Current balance	3,809	-4,443	1,205	3,788	-2,069	3,991	1,974	-1,496	941	-2,227	-1,945	-925	5,695	-358	-68	-6,336

Source: Balance of payments Eurostat, 1983; IMF Supplement to Trade Statistics No. 4, 1982.

* The current balance is made up of balances that are by their nature subject to variations according to economic circumstances. In order to compensate for this instability without presenting whole sets of annual balances, the years 1973 and 1979, in both of which the world economy experienced major shocks, were chosen to represent the 'structure' of the current balance of payments. Explanations of the headings are given in Appendix VI.

1 ECU 1973 = $1.23   1 ECU 1979 = $1.37

coined to describe the current weak state of manufacturing industry in both these countries (Bruno, 1982, p. 1). In the case of Holland and the United Kingdom, the initial income effect works in partial conjunction with a price effect. At the end of the 1960s, the external constraint manifested itself in the need to put a brake on growth in order to reduce the level of imports. Harrod's account of the unfavourable evolution of income elasticities seemed to apply very well. At the end of the 1970s, the income from natural gas and oil had the effect of increasing domestic demand; however, this new demand tended to be directed more towards services and imported manufactured goods than towards the products of domestic manufacturing industry. This new shift in the composition of the domestic market reflects the unfavourable trend in price elasticities which greatly reduces the opportunities for growth offered by the new energy sources. This shift is not simply the result of income elasticities of demand that favour the service sector rather than manufacturing industry. The price effect of the higher levels of profitability for investment in the energy and tertiary sectors must also be taken into account. This is analogous to the crowding-out effects mentioned by Bacon and Eltis (1976) in relation to the shift in financial investment in the United Kingdom towards non-industrial activities.

Appendix VI presents an estimate for the period 1960–79 of the elasticity of each economy to variations in world growth (income effects). Of particular note is the great difference over this long period in the capacities of the Dutch and British economies to react to world trade. The same is true of Japan and the United States. These differences may reflect the importance of price effects.

IV   The fall in productivity and changes in the conditions of production

The evolution of the profitability of industrial capital lies at the heart of those analyses that link the relative decline of manufacturing industry to a change in the conditions of production. Studies that see this change as the cause of the reduction in productivity gains refer either to the immediate shock effects or to long-term changes in the price of inputs or of labour and capital.

The sudden increase in the price of raw materials at the beginning of the 1970s belongs to the first category. The impact of these various shocks on the price of inputs affected the relative advantage of different production sectors and thus productivity in the manufacturing sectors.

But the fact that these shocks occurred almost simultaneously at the beginning of the 1970s and were closely linked to the disappearance of the international monetary system means that they cannot be seen as the sole cause of a relative industrial decline, the first indications of which were observed as early as the 1960s in many countries (Bruno, 1982, p. 2).

It is thus all the more interesting to compare the signs of a weakening of the industrial sectors with the fall in profitability that began to appear during the 1960s. Appendix VII shows that the fall in profitability occurred at roughly the same time as the weakening of the manufacturing sectors (as shown in Table 3.2). Such a lasting fall in profitability is, a priori, the result either of changes in the conditions of investment or of changes in the nature and payment of labour.

Most analyses of the fall in profitability have attempted in particular to clarify the changes in the conditions of investment.

According to one set of hypotheses, conditions of investment were particularly advantageous during the 1950s and 1960s, both in terms of fiscal policy (Sargent, 1982) and in terms of industrial structures (importance of monopolies, introduction of machinery leading to great savings in manpower (Glyn, 1982)).[4]

According to another set of studies, the geopolitical and technological upheavals of the 1980s should be implicated: the steep rises in the price of inputs, technological progress and the instability of the financial situation have contributed to the reduction in the life of machinery and the disruption of financial calculations. According to Baily (1981), this acceleration in the depreciation of capital, which is not taken into account by statistics and economic studies, affects the profitability of capital.

It is thus very difficult to assess the various factors which may have influenced investment decisions and led to the weakening of manufacturing industry. Yet these arguments underlie the various policies for assisting investment.

On another level, changes in the conditions of labour utilization have often been put foward as a primary cause of the fall in the profitability of manufacturing industry. This concerns both the payment of labour and its efficiency.

One of the most frequently mentioned factors, the sharp rises in wage levels at the end of the 1960s and beginning of the 1970s, cannot be used as a general explanation (cf. Sachs, 1979). On the one hand, this rapid growth in wages was of real significance in only a few European countries, such as France and Italy, where deindustrialization appeared later than in most other countries. On the other hand, the anti-inflation policies of the 1970s and 1980s, the aim of which has been to restrict the increase in the share of wages in value added, have not led to the restoration of earlier growth rates in productivity. However, wage costs are still regarded as a major problem in many industrial policies.

In complete contrast, Weisskopf, Bowles and Gordon (1983) see the relatively low growth of wages in the United States as an explanation for decreases in productivity. In this study, wages are only one of the factors determining the motivation to work, and it is the lack of motivation on the part of American workers, linked to a worsening of the balance between advantages and disadvantages in the situation of wage earners since the mid-1960s, that accounts for a large part of the reduction in productivity (once the changes in capital labour ratios have been taken into account). This questioning of workers' motivation suggests an interpretation of the reduction of growth in the economy as a whole that is usually applied only to single sectors in decline.

The main characteristics of the slowing down of industrial growth

This survey of the various analyses of the weakening of manufacturing industry strengthens the hypothesis that the cause lies in specific combinations, different for each country, of income effects and price effects. This may well call into question our hypothesis that income effects played a dominant role in the European economies and that price effects played a leading role in the United States.

This variety of causes of the present reduction in productivity gains shows through in all the analyses. Nordhaus (1982), starting from a simple formalization, highlighted the possibility that considerable demand effects may explain the reduction in productivity gains. According to these estimates, the demand (or income) effects vary widely from one country to another; they are particularly predominant in France, West Germany and Japan, but of little significance in the United States. Nordhaus's estimates tend to confirm the hypotheses set out above, but other estimates suggest that these conclusions should be qualified. Bruno (1982, p. 2), with the same aim in mind, used a more sophisticated production function to estimate the respective shares of price factors and demand in the fall in productivity gains. According to these studies, the average fall of 2.16 per cent in productivity gains in the OECD countries over the period 1974–80 is made up of an income effect of 0.87 and of a price effect of 1.24 per cent. These results confirm the importance of the two types of effects but also reveal that

Table 3.4 Slow growth of demand and the slowing down of productivity gains: some estimates

	Source	W. Nordhaus (1982)		M. Bruno (1982b)	
	Period	Evolution between 1960–73 and 1973–8		Evolution between 1955–73 and 1974–80	
	Concept of productivity	Total factor productivity		Total factor productivity	
	Method	Cobb–Douglas production function with assumptions on coefficients of returns to scale		Production function with factor inputs	
	Country	Estimate for all countries		Estimate for all countries	
Country		Slowdown of productivity gains	Share attributable to the evolution of demand	Slowdown of productivity gains	Share attributable to the evolution of demand
			(a) / (b)		
W. Germany		−1.0	30% / 90%	−0.95	69%
France		−1.7	18% / 53%	−1.84	47%
Italy		−4.3	9% / 28%	−2.37	39%
UK		−2.4	13% / 38%	−2.05	32%
USA		−1.9	11% / 26%	−1.34	46%
Canada		−2.1	14% / 38%	−2.66	27%
Japan		−5.6	14% / 41%	−3.30	66%
Belgium				−1.96	30%
Netherlands				−1.79	46%
Sweden				−3.38	19%

(a) with coefficient of return to scale of 1.1
(b) with coefficient of return to scale of 1.3

the income effect is very similar in all countries (except for Japan, where this income effect is 2.19 per cent) and that the price effects are very different, ranging from 0.69 per cent in the United States to 1.34 per cent and to 2.31 per cent in Italy (see Table 3.4). The links of causality are so intertwined that it is difficult to sort out which type of effect takes precedence over the other. It has to be assumed that the two types of effects came into operation in different ways in each country.

It is a characteristic of the great structural crises that they involve, in addition to the common factor of a reduction in growth, factors specific to each country. This partly explains the diversity of the research into the causes of the reductions in productivity gains in manufacturing industry.

It is sufficient to note here that our initial hypothesis, according to which the reduction in productivity gains was caused by income effects in the European countries and by price effects in the United States, must be qualified. The possible causes of the weakness of manufacturing industry are a priori more varied. Consequently, the effects on economic growth of a reallocation of resources towards the tertiary sector will also be more diverse. This diversity will be examined further in Chapters 4, 5 and 6, when the constraints on the extension of the markets for services and on their profitability will be discussed.

It will be useful beforehand to complete our survey of the multiple dimensions of the phenomenon of deindustrialization by considering the contrasts that arise within the manufacturing industry of a single country as the result of the coexistence of declining and expanding sectors. To the essentially macroeconomic analyses discussed above must be added analyses based on a sectoral approach to industrial decline. They start from the premise that the various sectors within the manufacturing industry of any one country evolve in different ways.

V Declining and expanding sectors

Sectoral analyses of deindustrialization often see the primary cause of the decline of manufacturing industry in changes in the conditions of production. These approaches occupy an important place in the analyses of the rate of industrial growth in countries like the United States, where there are few signs of a decline in manufacturing industry as a whole (cf. Table 3.2). Indeed, the Economic Report of the President of February 1984 denied the existence of the phenomenon of de-industrialization and stressed instead the coexistence of declining and expanding sectors, seeing this as a stage in the process of reallocating resources.

The arguments that locate the role of manufacturing industry as an engine of growth at the level of the economy as a whole have been discussed in full. Sectoral analyses do not invalidate the conclusions reached above on the dual origin of the reduction in the growth rate of manufacturing industry. However, studies of declining industrial sectors tend to concentrate particularly on the link between industrial decline and changes in the conditions of production. They make it possible to distinguish between those changes in the supply side that apply to the economy as a whole and those that reflect the ability of each industry to adapt to the new conditions of competition in the world economy.

The decline or expansion of industries must be linked to the development of the international division of labour. In the developed economies, which have high labour costs but also a high level of technological know-how, specialization works in favour of high technology production. This concerns both the production of new products and the use of new production processes.

The product cycle highlighted by Vernon (1966) provides a basis for analysing this specialization in the case of the manufacture of new products. According to Vernon's product cycle, there is an initial phase of innovation, in which markets expand quickly and developed countries keep most of the production process on their own territory. In a later stage, when production has become a matter of routine and when products have been standardized and markets stabilized, production tends to be shifted to developing countries where salaries are lower and the production equipment more recent. The industries in question then enter a phase of maturity, in which competition, based essentially on prices, leads to their decline.

But the specialization in the developed economies, made possible by their expertise in new technologies, means not only that they can produce new products (electronic goods, new materials, etc.), but also modernize old products and develop and transform old production techniques. The capacity for innovation thus affects all products and production processes. Hence, Vernon's product cycle would appear to be partially reversible. This considerably reduces the validity of an a priori distinction between declining and expanding industries. Indeed, from this point of view, it is impossible totally to write off an industry. The opportunities opened up by changes in products and production processes must first be assessed. Studies like those by Abernathy *et al*.

(1983) on the American car industry or those by CEPII (1983) on all the developed countries have attempted to show that new production methods or the modernization of products could lead to new growth in declining industries. The notion that these industries no longer have any future once they have reached their stage of maturity is thus partially refuted. For Abernathy *et al.* (1983), the product and the method of production cannot be separated. Product standardization is followed by the standardization of production processes. But, conversely, a transformation of production techniques brought about by a major technological revolution like computerization facilitates innovation and product modernization. This leads not only to lower costs but also to renewed product differentiation, through which technological advantages become obvious. This constant regeneration of products, which is the fruit of overall specialization in high technology products, would make it possible to reproduce at least partially the conditions for growth in the initial phase of Vernon's cycle.

These studies do not claim that it is possible totally to revitalize declining industries. The opportunities for extending markets opened up by the modernization of 'old' products are a priori variable. For this reason, it is necessary to distinguish between major and minor innovations, judged in terms of their impact on the growth of the economy as a whole. Nevertheless, these studies reduce the significance of those analyses that attribute the difficulties of manufacturing industry to a phase of adaptation to an international division of labour which is presented as an exogenous factor for each national economy.

This questioning of the dualist theories that reduce deindustrialization to a simple contrast between declining and expanding sectors is strengthened if the difficulties encountered by the new industries in the past ten years are taken into account. The relatively few opportunities for employment, growth and productivity offered by these industries indicate the reality of industrial decline. Table 3:5 underlines both the extent of job losses in the declining industries and the relatively few jobs created in the so-called expanding sectors.

The massive decline in employment during the 1960s in traditional industries such as textiles, clothing and leather affected between a quarter and a third of those employed in those industries in Europe (but more than half in Belgium and less than a tenth in Italy). The loss of jobs in the iron and steel industries had also begun in West Germany and the United Kingdom. During the same period, the capital goods industries (industrial and office machines, electrical machinery and means of transport) created enough jobs for there to be a net increase in employment in manufacturing industry as a whole, except in the United Kingdom and the Netherlands (in the first case, this was the result of the early decline of the motor industry and in the second of huge job losses in the textile industries). Manufacturing industry in the United States has created a particularly large number of jobs (3,335 million in thirteen years).

As far as the period after 1973 is concerned (although the reversal of trends took place at different times in different countries, cf. Table 3.1), job losses in the declining sectors have continued and employment in the capital goods industries has also fallen, except for certain products in the United States. This new conjecture is reflected in a marked decline in employment in manufacturing industry as a whole (cf. Section 1).

These two stages in the development of employment in manufacturing industry cannot thus be reduced to a simple reallocation of the work force from declining to expanding industries. The entire process of industrial growth is affected.

These sectoral analyses also have the advantage of bringing out the local aspects of the problem of manufacturing industry. The decline of a particular sector tends to be geographically very concentrated in a few areas. The impact of changes in one sector on other activities becomes clear at the local level. It is estimated that the direct job losses in manufacturing industry should be multiplied by 2 or 3 in order for the indirect effect on employment in local subcontracting firms and service industries to be accurately assessed. The problems in the iron and steel, textile, shipbuilding and motor industries have laid waste entire local labour markets, while the jobs created may well be in very different areas. This local dimension tends to exacerbate employment problems.

On the sectoral level, it is as if what is known as the labour market is no longer capable of carrying out in a socially acceptable way the traditional reallocations of labour. In a stage of growth in which manufacturing industry is playing its role as an engine of growth, the medium to long-term reductions in employment in the sectors undergoing reorganization are carried out either by natural wastage or by attracting labour to the expanding sectors. Redundancies are the exception rather than the rule. The following examples of such changes are remarkable in retrospect for the number of job losses involved. Between 1963 and 1973, the number of British Rail employees fell from 477,000 to 230,000, with two-thirds of the losses being accounted for by natural wastage and retirement. Between 1960 and 1970, the number of British miners fell by more than 300,000 (from 602,000 in

Table 3.5 Changes in employment over the years: all manufacturing sectors are affected (in thousands)

	Code NACE-CLIO	30 Manufactured products	13 Minerals and ferrous and non-ferrous metals	21 Industrial and agricultural machinery	23 Office and data processing machines	25 Electrical equipment and supplies	28 Means of transport	42 Textiles, leather goods, shoes, clothing
W. Germany	1960	9,242	590	1,016	237	904	484	1,565
	1960–73	+221	−134	+150	+72	+267	+240	−461
	1973–82	−1,526	−106	−117	−51	−165	+47	−429
	1982	7,937	350	1,049	258	1,006	771	675
France	1960	5,189	273	374*	118*	367	612	1,120
	1960–73	+575	−12	+15	+12	+106	+77	−252
	1973–82	−743	−66	−58	−1	−8	−36	−270
	1982	5,021	195	331	129	465	653	598
UK	1960	8,055	489	884	195	678	1,090	1,381
	1960–73	−593	−79	+14	+19	+48	−192	−318
	1973–82	−2,057	−165	−181	−50	−150	−199	−364
	1982	5,405	245	717†	164†	576†	699†	699†

	Code NIPA	13	18	20		21 + 24	22 + 23	29 + 36 + 30
Italy	1960	4,947	216	275	66	220	225	1,555
	1960–73	+563	+42	+95	+17	+146	+145	–95
	1973–82	–51	+19	+20	–3	+6	–15	–66
	1982	5,459	277	390	80	372	355	1,384
Netherlands	1960	1,163	26	80*	18*	131*	87*	254
	1960–73	–12	+12	–2	0	–8	+1	–133
	1973–82	236	–4	–10	–2	–19	–17	–70
	1982	915	34	68	16	104	71	51
Belgium	1960	1,056	98	87*	5*	81*	80*	250
	1960–73	+59	–5	+2	0	+7	+4	–44
	1973–82	–301	–27	–24	–1	–18	–2	–101
	1982	814	66	65	4	70	82	105

	Code NIPA	13	18	20	21 + 24	22 + 23	29 + 36 + 30
USA	1960	16,755	1,169	1,472	1,853	1,674	2,516
	1960–73	+3,335	+95	+619	+672	+250	+219
	1973–82	–1,230	–336	+162	+211	–181	–598
	1982	18,860	928	2,253	2,736	1,743	2,137

Sources: SOEC; U.S. Department of Commerce
* 1970 † 1981

1960 to 287,000 in 1970), with about 60,000 redundancies. Finally, between 1950 and 1970, the number of railway employees in the United States fell from one million to half a million, with hardly any redundancies (cf. OECD, 1982).[5] In the period of full employment in the 1960s, job losses in the traditional sectors such as textiles, clothing and leather were high: 50 per cent of jobs in these sectors were lost in Holland, 33 per cent in West Germany and the United Kingdom and 20 per cent in France.

In a period of economic stagnation, when manufacturing industry is no longer able to redistribute the labour force from declining to expanding sectors, the reallocation of manpower is going to be slowed down in relation to needs and will also be carried out to an increasing extent by means of redundancies. This new inability of manufacturing industry to guarantee the mobility of labour between sectors is thus a characteristic of deindustrialization.

The mobility of labour and of capital is fundamental to any explanation both of regional imbalances in employment and overall employment needs. Changes in this mobility are both a cause of the reduction in productivity gains and a consequence of economic stagnation. Once again, two arguments oppose or complement each other, calling into question the low level of labour mobility or the excessively high level of capital mobility.

From one point of view, one of the major characteristics of economic growth in the post-war period is the increasing rigidity of employment conditions. According to this argument, this increased rigidity, linked to the development of social welfare systems and the contractualization of industrial relations, reduced the opportunities for reallocating manpower between sectors and between firms. In the crisis, faced with fluctuating markets in which the need to adapt is even stronger, the need for greater flexibility is stressed even more. The low level of labour mobility is considered to be one of the causes of unemployment. Set out in this direct way, this argument has certain similarities with the debates of the 1920s and 1930s on the damaging effects of unemployment benefit. This historical reference is a warning not to put too much emphasis on the real impact of a lower level of labour mobility on the general level of unemployment.

On the other hand, the main cause of the lack of equilibrium in the labour market is linked to the increased mobility of capital. There are several reasons for this increased mobility. The first one is connected to Adam Smith's law and the development of new technologies. The development of transport, communication and financial intermediation increased the size of the markets, facilitating the division of labour and thus the transfer of production to other locations. The second is linked to the history of industrial relations and the attempts of entrepreneurs to escape from restrictions on the utilization of labour by constantly diversifying their sources of supply in the labour market as soon as stagnation in the markets leads them to look to reduced costs in order to maintain their market shares.

In a way, this aspect of the utilization of the labour force in a crisis brings us back to the remarks above on the lower level of mobility in the labour force. The increased instability of employment and the development of non-standard job forms, such as temporary or casual work, are part of this strategy. In purely sectoral terms, it is interesting to note to what extent certain practices of labour utilization which were used exclusively in the 'competitive' sectors have tended to be extended to other, more monopolistic activities.

According to Bluestone and Harrison (1982), the increased mobility of capital is one of the prime causes of the serious employment problems in traditional industrial areas. The new technical possibilities offered by a greater division of production processes and their transfer to new locations open the way to the internationalization of production. These authors cite the case of the Ford Escort, which is made from parts produced in sixteen different countries. The choices of production location made by multinational firms are based on slightly contradictory criteria: they need to remain close to the large consumer markets, while at the same time protecting the autonomy of their production lines from the uncertainties of national economies and exploiting the advantageous conditions of labour utilization offered by certain countries or areas. It is within this context that Bluestone and Harrison account for the shift in employment from the north-east of America towards the Mexican frontier, where wages are a third of those in the north. There is thus a cumulative process in which the increased mobility of capital exacerbates the problems caused in the traditional industrial regions by changes in the markets.

However, the analysis of the crisis in manufacturing industry based on the contrast between declining and expanding sectors should not simply be replaced by an analysis based on the contrast between declining and expanding regions. The studies by Hulten and Schwab (1984) have shown that the reduction of productivity gains in the United States affected manufacturing industry in the north-east (the 'Snow Belt') as well as those in the south (the 'Sun Belt'). In fact, the transfer of manufacturing industry towards the south, through the impetus given by interest groups in the north-east and Midwest (cf. also Olson, 1982), is part of the permanent search for cheap labour within the United States. The development of modern communications and the world economic crisis accelerated the transfer of manufacturing industry towards the south rather than initiated it.

Service industries are playing a new and major role in this attempt to increase the mobility of capital and labour. At the same time, the extension of service activities offers an opportunity on the local level to use capital and labour in a situation protected from external competition. In this sense, the development of profitable service industries might seem to be a means of recreating the conditions for growth in the developed economies. It remains to be seen to what extent the development of the service economy may actually provide a solution to the stagnation of demand and the apparent inability of productive systems to adapt to new conditions, problems which are reflected in the phenomenon of deindustrialization. The next two chapters will be an attempt to clarify these points. Firstly, however, this analysis of the diverse forms of deindustrialization will be concluded with an examination of the opportunities for industrial policies to solve the problems.

VI   Renaissance or decline of industrial policies?

The slowing down of the growth process in the industrial economies is not the only effect of the decline of manufacturing industry as an engine of growth. It also undermines the foundations of past economic development through its effects on the formation of demand and the organization of production. These changes, which affect for example the distribution of purchasing powers and the opportunities for using economies of scale to create large productivity gains, cannot easily be reversed. The concern expressed, particularly in the United States (cf. Kuttner, 1983 and Thurow, 1984), about the decline of the middle income class and the argument that there are physical limits to the scale of production (cf. Gold, 1981, Giarini and Louberge, 1978) reflect anxieties of this nature.

In this context, the use of limited or *ad hoc* industrial policies in an attempt to halt the relative decline of manufacturing industry can be of only limited effectiveness in stimulating economic growth. Everything depends in fact on what is understood by industrial policy.

A problem of definition

The most widely accepted definition of industrial policy, found for example in the work of the various OECD working parties on the question, includes the whole range of microeconomic structural adjustments, i.e. all interventions made in favour of expanding or declining economic activities. This definition stresses the microeconomic nature of the measures taken and the conjunctural conditions under which decisions are taken. However, there is not always a very clear distinction between the interventions made as a result of industrial policy decisions and certain normal macroeconomic policy measures. This is particularly true in the case of fiscal and trade policy. But this approach to industrial policies is strictly pragmatic. Industrial policies can also be described in terms of their prospects for action in the long term. Whatever the initial intentions may be, the full effects of a transformation in the structures of an economy will be fully felt only in the long term and will be difficult to identify. Hesselman (1983) rightly stresses this dual characteristic of industrial policies: they are essentially long-term measures and their results are uncertain. Moreover, a certain degree of confusion is inevitable if the whole rag-bag of state interventions in manufacturing industry is classified as industrial policy. It is thus widely accepted that the notion of industrial policy refers to active and coherent policies affecting the entire relationship between state and manufacturing industry. Magaziner and Reich (1982) and Thurow (1983), for example, use the term in this sense to advocate an industrial policy for the United States based on a genuine decision on sectoral development. However, we should not allow this line of thinking to lead to confusion between industrial policy and economic planning, even indicative planning. Certain authors have thus suggested that industrial policy was the weak link in indicative planning in France (cf. Armstrong, Glyn and Harrison, 1984). In the final analysis, only the Japanese experience gives rise to complete agreement on the actual existence of a true industrial policy (if not on its effectiveness, cf. Schultze, 1983). The relative heterogeneity of these approaches to industrial policies is reduced as soon as an attempt is made to link macroeconomic and sectoral policies in an historical context.

Industrial policies in their historical context

The pattern of state interventions in manufacturing industry during such different periods as the immediate post-war years, the booming

1960s and the present time of crisis cannot be understood in the same way. In the post-war period of reconstruction, general policy and industrial policy were closely linked in most of the countries that had suffered great destruction during the War. The aim of the general policy of the time was to rebuild the productive capacity of each country.

In the 1950s and 1960s, on the other hand, Keynesian policies of regulating internal demand dominated; measures to stimulate demand alternated with measures to control inflation (cf. Maddison, 1967). The limited and localized nature of state interventions in manufacturing industry was common to most countries, even if in a few countries such as France and Italy regional development policies were more wide-spread. It was largely during this period of transition that industrial policies acquired their present image. The increasing openness of economies to foreign trade within the framework of GATT and the Treaty of Rome gradually altered the initial conditions. Nation states found themselves forced, in the face of the strengths and weaknesses of their economic partners, to draw up industrial strategies.

The beginning of the world economic crisis in 1973 marked a turning point. It had become obvious that the openness of economies to foreign trade and the collapse of the system of fixed exchange rates set up at Bretton Woods had made it impossible to operate strictly national policies for sustaining demand. Structural adjustments became, *de facto*, important elements of economic policy. However, they were microeconomic and conjunctural in nature, which, together with the impact of sudden, sharp rises in the price of oil, made it impossible for any overall consistency to emerge. An OECD committee was set up at the time to compare the adjustment policies of member countries, but found itself unable to make an overall assessment of these policies (OECD, 1975), because the measures taken were so diverse and over-lapped to a large extent with the fiscal and trade policies.

As the crisis deepened, the need was felt to make adjustment policies more consistent. Studies carried out by the OECD led in June 1978 to a recommendation by the Council entitled 'Some general guidelines for a gradual transition to more positive adjustment policies'.[6] This was reflected at the beginning of the 1980s in explicit attempts to incorporate into a coherent, overall strategy the structural changes made necessary by the new conditions of trade and the opportunities opened up by new technologies. Two types of economic policy emerged as a result. One was based essentially on macroeconomic policy measures (supply side policy), while the other attempted to draw up an overall industrial policy based on the development of chosen sectors.

In order to understand the reasons for the polarization of economic policy options after ten years of economic crisis, it is necessary to recall the main elements of the debate on industrial policies that took place at the end of the 1970s.

Industrial policy choices in a time of crisis

As early as the beginning of the 1970s, when manufacturing industry in certain European countries was already beginning to decline relatively, it became apparent that it would be necessary to adapt various manufacturing sectors to the new world market.

Many different measures have been adopted under these industrial policies. Specific aids to investment are the ones most commonly used: the practices of directly subsidizing running costs, of guaranteeing markets by means of preferential state purchasing and of taking protectionist measures are more constrained by the international agreements on free trade such as GATT and the Treaty of Rome.

Nationalization and the acquiring of state interest in firms, which were measures favoured in the immediate post-war period in public utilities such as transport, communications and energy and in financial intermediation, have been the exception rather than the rule in the early stages of a crisis that is largely perceived as being caused by temporary present economic conditions.

Two basic concepts underlie decisions on industrial policy. The first is that the decline of manufacturing industry represents a transitional phase, in which the developed economies will withdraw from the declining sectors and develop the sectors of the future. In this case, the aim of an industrial policy is to facilitate a rapid withdrawal from the declining sectors and to encourage the growth of new industries.

The second is that all sectors of manufacturing industry need renovation and expansion. In this case, the aim of an industrial policy is to establish the conditions for this modernization, in particular in those industries in which market forces mean that there is not enough time for 'spontaneous' modernization.

In both cases, there is a desire to accelerate or slow down the process of structural change in manufacturing industry within a general framework regulated by market forces. These two policy directions result in fairly similar measures as far as the 'new' industries are concerned. The question of these 'new' industries is in fact the only one on which there is at least some degree of unanimity in favour of an industrial policy. Nevertheless, it implies, as do most industrial policy measures, that there is a fault in the mechanisms of the market, as is underlined in a critical fashion by Lawrence (1984).

The OECD working party on adjustment policies (which is not very favourably disposed towards anything that disturbs the smooth functioning of the markets) recognizes four reasons for intervening in support of the new industries:

(1) the ineptness of private capital in taking into account the long-term interests of society;
(2) the wide diffusion of the advantages of an innovation without any great benefit for the innovator;
(3) the uncertainty and scope of plans for innovation;
(4) the need to end an international monopoly in an area of high technology.

However, it might be pointed out that in economies in which large firms play a dominant role, the private sector would, a priori, seem capable of taking a large share of the risks involved in the development of new industries (points (1), (2), and (3) above). Thus, the main reason for state intervention would appear to be the desire to provide the foundations for the development of high technology industries on a national level.

The universal nature of the measures taken in support of the new industries reflects the persistence of industrial nationalism.[7] But for the institutions that co-ordinate the workings of the international markets (GATT, EEC, OECD), structural adjustment policies, particularly those directed at declining industries, are little short of heresy.

The two policy orientations discussed above are also to be found in policies towards declining industries. From one point of view, the measures taken should above all be aimed at reducing social costs in order to hasten the disappearance of declining industries. From the other point of view, the main purpose of any measures taken should be to modernize the industries under threat.

In practice, two considerations tend to lead to a certain degree of similarity in the industrial policies that are actually followed. The first is geopolitical in nature: it is very rare for a national economy totally to abandon industries considered to be of strategic importance. The iron and steel industry is a striking example, both in Europe and the United States. This is an indication of the economic nationalism mentioned above. The second consideration takes into account the scale of job losses and social changes caused by the modernization of traditional industries. In fact, when the crisis affects traditional manufacturing areas (such as the north and east of France, the Midlands and west coast of Scotland in the United Kingdom and the north-east of the United States) or highly concentrated activities such as the car industry, the direct and indirect effects in terms of unemployment and income go far beyond the local level. Faced with such serious situations, governments initially tend to intervene in support of the ailing sectors. Examples of this approach include the protection of markets for steel, the multifibre textile plan in Europe and financial subsidies for Chrysler in the United States and British Leyland in the United Kingdom. The persistence of the crisis and the pressing needs of the moment had led by the end of the 1970s and the beginning of the 1980s to a rethink of these interventionist measures.

Towards a polarization of policies on structural change

The OECD report mentioned above is evidence of this new attitude. It both recognizes that economic crisis leads to greater state intervention in manufacturing industry and also recommends that the number and scope of such interventions should be reduced to the minimum.[8] This is a particular reference to support for declining industries. Macroeconomic policies are held to be more consistent and thus preferable to industrial policy measures whose microeconomic and conjunctural nature is stressed. It was within this context that positive adjustment policies were recommended (OECD, 1983a). In fact, the scope left for both policies on structural change depends on the forcefulness of a new political context and on the weight of past relationships between state and manufacturing industry.

It should be noted first of all that the general tendency in the initial stages of a crisis to increase state intervention both in the new industries and the declining sectors was accompanied by clear differences between countries in the scope and nature of these interventions. It is true that it is very difficult to compare the various measures taken. The levels of intervention differ largely according to the degree of centralization in state decision-making, for example. There is a high degree of decentralization in West Germany and, in particular, in the United States, where the variety of industrial policy measures from one state to another limits the significance of any overall assessment of industrial policy (cf. Bellon, 1984).

State intervention in manufacturing industry is generally the result both of a national tradition (or historical experience) of relationships between state and industry[9] and of the degree of 'liberalness' in the particular government of the time.

The present period of economic stagnation has lasted so long that it has created the conditions for a questioning of earlier relationships between state and manufacturing industry. As a result, past practices and traditions seem to have less influence in political decisions. The destructive effects of stagnation have opened the way to a reformulation of the role of the state in the economy. The nationalization of new industries in France by the first Socialist Government and the privatization of public utilities such as British Telecom by the Thatcher Government in the United Kingdom are examples of this. In other words, the extent of state intervention in manufacturing industry has increased in France while it has decreased in the United Kingdom. This degree of variability has not been seen before. It is evidence of the latitude that exists for policy options in this second phase of the crisis; it may also reflect a desire to stop industrial policy being simply a response to immediate needs, whether this means solving a local employment problem or maintaining a national production capacity in a particular industry.

The decisions taken on industrial policy in the United Kingdom and France (if such different approaches can both be covered by this term) thus reflect in two very different ways the same desire to escape from this pragmatism. This desire to change the purely conjunctural nature of industrial policy and to gain control over the changes taking place in manufacturing industry was the main motive for the nationalization programme in France and the preparation of the Ninth National Plan. This experiment will be discussed in more detail later. In contrast, the British Government passed the Industrial Development Act of 1982, which put restrictions on the scope for state intervention in manufacturing industry. This withdrawal by the state is in sharp contrast to the growing interventionism of the Labour Government after 1975 (cf. Stout, 1979).

The same is true of President Reagan's supply side policy. It is presented as a consistent response, based on market mechanisms, to the need to adjust the productive system. However, nothing has been done to alter one of the main characteristics of 'industrial policy' in the United States, which, as is stressed by Reich (1983), is still based on a research and development programme of which the Federal administration pays half the cost. The desire to make adjustment policies more consistent is often accompanied by changes in the ideological framework (Reaganomics in the States, Thatcherism in the United Kingdom, 'modernism' in France). This search for consistency raises the question of harmonizing structural adjustment policies and general macroeconomic policies.

Industrial policies and their critics

For the advocates of the market economy, it is all the more imperative for governments to resist local and conjunctural pressures to intervene in manufacturing industry since the remedy may well be worse than the sickness.

This is a classic criticism and questions in particular the ability of governments to choose which industries to help (see, for example, Schultze, 1983). The problem is not simply that of choosing between those industries that should gain and those that should lose, but of an inability to make explicit the criteria on which the various measures of support are based, while market mechanisms dominate at the level of the world economy. Any new infringement of the regulatory principles of the market can only, according to these criticisms, increase the costs of adapting to the specializations forced on the economy by the world economy. State intervention in manufacturing industry should be carried out only by means of the standard macroeconomic mechanisms used in economic policy for intervening in the markets. Advocates of a restructuring of the supply side based directly on market forces thus give greater importance to fiscal and monetary policy. These more radical positions are reflected less in the macroeconomic measures taken than in the ability of the governments in question to resist demands for intervention made by protectionist lobbies or local political authorities.

Paradoxically, a similar demand for a long-term strategy could be used to assess the more radical approaches to active industrial policies. The aim of those who advocate an active industrial policy is to draw up an overall plan for sectoral development, and then use it as a basis for decisions on intervention. Local pressures and current economic difficulties, therefore, should not be the main reason for government support. Reich (1983) has suggested as an alternative to Reagan's adjustment policy an industrial policy that would be drawn up in discussions between workers and management within the framework of a National Economic Policy Board (cf. Richet, 1984).

The French experience after 1981 has revealed the difficulties of initiating and then developing such a debate. The list of companies to be nationalized and the ways in which the programme was to be carried out had been the subject of an earlier political agreement.[10] The implementation of this agreement in 1982 was not based on a redefined industrial policy. Indeed, such a policy had not been drawn up, not even to the extent of laying down guidelines for the newly nationalized companies or drawing up plans for sectoral development.[11] The needs of struggling industries such as iron and steel, shipbuilding, chemicals and the motor industry could not be disregarded simply because of the priority given to the electronics industries. In the spring of 1983, the Government declared that the only aim of the new nationalized concerns was to be profitable and that the resources of the sectoral plans would be mobilized for interventions in response to the immediate needs of those sectors in difficulty.

Obviously the conditions underlying the indicative planning of the period between 1950 and 1965 had altered significantly by 1982. The modernist ideology, which had at the time succeeded in coordinating efforts in support of a well-defined development plan, was no longer able to direct industrial policy in a medium-sized economy largely integrated into the system of world trade (cf. Petit, 1984). The French experience is not a condemnation of active industrial policies, but it has revealed the limits of such policies for a number of industries subject to the essentially commercial logic of international trade.

An active policy of intervention may lead to a reshaping of the fabric of industrial activity, including changes in management, redefinitions of the boundaries between industries and changes in investment opportunities. These upheavals constitute a new deal. However, the logic behind the development of these activities remains commercial. In the event, it will be the foreign markets which will determine whether the decisions made were in fact well founded.

In particular, these industrial policies do not appear to provide a direct solution for unemployment. By any calculation, the growth in employment in manufacturing industry is still very modest and is more likely merely to fall less rapidly or to stagnate. As a result, it is difficult to gain national agreement on policies that will no longer guarantee employment.[12] The alternatives are not sufficiently well defined to make job losses acceptable.

In order to obtain widespread support for any sectoral development plan, its direct and indirect implications for employment must be made clear. Industrial policies often go no further than offering faster growth, without specifying their link with the service activities that create jobs. On the other hand, certain employment policies put forward by the IFO in Germany or the Industrial Development Act in the United Kingdom rely solely on a reorganization of tertiary employment. It is nevertheless obvious that employment policy cannot rely solely on a plan linking the growth of the various sectors of the economy. To a certain extent, the success of industrial policies depends on their being extended to spheres of activity that are less directly constrained by the workings of the international markets.

This would enable supply side measures and those taken to stimulate demand to be linked. The analysis of the demand for services in Chapters 4 and 5 will make clear the conditions for this coordination of sectoral policies (Chapter 6).

Notes

1. The theories of export-led growth initially concerned the problems of developing economies (Myrdal, 1957, Nurkse, 1959) or referred to the history of industrialization in the developed countries (Lewis, 1957; Habakkuk and Deane, 1963; Kindleberger, 1961).
2. The multiplier effect of foreign trade suggested by Harrod can be formalized in a simple way: let Y be national income, m the propensity to import and X the volume of export demand; the equilibrium of the trade balance results in the medium-term relationship $mY=X$, and hence the export multiplier which determines the volume of realizable production $Y=(1/m)^*X)$.
3. Rapid changes in the terms of trade in 1974 nevertheless led West Germany and Japan to retain severe austerity policies.
4. The period between 1950 and 1975 saw extraordinarily high levels of productivity gains and growth in the developed industrial economies. According to a study by Maddison (1982), total output per capita in sixteen OECD countries increased by an average of 1.6 per cent per annum between 1870 and 1913, by 1.8 per cent between 1913 and 1950 and by 4.5 per cent between 1950 and 1973. From this historical point of view, the growth rate of 2.7 per cent for the period from 1973 to 1979 does not seem exceptional. However, the debate on the fall in productivity gains cannot be considered to be the result of simple 'shortsightedness', to repeat the expression used by Darby (1984). The question of whether there will be a return to the former pattern of growth or whether a new one will emerge is of major concern to societies that have undergone considerable transformations as the result of twenty-five years of high growth-rates.
5. It should be pointed out, however, that most of these examples are taken from nationalized or government subsidized industries, which may explain the relatively low proportion of redundancies in the job losses.
6. These general guidelines were developed subsequently by an OECD working party. This led to the publication of two reports on positive adjustment policies (OECD, 1979; OECD, 1983a). The basis of these reports is 'the hypothesis that a competitive market economy normally constitutes the best mechanism for channelling, in a flexible and constructive manner and without excessive costs, reactions to social, economic and technological developments' (OECD, 1983a, p. 9).

7. From this point of view, the revival of industrial policies in the 1970s would appear to be a response by nation states to a supranational crisis (cf. de Bandt, 1983 and Thurow, 1984).

8. Michalski (1983), coordinator of the OECD working party on industrial policies, stresses the link between local pressures and the general atmosphere of crisis: 'For governments faced with situations in which high unemployment, excessive labour costs, an overvalued exchange rate and excessively high interest rates all come together, there is a strong temptation to resort to microeconomic policies in order to reduce the pressure on sectors and firms to adjust to the new situation.'

9. It is wrong simply to refer to a supposed interventionist tradition in order to describe the relationships between state and manufacturing industry. History shows that what appears to be deterministic often turns out to be dependent on contingencies. The development of the relationships between state and manufacturing industry in the leading developed countries is not uniform in character, as is shown by the changes that took place in the immediate post-war period. The important role played by the state in the industrialization process in Germany, France and Italy developed in very different ways after 1945. In Germany, where Nazism had left the state discredited, there was a great reduction in state inter-vention; in Italy, where agriculture was still a very large sector, the state maintained its high level of intervention in manufacturing industry, and in France, where the liberal capitalism of the 1930s was blamed for the weak-ness of the economy, the state increased its intervention. At the same time, the reconstruction of the previously very liberal British economy increased the role of the state in the basic industries, while indicative planning in the French style was envisaged. In the United States, the war economy reverted to its normal state, although the defence industries retained considerable importance. The present debate on industrial policy in the United States thus tends to refer to the New Deal of the 1930s (e.g. the Reconstruction Finance Corporation).

   An historical and international perspective on these developments will be found in recent studies by Delorme and Andre (1983), Hesselman (1983) and Armstrong, Glyn and Harrison (1984).

10. Within the framework of the joint programme drawn up by the socialist and communist parties in the mid-1970s.

11. The degree of latitude that remains for drawing up an active and coherent industrial policy can be judged from the proceedings of the conference on the subject organized by the French Government in 1982. (cf. 'Une politique industrielle pour la France', *Documentation Française*, November 1982).

12. According to Cohen (1983), it is political nonsense to aim for consensus on an industrial policy which does not go beyond the conflict of interests between workers in the expanding industries and those in the declining sectors.

4
The demand for services: the extension of foreign markets

Is it possible for the development of service industries, in the sectoral growth model previously assessed at the end of Chapter 2, to open the way for a revival of the developed economies? One of the first questions to be asked concerns an assessment of the opportunities opened up for foreign trade in services. Can the developed industrial countries redirect their trade towards services and thus relax the constraint on growth caused by their difficulties in creating a large enough manufacturing surplus?

When the manufacturing sector and the exploitation of natural resources are no longer able adequately to balance import requirements, many developed industrial countries are forced to restrict domestic demand in the medium term. The deficit of their current balance of payments is limited by their opportunities for borrowing. In this situation, greater specialization in the export of services might lead to economic revival. According to the advocates of this argument, the capital available to these countries, their technological capability and the skill levels of their labour force should guarantee them a comparative advantage in the market for services. It remains to be discovered whether these advantages can compensate for those that they have lost in some markets for manufactured goods.

Growth opportunities in doubt

There are several factors limiting the benefits that the developed industrial countries might expect from this specialization. Firstly, the development of a high proportion of the trade in services appears to be very closely linked to that in manufactured goods. Growth in the market for services is thus affected in the same way as the market for manufactured goods by the recession in the world economy. This link is a direct one in the case of the traditional services such as transport, insurance and finance, which go hand in hand with trade in manufactured goods. It is equally direct in the case of the newer services that are equally closely linked to the organization of production and the distribution of goods; these services include leasing, maintenance contracts for equipment, consultancies and engineering. Most of the interest shown in the international trade in services is linked to the great opportunities for expansion offered by these new services. Nevertheless, up until now, the new expenditure they have created has merely compensated for the lower rate of growth for more traditional services.

The link between trade in manufactured goods and that in services is reduced only in the case of income from factors (investment income and payment for work carried out abroad, including diplomatic and military activities), listed under the heading of services in the balance of payments. Even then, a distinction must be made between income from direct investments and that from purely financial investments. The motive behind the first type of investment is often a desire for direct involvement in foreign markets. This type of investment may thus be a direct consequence of strategies for trade in manufactured goods (cf. Section IV of the present chapter). If the income from these factors is disregarded, it is impossible to discern within the last decade any shift towards service activities within the trade structure of the developed countries.

The stability of certain established positions gives rise to a second set of reasons which, a priori, limit the opportunities for a given country to expand its exports of services. There are wide basic differences from one country to another in terms of trade in services. In particular, the distribution of the markets for services among the developed industrial countries differs significantly from the distribution of the markets for manufactured goods. The advantages enjoyed by countries like the United States or the United Kingdom in certain markets for services have diminished only slowly in the course of the 1970s and 1980s.

Finally, the invisible nature of the products, the volatility of financial activities and the strategic importance of services such as transport and communication all contribute to the maintenance of a considerable regulatory framework. As a consequence, the markets for services are to a large extent protected from foreign competition. This partly explains the modest scale of imports and exports of services compared to the size of domestic markets. The difficulties in liberalizing the exchange of services underline the extent of these protectionist tendencies.

These three aspects of the foreign trade in services will be analysed:

(1) the development of the world markets for services compared with those for goods (Section X);

Table 4.1 'Invisibles' in the current balance of payments

The invisibles		SOEC headings	Numbers of IMF headings	Description	General observations
Services, excluding income from factors	Transport	A 21	3, 4, 5, 6, 7, 8	All transport, insurance and loading costs	Underestimation of income from flags of convenience
	Travel	A 22	9, 10	Expenditure by business travellers and tourists	Journeys lasting less than a year
	Other services and income	A 27	29, 30, 31, 32	Fees from rights and patents, commercial and financial activities, engineering, consultancy, communications	— Heterogeneity of the various items — Inclusion of residues not broken down elsewhere
Services from factors	Investment income	A 24	13, 14, 15, 16, 17, 18, 19, 20	Income from direct or financial investment	These financial flows are systematically underestimated
	Income from work	A 25	27, 28	Direct payment for work done abroad or for foreign concerns	Statistics rarely provided. Difficult to distinguish from transfers of migrant workers
	Government transactions	A 26	21, 22, 23, 24, 25, 26	Military and diplomatic expenditure	Statistical uncertainty due to the confidential nature of some expenditure
Unrequited transfers	Private transfers	B 1	33, 34, 35, 36, 37, 38	Transfers connected with the migration of private individuals	
	Official transfers	B 2	39, 40, 41, 42, 43, 44	Gifts and contributions to international organizations	

Headings: IMF, cf. *Fourth Balance of payments manual*, 1977; SOEC, cf. Balance of Payments, Eurostat, 1983.

(2) the development of market shares and analyses of dominant positions (Section III);
(3) the restrictions on trade in services and liberalization strategies (Section III).

These analyses will bring out the limits of any extension of foreign markets for services. Table 4.1 gives the current definitions of invisible earnings, current balance of payments, 'real' services, etc.

I The expansion of trade in services: from the visible to the invisible

The international trade in services is an heterogeneous mixture of 'real' services, such as transport and consultancies, for example, and more 'fictitious' services associated with the provision of production factors. The terms currently used to describe trade in services in the balance of payments[1] distinguish between transport, travel, investment income, earnings from work, government transactions and a heading for other services. Of these six headings, three correspond to activities that produce 'real' services: transport, travel and other specialized services under the heading of other services; two others refer to factor income: investment income and payment for work abroad. The remaining heading covers government transactions and refers to non-commercial products: diplomatic and military activities abroad. These last three categories which are somewhat fictitious in character, account for almost half of all trade in services. This distinction between 'real' and 'fictitious' services is fundamental to any attempt to assess the possibilities for extending markets. Our first task, therefore, is to examine the structure of the trade in services between the ten EEC countries (cf. Table 4.2).

The structure of the markets for services

About a third of the foreign trade in services is accounted for by passenger and freight transport (32.4 per cent of the export of services within the EEC in 1981). This service is linked directly to trade in goods or to tourism. A varied assortment of services, usually services to firms and classified under the heading 'various services' in Table 4.1, represents a quarter of all trade (24.7 per cent of the exports of services within the EEC in 1981). This category includes engineering, advertising, brokerage, financial management, leasing arrangements, the sale of newspapers and films, maintenance contracts, etc. Royalties, patents, licences, etc. are also included in this category.

Investment income, earnings from work and government trans-actions (except for the unrequited transfers not included under services and accounted for in another section of the balance of payments) account for the remaining trade in services (40 per cent of the exports of services from the ten EEC countries in 1981). Within this last category, investment income and profits from financial investment and direct investment abroad account for a large share of the total (36 per cent of the exports of services in Europe in 1981, 62 per cent in the United States). In order to distinguish these fictitious services from the other services in the balance of payments, the terms 'income from factors' and 'services excluding income from factors' or 'real services' will be used from now on.[2]

The heterogeneous nature of the item 'services' in the balance of payments often means that the scope of analysis is extended to all invisible transactions. This last category adds unrequited transfers to the services mentioned above. These are direct, unilateral payments between governments and international institutions, or transfers between private individuals (including the remittance of wages and salaries of employees working abroad). These unrequited transfers are thus linked to the structural and geopolitical characteristics of each economy: the presence of foreign workers, membership of inter-national organizations such as the EEC or the UN and its specialist agencies (UNICEF, UNESCO, FAO, BIT, etc.) and policies on direct aid to developing countries. For the developed countries, these transfers are largely a debit item. This is the case for a country like the United States, for which the debits ($10.7 billion in 1981) represent 10 per cent of the imports of services and the credits ($1.7 billion) only 1.1 per cent of the exports of services. But this is less true for the ten EEC countries, since the system of redistribution within the Community increases the total amount of debits ($42.8 billion) and of credits ($24.2 billion); these transfers correspond in 1981 to 9.5 per cent of the exports of services and 17.6 per cent of the imports of services (cf. Table 4.2a and 4.2b).

Finally, invisible items of trade are distributed almost equally between services, excluding income from factors (54.4 per cent of invisible earnings within the EEC in 1981 and 49.7 per cent of debits) and income from government transactions and unrequited transfers. The next section is an attempt to make a clear distinction between these two types of services, for which the notion of market opportunities has radically different meanings.

Table 4.2 Services in the current balance of payments (million ECUs)

(a)

+: credits −: debits Balance		West Germany 1973	1979	1982	France 1973	1979	1982	Italy 1973	1979	1982	Netherlands 1973	1979	1982
A. Goods & services	+	65,781	152,263	225,423	42,960	117,518	178,383	25,308	69,322	100,951	24,830	59,019	89,884
	−	57,215	148,241	210,124	40,347	110,793	186,002	27,579	65,668	107,461	22,807	59,023	85,067
of which services	+	13,417	32,049	50,556	12,213	36,086	66,158	7,422	17,272	26,940	7,015	16,275	28,081
	−	17,022	39,747	60,071	10,010	27,836	57,903	6,471	12,935	25,319	5,805	16,152	27,159
as % of Goods & services	+	20.4	21	22.4	28.4	30.7	37.1	29.3	24.9	26.7	28.3	27.6	31.2
	−	29.8	26.8	28.6	24.8	25.1	31.1	23.5	19.7	23.6	25.5	27.4	1.9
of which income from factors*	+	6,250	13,691	23,007	3,205	10,829	26,956	2,238	4,181	7,905	2,079	5,729	12,208
	−	4,300	10,225	19,624	2,939	9,559	26,665	1,824	2,531	10,835	1,726	5,814	12,311
as % of services	+	46.6	42.7	45.5	26.2	30.0	40.7	30.2	24.2	29.3	29.6	35.2	43.5
	−	25.3	25.7	32.7	29.4	34.3	46.1	28.2	27.3	42.8	29.8	36.0	45.3
B. Unrequited transfers	+	1,587	4,523	4,764	1,834	4,035	5,027	1,284	2,647	4,817	899	2,281	2,213
	−	6,344	12,988	16,591	3,242	6,973	9,740	1,083	2,310	3,937	949	2,874	3,512
C. Current balance	+	67,368	156,786	230,186	44,794	121,553	183,409	26,592	71,969	105,768	25,729	61,300	92,096
	−	63,559	161,229	226,715	43,589	117,766	195,742	28,662	67,978	111,397	23,755	62,797	88,579
(A + B)	=	3,809	−4,443	3,472	1,205	3,788	−12,333	−2,069	3,991	−5,629	1,974	−1,496	3,517
Value of 1 ECU in national currencies		3.27	2.51	2.38	5.47	5.83	6.43	716.5	1,138.5	1,323.8	3.43	2.75	2.61

(b)

+: credits −: debits Balance		Belgium			UK			USA			The 10 EEC countries		
		1973	1979	1982	1973	1979	1982	1973	1979	1982	1973	1979	1982
A. Goods & services	+	19,945	55,716	87,063	39,878	97,928	150,070	89,402	209,193	358,400	229,936	579,152	800,761
	−	18,750	57,235	88,532	40,942	95,353	136,635	80,376	205,149	358,016	221,379	571,332	794,812
of which services	+	4,747	18,744	34,931	16,121	34,845	50,996	31,467	74,615	142,503	64,451	164,084	251,200
	−	4,562	16,790	34,327	12,073	26,995	41,330	23,147	50,648	104,647	58,662	147,825	237,670
as % of Goods & services	+	23.8	33.6	40.1	40.4	35.6	34.0	35.2	35.7	39.8	28.0	28.3	31.4
	−	24.3	29.3	38.8	29.5	28.3	30.2	28.8	24.7	29.2	26.5	25.9	29.9
of which income from factors*	+	2,223	9,389	24,630	6,189	13,750	21,836	20,039	52,949	103,844	20,488	54,061	101,513
	−	1,818	8,336	23,831	4,140	12,495	18,995	12,106	31,527	72,987	15,578	48,404	98,781
as % of services	+	46.8	50.1	70.5	38.4	39.5	42.8	63.7	71.0	72.9	31.8	32.9	40.4
	−	39.9	49.6	69.4	34.3	46.3	46.0	52.3	62.2	69.7	26.6	32.7	41.6
B. Unrequited transfers	+	548	1,350	1,210	767	2,093	5,617	571	1,009	1,628	8,073	19,656	23,742
	−	801	2,058	2,460	1,648	5,593	9,390	3,903	5,412	10,482	14,266	33,605	41,912
C. Current balance	+	20,493	57,066	88,273	40,645	100,021	155,686	89,974	210,202	360,029	238,009	598,808	824,503
	−	19,552	59,793	90,992	42,590	100,946	146,025	86,274	210,560	368,498	235,645	604,937	836,726
(A + B)	=	941	−2,227	−2,720	−1,945	−925	9,662	5,695	−358	−8,469	2,364	−6,128	−12,221
Value of 1 ECU in national currencies		47.8	40.2	44.7	0.502	0.646	0.560	1.23	1.37	0.98	—	—	—

Source: SOEC, Balance of Payments—General Data, 1979–1982.
* Investment income, income from work, government transactions.

Table 4.3 Trade in services, excluding income from factors—comparison with trade in goods (millions of ECUs)

(a)

	West Germany				France				Italy				Netherlands			
	Exports		Imports		Exports		Imports		Exports		Imports		Exports		Imports	
	Value 82	Growth 82/73	Value 82	Growth 82/73	Value 82	Growth 82/73	Value 82	Growth 82/73	Value 82	Growth 82/73	Value 82	Growth 82/73	Value 82	Growth 82/73	Value 82	Growth 82/73
Real Services* as % of goods	27,555 *15.8*	385	40,447 *26.9*	320	39,202 *34.9*	435	31,236 *24.4*	442	19,035 *25.7*	367	14,484 *17.6*	312	15,873 *25.7*	322	14,848 *25.6*	364
Transport as % of goods†	9,504 *5.4*	334	9,804 *6.5*	260	10,834 *9.7*	390	12,172 *9.5*	381	4,958 *6.7*	306	6,002 *7.3*	321	3,038 *14.6*	337	6,496 *11.2*	332
Travel as % of goods	5,745 *3.3*	288	16,648 *11.1*	310	7,127 *6.3*	367	5,251 *4.1*	299	8,513 *11.5*	389	1,774 *2.2*	206	1,576 *2.5*	201	3,373 *6.8*	352
Other services as % of goods	12,310 *7.1*	528	13,994 *9.3*	391	21,241 *18.9*	495	13,815 *10.8*	343	5,565 *7.5*	404	6,708 *8.2*	350	5,259 *8.5*	357	4,979 *8.6*	427
Goods	174,856	334	150,053	373	112,224	365	128,099	422	74,011	414	82,141	389	61,803	347	57,908	341

* Not included under this heading are investment income, income from work, government transactions (*Source*: SOEC, 1984, Balance of Payments).
† Including transport insurance.

(b)

	Belgium				UK				USA				The 10 EEC countries			
	Exports		Imports		Exports		Imports		Exports		Imports		Exports		Imports	
	Value 82	Growth 82/73	Value 82	Growth 82/73	Value 82	Growth 82/73	Value 82	Growth 82/73	Value 82	Growth 82/73	Value 82	Growth 82/73	Value 82	Growth 82/73	Value 82	Growth 82/73
Real Services*	10,301	408	10,496	383	29,160	294	22,335	282	38,659	338	31,660	287	149,687	340	138,885	322
as % of goods	19.8		19.4		29.4		23.4		17.9		12.5		27.2		24.9	
Transport	4,505	491	3,912	455	10,775	214	10,689	209	15,321	347	15,728	298	50,773	300	49,860	284
as % of goods†	8.6		7.2		10.9		11.2		7.1		6.2		9.2		8.9	
Travel	1,613	307	2,239	257	5,696	398	6,536	477	11,658	419	12,664	283	30,498	308	36,089	306
as % of goods	3.1		4.1		5.7		6.9		5.4		5.0		5.5		6.5	
Other services	4,185	390	4,346	435	12,689	366	5,106	353	11,680	276	3,268	254	62,040	419	46,275	397
as % of goods	8.0		8.0		12.8		5.4		5.4		1.3		11.2		8.3	
Goods	52,132	343	54,205	382	99,074	417	95,305	330	215,897	373	253,369	443	549,561	332	557,142	342

* Not included under this heading are investment income, income from work, government transactions (*Source*: SOEC, 1984, Balance of Payments).
† Including transport insurance.

Trends in world markets for services

Trends in the various world markets for services will be analysed by comparing their development with that of the markets for goods. This comparison only has a precise meaning for services excluding income from factors. The factors that determine this trade are a priori similar to those that determine trade in goods. More precisely, this trade in services not linked to the utilization of factors may appear to be a substitute for or a complement to trade in goods. Table 4.3 shows the relative share of this trade in services in comparison with the imports and exports of goods, together with their respective rates of growth for the period 1973–82.

The first observation to be drawn from this comparison is that there is a similar rate of growth for trade in goods and trade in all services (cf. Table 4.3, which gives data for all ten EEC countries). In 1973, the trade in services represented on average one-quarter of the trade in goods, as it did in 1982. However, this stability hides very different patterns of development for different types of services.

In general, transport and travel services have grown less rapidly than trade in goods. The cause of this relative decline is different for transport and for travel. In the case of transport, high productivity gains have made it possible to make long-term reductions in expenditure on transport relative to the value of trade in goods. There are several reasons for these productivity gains: the development of road and air transport, the improvement of port facilities, the use of containers and the economies of scale associated with the introduction of supertankers and jumbo jets. The rise in energy prices has not had the effect of reversing this long-term trend towards a reduction in the relative costs of international freight transport. Moreover, excess capacity, particularly in merchant shipping, has had the effect of lowering prices. There has been a continuous fall in the relationship between the total cost of imports including and excluding transport and insurance costs: between 1950 and 1981, this ratio fell in world terms from 1.10 to 1.07.[3] This reduction in the share of transport costs is largely a feature of the trade of the industrialized countries, where the productivity gains mentioned above have been of particular importance.

Expenditure on tourism has been more affected than that on goods by the slowing down of growth in the developed economies. From 1963 to 1973, the average annual growth rate of expenditure on travel in the OECD countries was 14.9 per cent, slightly higher than the growth rate for imports of goods (14.6 per cent). Between 1973 and 1982, this differential was reversed, with annual growth rates of 11.3 per cent for travel and 13.1 per cent for goods. This reduction in expenditure by tourists from the developed countries can be directly explained by the net reduction in the growth of household incomes. The income effect is thus greater than the effect of any internal shift in expenditure on tourism towards foreign travel, which is a social phenomenon in the developed countries.[4]

The remaining heading is specialized services, mainly services to firms (presented under the heading 'other services' in Table 4.3), the expansion contrasts with the stagnation of other services. Over the past decade, the average of exports of goods in the EEC has increased at an annual rate of 16.2 per cent per annum, while 'other services' have grown at a rate of 19.6 per cent per annum; the corresponding figures for imports are 16.6 and 18.8 per cent.

These figures have not yet had more than a modest effect on the balance of payments, since in 1981 they represented on average only 11 per cent of exports and 8 per cent of imports of goods. Nevertheless, their high growth rate encourages more detailed analysis of the activities concerned. If the differential in growth rates of almost 3 per cent per annum, according to the estimates above, were maintained throughout the 1980s, these services would by 1990 be equivalent to a third of the value of trade in goods. In the absence of standardized statistics, it is difficult to follow closely the major trends in the world market for these varied activities, which include management, engineering, communications, financial, business and insurance (excluding transport) services.

It is possible, by using the available figures on the development of the trade in services for a few countries which have a credit balance in this trade (e.g. the United States, France and the United Kingdom), to gain some idea of the trends for these various activities. Table 4.4 underlines the importance of a few well-defined activities for each country: patents and fees in the industrial and cultural fields for the United States, engineering and public works in France, the financial activities of the City for the United Kingdom. It should be noted, as we shall see later, that the share of these three countries in the world market for 'other services' fell in the 1970s. Thus, the trends mentioned above probably underestimate the development of world markets.

If account is only taken of services, excluding income from factors, the overall growth in these services since 1973 is very similar to that of the trade in goods. This stability is the result of contrasting trends in transport and travel services, the relative share of which is decreasing, and in specialized services, the share of which is increasing.

Income from factors

The net growth in the share of all services in the balance of payments (from 28 per cent in 1973 to 31.4 per cent in 1981 for the ten EEC countries, cf. Table 4.2) is thus essentially the result of the increase in investment income, earnings from work and government transactions. Their share in the balance of payments of the major European countries and the United States has continued to increase, particularly towards the end of the period in question. The preponderance of investment income, and particularly of income from financial investment, in the share of all services in the balance of payments, makes the sharp rise in interest rates a plausible explanation for this rapid growth. This would partly explain why debits and credits have often increased at similar rates.

Interest payments in fact constitute one of the most rapidly growing items in the balance of payments. Between 1970 and 1980 they increased from 0.5 per cent to 2 per cent of total world output; during the same period, income from direct investment remained constant at 0.4 per cent of total world output. This growth in interest payments did not really take off until 1978, when interest rates began to rise to the record level reached in 1981. Between 1977 and 1981, income from the export of capital in the ten EEC countries increased by 350 per cent, whereas the value of exports of goods increased by only 170 per cent in the same period. The difference is all the more striking in the case of imports of the same products (370 per cent compared with 170 per cent). During the same period, the value of imports of other 'fictitious' services in the balance of payments (earnings from work and non-market public services) increased less rapidly than the value of imports of goods (40 per cent compared with 70 per cent).

It is only the growth in income from financial investment therefore that has made any significant contribution to the increase in the share of services in the balance of payments. The fact that two very different entities are amalgamated under the heading 'services' leads to often very mistaken generalizations about the opportunities for extending markets. Financial markets cannot be thought of as opportunities for specialization on a national level. The strategy adopted by the investor requires first and foremost that the capital invested be highly mobile. The growth of investment income poses problems of development of a very different kind from those discussed in the present analysis of the opportunities for 'real' trade in products. Not only does the time horizon of investment income combine the long-term considerations of

Table 4.4 Growth in income from the 'various' services:
specializations of countries with a balance of payments
surplus*

(millions of US$)	1970	1973	1979
OECD total income from other services	18,253	30,149	86,203

(a) USA: patents and fees

	1970	1973	1979
Market share of USA	3,668	5,125	10,430
(%)	(19.8)	(17.3)	(12.1)
of which income from:			
Patents and fees, consultancy, film and distribution	2,331	3,225	6,048
Engineering	258	384	1,004
Reinsurance	77	155	207
Communications	304	498	1,109

(b) UK: financial services

	1970	1973	1979
Market share of UK	3,012	4,462[†]	11,465
(%)	(16.5)	(14.8)	(13.3)
of which:			
Financial services (millions £)	1,053	2,268[†]	3,392
Engineering, public works, consultancy, research and development (millions £)	415	1,248[†]	2,627

(c) France: public works and technical co-operation

	1970	1973	1979
Market share of France	1,771	3,045	10,431
(%)	(9.7)	(10.1)	(13.6)
of which:			
Public works and technical cooperation	637	1,078	5,013
Patents and fees	68	138	428
Other services	766	1,233	3,522

Sources: (a) *Survey of Current Business*, November 1981
(b) Bank of England, *Quarterly Bulletin*
(c) *Statistiques et Études Financières*, Ministère de l'Économie
* This table breaks down the total income for various sources, taken from OECD
Balance of Payments Statistics, 1984, into their main components, figures for which are
taken from national statistics.
† 1975.

direct investment with the very short-term considerations of speculative movements of capital, but, moreover, the extremely fluid nature of these transactions limits the relevance of any analysis taking a national perspective. The internationalization of capital tends to weaken the community of interest that links the accumulation of capital to the prosperity of the national economy. Moreover, it will be shown in Section IV that this kind of investment strategy is far from offering a solution to the chronic balance of payments problems of most of the older industrialized countries.

The uncertainty and heterogeneity of invisible transactions

The heterogenous nature of these transactions is increased if account is taken not only of services but also of all invisible transactions. This item in the balance of payments combines the services mentioned above with unrequited transfers.

The contribution of these invisible transactions to the current balance of payments brings into play a variety of different factors: commercial competitiveness in the case of 'real' services, financial operations and the long-term strategies of the internationalization of national capital in the case of investment income, the structural and geopolitical conditions for growth of unrequited transfers. This diversity makes it impossible to make a uniform and static assessement of the role of invisible earnings in the current balance of payments. This raises many economic policy questions. Trade in services excluding income from factors raises the classic medium-term problems of competitiveness with which any trade policy is always confronted. Unrequited transfers raise ethical problems and questions about development in the very long term. Income from factors, and more particularly investment income, raise much more complex questions. It is thus difficult within these movements of capital to make a distinction between very short-term financial speculation and investment aimed at facilitating the expansion or maintenance of markets for goods. This is all the more true since these invisible transactions are difficult to check, as is shown by the growing uncertainty as to how to measure such transactions.

Statistics on the level of the world economy reveal a 'black hole' between the balances of debtor countries and those of creditor countries. This gap, which represented 1 per cent of trade at the end of the 1970s, is continuing to grow. By 1983, it had reached $80 billion, or 3 per cent of world trade. For the United States alone, the heading 'errors and omissions' had reached $38 billion by the same time.

Experts attribute these accounting imbalances to errors in the recording of trade in 'invisibles' (cf. Brender and Oliveira-Martins, 1984; Veil, 1982). According to the OECD,[5] statistical errors in the trade in goods led in 1983 to a surplus on the world level of $20 billion, or just over 1 per cent of all trade. The world balance for services excluding income from factors, by comparison, shows a larger degree of error, of the order of 3 per cent of total trade. The source of this error seems largely to be found in the trade in 'specialized' services (building, engineering, consultancy, etc.), particularly with the OPEC countries. This statistical gap jumps to 8.5 per cent in the case of investment income, which represents more than a third of the trade in services. According to the OECD experts, this deficit is attributable to the increasing use of tax havens.

These difficulties in measuring the trade in services make it all the more necessary to maintain the obstacles to greater freedom of trade in services.

II Market shares and the orientation of trade

The trends observed at world level are not reflected systematically in the development of the foreign trade of each country. Thus there are countries like West Germany, France and Holland, where the value of exports of transport services has kept pace with that of goods, or even, in the case of Belgium, exceeded it. Similarly, there are countries where the value of exports of services to firms (classified under 'various') has increased less slowly than that of goods. This is the case for Italy, the United Kingdom and the United States. These differences can be explained in various ways. The first is that initial differences in market shares are the result, in the case of tourism, of natural and historical resources, in the case of transport, of the particular traditions of each country in that area and, in the case of financial activities, of long-established specialities. Secondly, according to country and market, countries with a low market share have tended to increase that share in the past decade, while there has at the same time been a strengthening of former tendencies towards specialization.

These changes are themselves partly linked to the development of the trade in goods in each country. We shall attempt first of all, and in a very descriptive way, to examine in more detail the growth in the trade in goods and services respectively. In order to highlight any possible trends towards specialization or complementarity, this examination will be limited to services excluding income from factors.

Specialization or complementarity: the hypotheses

The ratio of trade in services to trade in goods is an initial step towards revealing any autonomous developments in the trade in services that may be taking place. An increase in these ratios is evidence either of increased specialization towards trade in services or of a change in the complementary relationship between trade in goods and trade in services. By means of a simple formula, the relationship of this ratio to market shares themselves can be discovered:

for a given country, the share of the world market, MSS, represented by its exports of a given service XS is the product of three ratios:
— that between the exports of services XS and the exports of goods XG;
— that between the exports of goods EG and the world market for goods GG;
— that between the world market for goods GG and that for services SS.
i.e. $MSS = XS/SS = (XS/XG)\,(EG/GG)\,(GG/SS)$.

The three factors specified above are not located on the same level for any given country.

The relative development of world markets for goods and for services, reflected in the ratio GG/SS, is a largely exogenous factor for most countries. On the other hand, for an individual country, the value of these exports of services in relation to those of goods, XS/XG, or its market share in trade in goods, EG/GG, is of direct importance for its position in international trade. It is possible that these last two ratios are interdependent.

The experience of thirty years of sustained growth in world trade rather invalidates the hypothesis that there is a simple link between trade in goods and trade in services. At least, this is the lesson to be drawn from the contrasting cases of the United Kingdom and West Germany as far as transport and financial activities are concerned. In the first case, a higher than average transport capacity (British exports of transport services in 1982 still represented 11 per cent of the exports of goods) has not prevented a marked reduction in market shares for trade in goods; in the other case, a lower transport capacity relative to total output and to exports (5.4 per cent in 1982) has not had any obvious braking effect on the significant growth in market shares. West Germany has largely resorted to importing services as its exports of goods have grown rapidly. In the mid-1960s, when the growth in world trade was accelerating, West Germany and the United Kingdom still had fairly similar shares of the market for goods, 10.9 per cent and 8 per cent respectively. At the end of the 1970s, the relationship between the two was 1:2: West Germany had slightly increased its market share (11.2 per cent in 1979), despite the arrival of new competitors, whereas that of the United Kingdom had fallen to 5.6 per cent.

In the light of this past experience, therefore, it is more likely that the development of the ratios (*XS/XG*) between trade in goods and trade in services are indicators of specialization. These orientations could then be explained by the theory of comparative advantages (to which we shall return).

Nevertheless, the hypothesis of a new complementary relationship between trade in goods and trade in services cannot be rejected. The recent growth in trade in 'specialized' services over the last decade may be both a contributory factor in and/or be caused by the maintenance or expansion of shares in the market for goods. This complementary relationship is obvious in the case of high technology capital goods, the installation, adjustment and maintenance of which require services which can often best be provided by the manufacturers of such goods (cf. Stewart, 1979). IBM is a typical example of this tendency; it is difficult to say whether the company is primarily a manufacturing or a service concern.

In conclusion, the opportunities for trade in services for a given country can be analysed as a combination of an exogenous factor linked to the development of world markets and of two factors between which there may be a correlation: the national share in the world market for goods, *XG/GG*, and the ratio between trade in goods and trade in services, *XS/XG*. Both the recent and past history of trade between nations suggests that this correlation would come into play only in the case of trade in various services to firms, while traditional specializations would be the main forces behind world trade in other services (excluding income from factors).

Specializations and complementary relationships in trade in services: observations

The development of world trade in services excluding income from factors does not show any general tendency towards specialization on the part of the developed countries: in 1982, as in 1973, this trade was equivalent to almost one-third of the trade in goods. We have already seen, in the case of the ten EEC countries, that this overall development could well conceal a substitution between trade in transport and travel and trade in specialized services. Analysis of each country's trade in goods and services leads to more detailed conclusions.

In order to be more precise about the specializations and comple-mentary relationships in each country's trade, we shall analyse the changes in the coefficients XS/XG (the ratio between trade in services and trade in goods) and XG/GG (shares of the world market). It should be noted firstly that the seven countries analysed here play very differ-ent roles in the system of world trade. Four of the countries are rela-tively similar in this respect: for West Germany, France, Italy and the United Kingdom, foreign trade represented at the beginning of the 1980s between a quarter and a fifth of total output. For the smaller economies of Holland and Belgium, foreign trade was equivalent to more than half of total output (50 and 60 respectively). On the other hand, and despite the continued growth in world trade, the share of imports and exports in the United States at the beginning of the 1980s was less than 10 per cent of total output. These structural differences obviously mean that the importance of foreign markets varies accord-ing to country. In this respect, the position of the European countries has changed a great deal in twenty years; in the mid-1960s, foreign trade accounted for no more than 10 to 15 per cent of the total output of the four largest European countries.

It might be thought a priori that the increased internationalization of these economies would have had the effect of reducing the comparative advantages inherited from a particular historical tradition or arising out of natural or cultural resources. In fact, according to country and type of service, these differences in the relative importance of foreign trade or in the balances arising out of such trade have both increased and diminished.

Let us look first of all at the markets for transport and travel, where growth is lower than in the market for goods. The first characteristic of the market for transport is that each country more or less balances imports and exports (cf. Table 4.3), with the exception of Holland, which has a sizeable positive balance: thus, the traditional trade co-efficient, which compares the balance of trade to the total amount of imports and exports, was close to zero in all the countries in 1973 and 1982, except for Holland, where it remained at 0.16. This stability goes hand-in-hand with a wide range of market shares in trade in goods. In two countries, the United Kingdom and Holland, transport services have a very high market share relative to trade in goods. There are obvious historical reasons for these situations, which are the result of a tradition of supplying overseas colonies, which was itself based on the existence of a large merchant navy.

The example of the United Kingdom in the years following its entry into the Common Market also shows how these historical characteristics may disappear rapidly. In 1973, transport services were equivalent to 21.2 per cent of exports of goods; by 1982, this percentage had fallen to 10.9 per cent. This is accounted for by a very rapid reorientation of the United Kingdom's foreign trade and also by a massive restructuring of the world transport industry. The upheavals in merchant shipping in the past twenty years, caused by competition from air transport and by excess capacity in merchant fleets, have played their part in these changes. In 1970, merchant shipping accounted for 39 per cent of the exports of services from the United Kingdom, and for 49 per cent of imports; by 1980, these proportions had fallen to 24 per cent and 32 per cent respectively. At the same time, the share of the British merchant fleet in world tonnage fell from 11.6 per cent in 1970 to 5.6 per cent in 1982.[6] In this situation, it is all the more remarkable that Holland has succeeded both in maintaining a high level of trade in transport services (15 per cent of exports in goods) and in achieving a sizeable positive balance.

The figures gathered under the heading of travel produce results that are more clearly differentiated with respect to a general trend characterized by a relative reduction in the growth rates achieved by tourism in the 1960s. In France and, particularly, in Italy, income from tourism remained at a high level and both countries enjoyed sizeable surpluses: in 1982 the trade coefficients were 0.16 and 0.66 for France and Italy respectively. The opposite is the case in West Germany and Holland. The reduction in the growth of expenditure on tourism abroad was as marked in these countries as anywhere else, but had an even greater effect on income from tourism, thus helping to increase the deficit in this trade. Between 1973 and 1982, the trade coefficients decreased from −0.46 to −0.49 in West Germany and from 0.10 to 0.36 for Holland. The long-term trend towards the internationalization of tourist industries already mentioned has thus been accompanied by a trend towards increased specialization. This development is not to the benefit of all those countries that used traditionally to have a positive balance on their trade in tourism. In the case of the United Kingdom, a rapid increase in expenditure on tourism abroad between

1973 and 1982 had the effect of turning a taditional surplus into a deficit.

In short, the development of trade in tourist industries, even though it has slowed down, leads to a fairly general worsening of the tourist balances of the developed industrial countries, with the exception of Italy and,[7] to a lesser extent, France. As is to be expected, tourism offers very few opportunities for new markets as far as the countries in question are concerned.

In fact, new trends towards specialization or complementarity may become apparent, particularly in the growth of trade in specialist services. The services included under the heading 'various' are heterogeneous in nature and vary from one country to another, which restricts the opportunities for more detailed comparison. The first thing to note is that between 1973 and 1982 imports and exports of these services increased relatively rapidly in all the countries (cf. Table 4.3). This gives credence to the hypothesis that the general growth in this trade is linked to the continuous expansion of trade in goods. If there is a trend towards specialization, it seems to be common to all the industrialized countries studied. The trade coefficients given in Table 4.5 largely confirm this hypothesis. In all cases, with the exception of the United Kingdom, these coefficients are close to zero, which reflects a reduction in overall specialization in trade in this type of service. This trend is a general one, but has very different effects on different countries. In the case of West Germany and Italy, it reduces their dependence on imports of this kind of service. Holland and Belgium lost the small surplus in this trade that they had in 1973. On the other hand, the large credit balances achieved by France and the United States were reduced. The prevailing impression, therefore, is that there has been a general catching-up process which has led to a high degree of uniformity in trade in specialized services.

However, this development does not mean that there are not considerable differences in the capacity of each country to export specialized services. In each country, these dominant positions concern particular activities. The United Kingdom is the best example of this. The immense importance of the City in all matters related to financial dealings is the main reason both for the United Kingdom's positive specialization coefficient and for the fact that it was held at this level between 1973 and 1982. This supremacy has a dynamic effect on the growth in income in an expanding market, but also reduces expenditure very significantly. It is estimated that by 1982 the City's net income from abroad had risen to £4.4 billion, or slightly more than the total balance for all trade in specialist services (£4.2 billion). Banks contributed £1.7 billion to this total, and insurance companies 1.2 billion.[8] The special position of the United Kingdom in the trade in services is thus due entirely to the City's historical position as a financial centre. In comparison, France's favourable position in terms of foreign trade in services is based on a completely different type of specialization. It is characterized by rapid growth in both income and expenditure in its foreign trade in 'various' services. In 1973, France, the United States and the United Kingdom had similar levels of income under this heading; by 1982, this income, which had increased fivefold, was almost twice as high in France as in the other two countries (cf. Table 4.3). During the same period, however, expenditure by France on these services had increased two and a half times, making it three to four times higher than in the other countries. This 'extrovert' growth in the trade in services (the opposite to what can be observed for the United Kingdom), in which the credit balance does not increase so quickly as the total volume of trade, explains why the trade coefficient indicates a reduction in the level of specialization. Nevertheless, the value of this trade did not cease to increase, and by 1982 it was equivalent to 19 per cent of the value of French exports of goods. The dynamism of both exports and imports is based on a limited number of activities. The banking sector has expanded its foreign activities in a remarkable way: four French banks now rank among the top ten in the world. But the fruits of this growth are still modest as far as the total trade under this heading is concerned: 0.7 billion frs. in 1973 and 2.7 billion in 1982. In particular, expenditure on banking activities increased even more quickly than income, reaching 3.6 billion frs. in 1982.

In fact, a large part of the surpluses recorded under the heading of specialized services is generated by 'public works' and 'technical co-operation'. Net income from these construction, consultancy and engineering activities increased from 2.7 billion frs. in 1973 to 17 billion in 1982 (cf. Table 4.4). This represents 36 per cent of the balance achieved under the heading of 'other services'. A large part of this technical co-operation was carried out in OPEC countries. Following the rapid redistribution of purchasing powers in the wake of the oil price increases of 1973 and 1980, the services offered by French firms were aimed at making available to these countries the technical skills that they lacked in order to carry out their investment. This situation did not guarantee market opportunities in the medium to long term. On the one hand, the price rises meant that the OPEC countries had quite extraordinary amounts of money to invest. On the other hand, these

Table 4.5 Development of trade in services and changes in market shares in goods

	West Germany 1973	1982	France 1973	1982	Italy 1973	1982	Netherlands 1973	1982	Belgium 1973	1982	UK 1973	1982	USA 1973	1982	The 10 EEC countries 1973	1982
Indices of specialization: $\dfrac{\text{Exports} - \text{Imports}}{\text{Exports} + \text{Imports}}$																
Services excluding income from factors	−0.27	−0.19	0.12	0.11	0.05	0.14	0.10	0.03	−0.04	−0.01	0.11	0.13	0.02	0.10	0.01	0.016
of which various specialized services	−0.2	−0.06	0.34	0.21	−0.16	−0.09	0.12	0.03	0.04	−0.02	0.4	0.43	1.88	0.56	0.12	0.15
Relative importance of trade in goods and services: $\dfrac{\text{Trade in services}}{\text{Trade in goods}}$																
Services excluding income from factors																
Exports	13.7	15.8	29.3	34.9	29.0	25.7	27.7	25.7	16.6	19.8	41.8	29.4	19.7	17.9	25.2	26.1
Imports	31.7	27.0	23.3	24.4	22.0	17.6	24.0	25.6	19.3	19.4	27.5	23.4	19.3	12.5	25.2	24.9

of which various specialized services																
Exports	4.5	7.0	14.0	18.9	7.7	7.5	8.3	8.5	7.1	8.0	14.6	12.8	7.3	5.4	8.9	11.2
Imports	8.9	9.3	7.0	10.8	9.1	8.2	6.9	8.6	7.0	8.0	5.0	5.4	2.3	1.3	7.2	8.3

Market shares and involvement in the world economy

Market share of exports from the industrialized countries*	16.8	15.2	9.2	8.4	6.1	6.4	6.1	5.8	5.5	4.6	7.8	8.4	17.8	18.3	—	—
Importance of exports of goods relative to total output	18.6	26.0	15.1	20.3	15.5	20.8	36.3	43.9	41.0	59.0	16.5	20.0	5.5	6.9	19.0	24.9

* According to the IMF classification of industrialized countries.

countries were in a position to acquire the necessary technical skills very quickly, even if they had to set up their own service companies, either by establishing them from scratch or by buying up existing companies (thus strengthening the link between trade in services and direct investment). Recent developments give cause for concern: the markets for engineering services fell by 50 per cent between 1981 and 1984. Despite this uncertainty, however, French firms may in fact have laid the foundations for a type of specialization which is perhaps less profitable than in the past but more lasting.

Trade in specialized services in the United States is a different case altogether. The credit balance under this heading is simply due to the fact that imports are even lower than exports. Compared with trade in goods, the trade in specialist services is very small: in 1982, it was equivalent to 5.4 per cent of the exports of goods and 1.3 per cent of imports; the figures for Europe were 11.2 per cent and 8.3 per cent respectively. Moreover, the trade is highly concentrated, with patents and other fees being by far the largest item (cf. Table 4.4).

Towards a new distribution of the international trade in services?

This descriptive analysis of the trade in services reveals the limits of hypotheses advocating that there should be an autonomous reorientation of trade towards services. As far as transport is concerned, countries tend to balance their trade, although at different levels. In the case of tourism, the modern cult of sun worship makes it very difficult for the Scandinavian countries to benefit from the development of foreign travel. And finally, the trade in specialized services reveals a widespread tendency towards despecialization. The City is simply the exception that proves the rule. It would seem that traditional specializations are breaking down. Nevertheless, this dominant characteristic conceals the heterogeneity that still exists within the heading 'various services', where the nomenclatures used in different countries are hardly comparable. The development of the activities in multinational firms is a key factor in the relative despecialization revealed by the rapid growth for all countries of both credits and debits in trade in services. The type of trade concerned (consultancies, technology transfer, advertising, financial operations, technical maintenance) is central to the tertiary functions of the production organized by these multinationals on a world scale. The expansion of computerized communications is a precondition for this division and externalization of labour on a world scale. The importance of a small number of multinational firms in this market should also be noted: according to a recent CNUCED report (1984), these firms have 'infiltrated the service sector' and constitute 'the driving force behind its internationalization, which has accelerated the disappearance of the small and medium-sized firms that used traditionally to dominate the market'.

It is tempting to conclude that a trend towards complementarity between trade in goods and trade in services is gradually replacing the traditional specializations. However, this conclusion needs to be qualified and supplemented in several respects. Firstly, only the developed industrial countries have been discussed here, whereas the markets that might make increased specialization possible are in the newly industrialized and developing countries. It is from this point of view that the opposition of the Third World to the liberalization of trade in services must be understood.

Secondly, the relationship between external markets for goods and services has still to be clarified: is a strict complementary relationship between the two becoming apparent, marking the beginning of a new phase in the development of world trade, or does a greater capacity for trade in services simply improve competitiveness?

Finally, only 'real' services have been discussed. As has already been stressed, income from factors does not fit into the strictly national framework within which the problem of external constraint was posed. This is obvious in the case of purely financial operations that are easily transferable from one part of the world to another. But this restriction does not apply to all sources of income from investments, such as, for instance, investment in the distribution of domestically produced foods or institutional investment, which, by its very nature, retains its link with the country of origin (this is the case, for example, for institutional investors such as pension funds). The following section will attempt to clarify these points.

III The liberalization of trade in services and comparative advantages

Competitiveness and participation in trade in services

The trend towards despecialization in the trade in services (particularly as far as specialized services are concerned) suggests that a new dynamic of trade is developing, in which there is a link between the extension of foreign markets for goods and of those for services. This type of relationship does not appear to have played a part in the establishment of trade flows in the 1950s and 1960s. The Japanese and German success in the export of manufacturing goods was accompanied by deficits in trade in services. Moreover, the period since 1973 has been characterized by a world-wide challenge to the shares of export markets held by the industrially developed countries. The redistribution of purchasing powers that followed the increases in oil prices and the emergence within the system of international trade of new trading partners has reduced the share of the industrialized countries in world trade: it fell from 76 per cent of world exports in 1973 to 68 per cent in 1982 (according to IMF statistics). As a result, it is an achievement for these countries simply to maintain their market shares. It is thus difficult to draw any firm conclusions from a simple comparison of the changes in market shares and the ratio of goods to services in total trade. Moreover, variations in the exchange rate of the dollar have a significant effect on market shares. It would be very deceptive to attempt to simplify this complexity by assessing markets in volume terms, since any estimate of the volume of services to firms is arbitrary. We shall thus confine ourselves to a few general remarks. Between 1973 and 1982, the economies under consideration increased their involvement in world trade, as measured by the development of the ratio of goods exported to total output; this process went hand-in-hand with an even more rapid increase in the exports of specialized services, except, notably in the United Kingdom and the United States, as Table 4.5 shows. At the same time as the structure of trade was changing, the market shares of each country within the industrialized countries as a whole were falling, except in the case of the United Kingdom and the United States, where trade in services grew less quickly than elsewhere.

These statements must be treated with caution. The growth in the import and export of specialized services has not led to an equal growth in net surpluses. Moreover, in a tertiary economy like the United States, the share of specialized services in exports, which was already relatively low in 1973, has fallen. In 1982, it was equivalent to only 5.4 per cent of trade in goods, which is only half of the average for the European countries. Their market share in the financial sector is also paradoxically low, in view of the key role played by the dollar. However, this assessment wrongly ignores the major importance for the American economy of income from factors (cf. Section IV).

A new campaign for the liberalization of trade in services

At the beginning of the 1980s, the campaign for the liberalization of trade in services was intensified; this was somewhat paradoxical since, at the same time, there was an increase in protectionist measures in the trade in goods such as steel, textiles, cars and electronic consumer goods. This liberalization of trade in services had been advocated by the OECD and in EEC agreements for the past two decades: the OECD Code of Liberalization for current invisible operations of the 1950s and the Treaty of Rome (Article 59) of 1957 were both aimed explicitly at services (cf. Griffiths, 1975). In the post-war period of reconstruction, the 'developed' countries were not favourably disposed towards the liberalization of trade in services, in particular, transport. This is one of the lessons that can be learnt from the failure of the Organization of International Trade project (cf. Shelp, 1981). The OECD recommendations on invisible transactions and freedom of establishment had long been dead letters. The cause of these relative failures, acknowledged by the OECD in 1975, lay mainly in outright opposition or lack of enthusiasm on the part of the various countries: the United States and the developing countries were still opposed to liberalization, while the European countries were preoccupied by Common Market negotiations.

The campaign, led mainly by the United States at the end of the 1970s during the GATT negotiations in Tokyo (which ended in 1979), marked a turning point. The use of the GATT negotiations in this way reflects the fact that the campaign for the liberalization of trade in services was aimed at world markets as a whole. The choice of these proceedings was presented as a compromise between the OECD, which is orientated towards the developed countries, and UNCTAD, which performs a similar function for the developing countries. Until this time, the GATT agreement, with one exception, referred only to trade in goods. This campaign launched by the United States in the mid-1970s (which implemented the principles laid down in the Trade Act of 1974)[9] should be viewed in the light of the transformation of the division of labour.

New countries had developed export capacities in the markets for goods and, as a result, the market shares of the industrialized countries fell from 75 per cent of world exports in 1966 to 68 per cent in 1982. The aim behind the liberalization of trade in services was to facilitate an increase in the specialization of trade. The loss of market shares in manufactured goods would thus be offset by increased market shares in trade in services. This argument was based on two factors. On the one hand, the theory of comparative advantages largely explains, on the world level rather than on the level of the industrially developed countries, specializations in the trade in services excluding income from factors (this will be examined in more detail later, using an econometric study by the World Bank). On the other hand, trade in services is subject to real restrictions, linked less to the invisible nature of such trade than to the expressed aims of governments wishing to retain strict control over such volatile and strategically important activities.

A general redistribution of market shares

The debate on the liberalization of the trade in services did not stop at the affirmation of a 'natural law' of specialization or at pointing out the obstacles to trade. However, opposition to the campaign did develop among the industrialized countries themselves. The redistribution of market shares among the industrialized countries was certainly greater than that between the industrialized and the developing countries. West Germany and Japan, having significantly increased their shares of the trade in manufactured goods while allowing a large deficit in their trade in services to develop, tended once again to balance their trade. They were forced into this both by the growing importance of services in their economies and by the entry of newly industrialized countries into the world markets for manufactured goods. This change in the trade structure of these two industrial countries was facilitated by the amount of foreign credit accumulated over the previous twenty years as a result of trade surpluses.[10] This new tendency towards balance in the trade structure of countries that used to run deficits is part of the relative trend towards despecialization revealed by the analysis of the trade in 'various' services. As a result, the relative position of those countries that used to achieve a surplus in this trade is threatened. As we have seen, these countries specialize in clearly defined types of trade: patents and other rights in the case of the United States, financial dealings in the case of the United Kingdom, public works and technical co-operation in the case of France, transport in the case of Holland and tourism in the case of Italy. General developments in world trade have thus caused all the developed countries to redistribute their trade in services. This redefinition of markets is less the result of far-sighted economic policies than of direct pressure from firms operating on an international scale. The American pressure in this direction is created largely by the international strategies of large banks and insurance or service companies.[11]

This intervention by governments and international institutions such as GATT in an attempt to redefine markets was made necessary by the permanence of the obstacles to trade. But these obstacles are not exclusive to the developing countries. The industrialized countries have retained a number of limitations, linked historically to the organization of transport, insurance and financial management services. The restrictions on merchant shipping and banks in the United States, insurance companies in West Germany and France are evidence of this. Thus the negotiations on the liberalization of trade in services also concealed differences among the developed countries.[12] Moreover, liberalization of the trade in services goes hand-in-hand with a liberalization of movements of capital. Indeed, service industries require a certain amount of facilities in the countries to which services are exported. This freedom to set up service activities, that the OECD recommendations had not been able to facilitate in 1975, is still very hypothetical on the world level. The UNCTAD conferences show that a number of countries intend to place severe restrictions on the use of foreign transport companies in their trade in goods. And in the economic climate of the 1980s, the GATT agreements on trade in goods are themselves broken by the developed countries as far as iron and steel, textiles and agriculture are concerned. The problems of liberalizing trade in services cannot thus be reduced to a conflict of interests between developed and developing countries.

Nevertheless, the debate on easing the restriction on trade in services should initially be put into this context of a trend towards specialization, as a result of which most trade in services would be carried out by countries with high incomes. The desire to extend the scope of trade agreements reflects a change in the structure of world trade.

Specialization based on the comparative advantages of the developed countries in trade in services

In an attempt to explain the basis of international trade, Ricardo's theory of comparative advantages quite naturally saw the origin of specialization in differences in production costs. This gave a direct explanation of the situation at any given moment, but left unresolved the original question of how these differences in comparative costs originated. As a result, all protectionist measures were justified by the desire to reduce comparative costs. Heckscher and Ohlin's 'theorem' was an attempt to reduce the scope for protectionism by attributing these variations in comparative costs to differences in factor endowment. This hypothesis still leaves room for a great deal of clarification. Factors of production can be said to include the various human, natural, material, technological and scientific resources available to a given country. The capital/labour ratio, the size of the country, the extent of the training system and expenditure on research and development are some of the characteristics most commonly used to analyse the distribution of factors. Most empirical studies have compared the composition of trade for each country to its factor endowment, rather than analysing the structure of trade in a given product (distribution of market shares or specialization coefficients). Services were usually excluded from the analysis. A study by Sapir and Lutz (1981) for the World Bank attempted to fill this gap. The authors showed that the structure of trade in services as indicated by the relationship between imports and exports correlates quite well with the distribution of factor indicators mentioned above. These studies are based on an examination of the trade in four kinds of 'real' services for fifty countries (including thirty-five developing countries) during the year 1977. The results of this research clearly complement the straightforward analysis of trade.

For the industrialized countries, the indicators of factor endowment, such as capital per head of population, the size of the economy or the level of training in the economically active population, do not appear to be correlated with a credit or deficit balance for trade in services. There is such a correlation for developing countries as far as trade in transport services, tourist expenditure and insurance services are concerned. On the other hand, no relationship is given between factor endowments and positions in the trade in specialized services, either for industrialized or developing countries. The beneficial role of these new services in facilitating technological transfers is mentioned indirectly by reference to the experience of a few countries, including India and Korea (cf. Stewart, 1979), although no connection is made between this and the theory of comparative advantages. These studies seem to suggest that the theory of comparative advantages is of only limited relevance to trade in services. Moreover, an examination of countries whose trade deviates significantly from the profile that would be expected if the theory held good underlines the importance of either historical specialization or of restrictive practices. Thus a higher than expected level of income from transport services reflects either long-established specializations, like those in Greece or Norway (to take two countries that have not been discussed until now) or obstacles to trade, in the case of Brazil, Korea and Taiwan. The campaign for the liberalization of trade in services would thus have the aim of encouraging the law of comparative advantage to be more widely applied. There is obviously still resistance to the removal of obstacles to trade.

Deep-rooted restrictions

The restrictions on trade in services do not affect all types of services in the same way. Detailed analyses of these restrictions will be found in studies by Griffiths (1975), Shelp (1981), Sapir and Lutz (1981) and Schott (1983). The main points of these analyses will be outlined here. In the case of each type of service, contrasting principles come into play in order to create a fairly stable equilibrium as far as restrictive practices are concerned, which leaves little scope for liberalization.

As far as transport is concerned, most of the controversy concerns the regulations governing merchant shipping. The developed and developing countries fail to agree on two points: flags of convenience and the use of contracts linking trade in goods and transport services. Ships sailing under flags of convenience as a means of avoiding national taxes and social security contributions provide strong competition for national fleets, encouraging them to transfer their activities. This internationalization of the capital invested in merchant shipping benefits only a limited number of developing countries. Thus the majority of these countries still support measures restricting the freedom of trade. It has been suggested by UNCTAD (a suggestion to which the United States is opposed) that the 40/20/20 rule should be made more widespread (according to this rule, 80 per cent of transport services would be divided between trading partners, leaving only 20 per cent of the market to third parties). It is certainly the case that the threat of liberalization leading to the development of flags of convenience helps to maintain restrictive regulations. Finally, the pressure of competitive mechanisms hardly seems to have reduced the practice of reaching agreement on the distribution of markets for merchant shipping and air transport (via IATA). The deregulation of internal transport in the United States seems in this respect to have had only limited effects on the organization of international transport. It is clear that this cartel system organized on an international scale by institutions such as the International Air Transport Association, the International Maritime

Organization and the Intergovernmental Organization for Maritime Consultation leads to relatively balanced trade in transport services between the various developed countries (cf. Table 4.2). Within this very particular system of market organization, technical standards, such as reliability, play an important role, as do operating obligations (route concessions linked to a schedule of conditions) and the concerns of military strategy. There thus appears to be little scope for a liberalization of trade in transport services.

In contrast, the obstacles to trade in services arising out of exchange control measures seem to be closely linked to current economic conditions. The IMF publishes an annual report on exchange control measures throughout the world; in 1977, for example, 9 of the 23 OECD countries used such controls, as did 101 of the 114 developing countries. Firstly, these very widespread measures limit tourist trade by restricting the expenditure permitted for each traveller. It should be noted that the heading 'Travel' also includes business travel, which is subject to restrictive practices implemented by means of simple fiscal measures. Since 1977, for example, American firms have not been allowed to include more than two conferences or seminars per person in their general expenses.[13] To this variety of restrictive practices can be added the publicity campaigns launched by governments to encourage tourism in their own countries. The impact of all these measures is difficult to assess, but they do have an obvious symbolic role as an attempt to keep alive economic nationalism, the effects of which rebound on all trade.

In fact, the most important effect of exchange control measures may well be to reduce the freedom of investors. These controls thus have a direct effect on the freedom of firms to establish branches abroad, which is one of the preconditions for a real liberalization of trade in services. Specialist services, which are the most dynamic element in the trade in 'real' services, often require the setting up of local branches, since the number of operations that can be handled on an international level is limited, although telecommunications and computerization have improved the situation considerably. However, many countries have introduced legislation that restricts the freedom of firms to set up branches abroad; these measures include stipulations on minimum percentages of national employees, limits on the repatriation of profits and on earnings from work (making it more difficult to employ foreign exports). Studies of these frequently used and varied practices are rare. However, one study carried out in 1976 for the United States government (and quoted by Sapir and Lutz, 1980) does give an indication of the obstacles encountered by American firms in foreign markets. The following is a summary of the nature of and reasons for the main obstacles to the diffusion of specialized services.

The international diffusion of cultural products (mainly firms) is often subject to quotas in an attempt to preserve and develop a national cultural heritage. The American dominance in film-making is the particular target of these measures, which are found in countries as diverse as Switzerland, Australia, France, Canada, the United Kingdom, Brazil and India.

Services that require the use of skilled personnel on the spot, such as auditing and accountancy, engineering and construction, are directly affected by restrictions on work permits and the repatriation of earnings from work. The aim of all these practices is to encourage the development of a skilled local labour force. These practices are fairly widespread in developing countries, which is precisely where there are large markets for these services (this is the case in Saudi Arabia, Brazil, Mexico, India, Argentina, Nigeria, etc.).

A similar desire to reduce comparative disadvantages by developing local factors of production is to be found in service activities linked to data processing. To the restrictions mentioned above on employment and the repatriation of earnings can be added limits on the freedom of foreign companies to set up local branches, on the granting of operating licences and on intellectual property. Moreover, governments, which are some of the main customers for these services, are in a position to favour national firms.

Finally, banking and insurance services, which are already subject to fairly restrictive regulations on the national level, are often the target of particular measures as soon as they are considered as foreign companies. The logic is simple, and is usually based, as far as the developed countries are concerned, on the experience of the depression of the 1930s. Bankruptcies, crises of confidence and financial scares characterized the fairly liberal systems of the 1920s and 1930s and were the reason for the relatively restrictive regulations of the 1950s and 1960s. The Banking Act of 1934 in the United States, which restricted the freedom of banks to open branches across state boundaries, is an extreme example. The development in the 1970s of financial operations on a national and international scale, within a very fluid system of free convertibility, encouraged a significant degree of liberalization. The opportunities for distance management opened up by computer technology and modern communications mean that the old regulations have become outdated, they also provide the basis for the new operating conditions within the sector (cf. Revell, 1983 and Petit, 1984). But this latter change has also encouraged these financial activities to be moved to tax havens. This trend, which has been rapid and unchecked, has aroused opposition to any further liberalization of these financial services. The threat of losing control of these services has led many countries, even the richest ones, to set up free zones where their domestic regulations do not apply (this is the case in New York) or to make significant changes to their approaches to foreign markets (e.g. the City after its computerized reorganization in 1986).[14] This reaction on the part of the richest countries, together with the fears of a financial crash caused by the growing crisis in the world economy, has restricted to a large extent the scope for liberalizing trade. This is the conclusion of two recent OECD studies on foreign trade in the banking and insurance sectors.[15] International banking and insurance activities are carried out either as international services (based in the large financial centres) or through local representatives. In order to establish a local presence, financial organizations can either open branches or set up subsidiary companies. The first option, which is preferred by firms because it retains their brand image and their management methods, is subject to many restrictive measures. Each of the OECD countries lays down its own conditions governing the freedom of companies to set up overseas branches. In seven of the member states, these restrictions go as far as a total ban (in Australia, Canada, Finland, Iceland, New Zealand, Norway and Sweden, as well as some states in the United States). In the EEC countries, where the restrictions are less overt, it must be pointed out that foreign penetration of national markets is still modest. Neither the existence since 1930 of a world organization, the Bank for International Settlements, nor the studies and recommendations by the OECD on the Code for invisible transactions in the 1950s has led to any significant liberalization of trade in this area. In the insurance sector, where there are no international organizations to facilitate any possible future organization of the conditions of trade on a world scale, the efforts of the present campaign for liberalization may turn out to be more promising. In fact, however, certain specific conditions, such as the fiscal advantages attached to some life insurance agreements, tend to reduce the opportunities for opening up national markets.

In conclusion, it seems unlikely that the present campaign for the liberalization of trade in services will be able to open up new market opportunities in an atmosphere of crisis which tends to encourage protectionist measures as far as trade in goods is concerned. The desire to liberalize trade usually comes up against the uncontrollable nature of tax havens and flags of convenience, which can be regarded as extreme forms of competition. It may be possible to avoid a spiral of 'competitive deregulation' if the countries with comparative advantages take the initiative and set up free zones. However, this is unlikely to lead to any significant reduction in the obstacles to trade in services.

These initial conclusions hardly provide grounds for regarding the trade in 'real' services as an opportunity for creating new specializations within the trade of the developed industrial countries.

IV Towards balanced development of trade in services

The slowing down of trade since 1973 has affected services as well as goods. However, this is an overall view of trade excluding income from factors. This section will provide a summary of the main conclusions of the previous sections and complement them with an analysis of income from factors. Although trade in goods and trade in services as a whole have developed at more or less the same rate, trade in traditional services has grown less rapidly than that in specialized services. However, even the rapid growth of this latter type of service is unlikely in the long term to create large surpluses.

The extension of these services has indeed been characterized by a well-defined trend towards de-specialization. Receipts and expenditure have increased at more or less the same rate. Net balances have fallen relative to the value of trade. It is true that the credit and debit positions of the developed countries are still very different, but the development of trade has gone hand-in-hand with a reduction in these differences.

The relative inability of the developed countries to generate stable and long-term surpluses in this trade in services cannot simply be blamed on the restrictions placed by the developing countries on the freedom of trade. In the first place, such obstacles exist even in the developed countries themselves. More particularly, however, these obstacles are not merely a legacy from the past. They are a response to contemporary problems raised by the conditions of trade. The international trade in services is actually carried out either on an international scales or through local companies. In the first case, excessive liberalization of trade leads to the development of uncontrolled internationalization; flags of convenience and tax havens act as a foil in this process, encouraging the maintenance of restrictive regulations. In the second case, the lasting agreements entered into when foreign firms are given permission to open local branches lead to equally permanent regulations guarding against any reduction in national sovereignty.

In the absence of any restrictions, such growth in the mobility of productive capital would represent a shift to a new stage of free trade at the world level. The liberalization of trade in services is not the only condition for this change; restrictive practices are still very widespread.

The trade agreements that governed the growth in the trade in goods during the 1950s and 1960s always contained safety clauses that guaranteed a certain degree of national control over the organization of foreign trade. Moreover, the reduction in tariff barriers often left room for a multiplicity of non-tariff barriers. Ray and Marvel (1984) estimate that the development of these obstacles after the Kennedy Round (GATT negotiations that preceeded the Tokyo negotiations) was equivalent to a doubling of actual customs duties.[16] The definition of standards and the practice of ratification play a discreet but effective role in the restrictive practices affecting trade in goods. More obvious are protectionist agreements (of which the Multi-Fibre Agreement is a famous example), self-imposed restrictions implemented after much persuasion (in the case of Japan) and quotas (for a recent summary of industrial protectionism, see Balassa and Balassa, 1984).

The freedom of companies to set up branches abroad and the free mobility of capital would make it possible to get round the restrictions on the freedom of trade. It thus seems unlikely that such changes will be implemented in the current circumstances. The experience of the EEC is revealing in this respect. In theory, directives issued by the Commission in 1960 and 1961 guarantee the freedom of companies to set up branches abroad and the free mobility of capital. However, they have been largely ineffectual due to the operation of safety clauses and the maintenance of restrictive national regulations. Indeed, it is possible for these recommendations to be implemented as long as individual countries retain very different legislation on trade.

It is thus very doubtful whether, in a period of economic stagnation, the transition to this phase of increased liberalization of trade can be achieved. The desire to benefit from foreign investment, both to support economic activity and to increase foreign exchange reserves, is not strong enough to persuade governments to give up their control over the organization of foreign trade. The unequal power of finance capital, which in each country can operate on a world level, only serves to reinforce the determination of governments. A simple analysis of income from factors will confirm these disparities and thus the lack of incentive for any relaxation of the restrictions on the mobility of capital and the freedom of firms to set up branches abroad.

Income from factors

Firstly, it should be remembered that this heading in the balance of payments, the development of which is outlined in Table 4.1, includes, as well as investment income, which is analysed below, individual earnings from work abroad (although the transfer of funds from resident foreign workers are included with private unrequited transfers) and government transactions for diplomatic and military activities.

It has already been stressed that the growth in invisible trade relative to trade in goods is due solely to increased income from investment. Between 1977 and 1982, the value of this investment income relative to that of the trade in goods almost doubled the ratio between the two at the world level (8.5 per cent in 1977, 15.3 per cent in 1982).

There are in fact two categories of foreign investment. On the one hand, there is direct investment in the productive system of the foreign country, while on the other there is financial investment, by means of which the receiving countries can meet their need for investment capital.

The factors that determine these two types of investment are very different (even though they may on occasion fulfil the same function of sustaining productive activities). Financial investments are made in accordance with differentials in interest rates and variations in exchange rates. Direct investment, on the other hand, reflects the strategies of firms wishing to internationalize their production.

According to Dunning (1979), there are three main reasons behind decisions to make direct investments, as opposed to direct exports or production under licence.

(1) Direct investment retains all the advantages of the parent company: brand image, organizational and technological capabilities and supply network.
(2) It enables firms to benefit from the particular conditions of access to local markets, whether this involves avoiding customs restrictions or tailoring their products more closely to the local market.
(3) Finally, it enables firms to reduce production costs by using cheaper labour and inputs and more convenient transport arrangements.

This 'eclectic theory' (to use the words of Dunning) of direct investment reveals the limits of any comparison between income from direct
investment and that from trade in specialist services. Know-how is
important but is secondary to size and financial power if a firm is to
become a multinational and achieve a sizeable income. It is thus a question of a long-term process which has until now been characterized by
flows of long-term investment, as is shown by the distribution by
country of this income. In 1983, income from investment (reinvested or
repatriated) in the world as a whole was equivalent to 5.4 per cent of
income from services (or 2.1 per cent of total exports of goods). The
United States held 60 per cent of the 'market' and the United Kingdom
16 per cent. Japan's market share (5.9 per cent) did not catch up with
that of Holland (5.3 per cent in 1983) until the beginning of the 1980s.
The market shares of the other countries was lower than 2 per cent.
Moreover, only the United States, with 13133 million SDRs (special
drawing rights: value defined by IMF from a basket of weighted currencies), and to a lesser extent Japan, with 1259 SDRs, had a significant
credit balance for income from investment. This distribution of income
from investment clearly underlines the amount of time it takes for
investment abroad to become profitable. It hardly reflects, in particular,
changes in the amount of capital invested.[17] This is evident in the case of
West Germany, whose industrial power has, since the 1960s, made it
easier for German firms to develop as multinationals. In 1983, however,
West Germany still had a deficit balance of 971 million SDRs for
income from direct investment. It is surprising that West Germany does
not have substantial surpluses in view of the level of its foreign holdings
(66 billion DM in 1982). The Bundesbank attributes this deficit to the
recent and less profitable nature of the investments compared to those
made in the past in West Germany by foreign investors, especially
American companies.

When all is said and done, income from direct investment not only
constitutes a persistently small proportion of the trade in services (8.6
per cent in 1977, 5.5 per cent in 1983), but is also the very long-term
result of dominant positions in the markets for goods. The '*rentier*'
strategy, at least as far as this type of direct investment is concerned, is
thus far from being an opportunity open to the various developed countries engaged in the system of world trade.

Other kinds of income from investment are significantly higher, since
they accounted for one third of invisible earnings in the world in 1983.
They are also subject to rapid variations. In 1977, their share of invisible
earnings was only 18 per cent. The rapid growth at the end of the 1970s

was directly linked to the rise in interest rates and the increased demand for finance capital from public and private agencies. Inflation, sudden distortions of relative prices and the redistribution of markets encouraged these developments. The balances that appear under the heading of income from investment thus reflects borrowings and loans made in the past. They thus depend on results achieved prior to the other items in the current balance of payments. The trade surpluses recorded in the past by West Germany and Japan explain their net income in 1983 (1,862 and 1,624 SDRs respectively). Similarly, the deficits in the trade balances of France and Italy are the cause of their debit balances for income from investment (987 and 3,662 million SDRs respectively). But it is particularly the role of the dollar as an international currency, and to a certain extent that of the pound as well, that is responsible for the gains on this item recorded by the United States (8,866 million SDRs), and the United Kingdom (1,358 million SDRs) in 1983.

In conclusion, it is even more difficult to speak of a possible future *rentier* strategy in the case of income from financial investment than in the case of income from direct investment. This former type of income arises out of past situations. It offers no opportunity for new markets, at least as understood in the theories on the new specialization in the trade of developed countries in service activities.

The general conclusions drawn from the analysis of the trade in 'real' services must be added to this analysis. This trade cannot be seen as offering scope for the creation of a new, autonomous external demand capable of helping the old industrialized countries to guarantee the long-term financing of the imports necessary to their growth.

Notes

1. Cf. *IMF Statistics on Balance of Payments, Users' Handbook*, 4th edn 1977. This nomenclature is used in particular in OECD and SOEC statistics.
2. This 'technical' designation corresponds to the English 'non factor services'. However, the IMF, OECD and SOEC statistics on the balance of payments do not make a clear distinction between 'real' services and income from factors. In particular, income from intellectual property rights is classified under 'various real services', and earnings from work are divided between income from factors and unrequited transfers. For a statistical analysis that makes a clear distinction between services related to factors of production and other services, see the study of invisible trade by major geographical zone by Brender and Oliveira-Martins, 1984.

3. Cf. *IMF Supplement on Foreign Trade*, 1981; import ratios CIF/FOB.
4. This phenomenon is reflected in the belated but sustained expansion during the recession of foreign travel in the United Kingdom: expenditure on foreign travel increased from £917 million in 1975 to £2,757 million in 1980, taking the share of such expenditure in imported services from 14 to 24 per cent.
5. In OECD, 1984e, 'the statistical gap in the current world balance of payments'.
6. In 1981, the British merchant fleet (24,417 million tons) was still the fifth largest in the world, after Liberia (74,754 million tons), Greece (41,862 million tons), Japan (38,900 million tons) and Panama (26,732 million tons).
7. The very positive effects of the tourist trade in Italy are also the result of a very low level of expenditure. However, the experience of the United Kingdom suggests that this expenditure ought to increase significantly in the next few years.
8. Cf. *European Economy*, **19**, March 1984, pp. 108–12.
9. This American pressure emerges clearly in the firm positions taken at the recent GATT meetings on this question in 1982 and 1984 (cf. *Journal of World Trade Law*, various editions). The various phases of this campaign can also be followed in the *International Services Newsletter*, a quarterly publication by the Office of the US Trade Representative. The origin of this campaign goes back to the new mandate given to the American Government in the Trade Act of 1974 to encourage the liberalization of trade in services. Nevertheless, the Nixon and Ford administrations were opposed to this extension of negotiations and it was not until 1977 that the United States began to pursue an active policy in this area (cf. Shelp, 1981, Chap. 6).
10. This is reflected in the development of the international role of the Japanese banking system. But the transformation does not stop there. Japan's industrial enterprise has created a technological capital that is just beginning to be exploited. Japan has had a positive balance in trade in patents and other rights since the beginning of the 1980s (cf. Saxonhouse, 1982).
11. However, different firms are far from agreeing on this struggle against restrictive practices. Many firms have been able to conquer and protect their market within the framework of existing regulations. On the other hand, firms that produce capital goods and that wish to develop their trade in maintenance services, consultancy and research are actively demanding greater liberalization of trade (cf. Stalson, 1982).
12. This antagonism among the developed countries on the question of the conditions of trade in services is clearly explained in an intervention by the American Chamber of Commerce before the Senate, quoted by Sapir and Lutz (1980, p. 61). Both the traditional preferences of governments and the discriminatory regulations on trade in services are called into question.

13. This market is far from negligible. It has been estimated that 25 million Americans take part each year in an average of four conferences or seminars. The industry has a turnover approaching $10 billion. The growth of the market is partly explained by the increased use of conferences and seminars as an incentive for employees. Over a period of two years, Paris, which is the most popular city in the world for international conferences, was host to 16,000 Japanese Coca-Cola distributors and salesmen! (cf. report by Verger, 1982).

14. The modernization of the London Stock Exchange is being accompanied by a radical change in practices. Supply and demand in the stock market can be controlled entirely by computer. London has adopted the most automated system, the one used in New York, the National Association of Securities Dealers Automated System (NASDAS), which in a few years has become as important as the New York Stock Exchange. This development has called into question the distinction between brokers, who receive commissions, and jobbers, who act as intermediaries between brokers.

15. The OECD has recently published three studies of trade balances for certain services: 'International trade in services: insurance (January 1984), banking (February 1984) and tourism (June 1984)'.

16. Ray and Marvel (1984) show that these obstacles have a particular effect on agricultural products and consumer goods. Protectionism on the part of the developed countries is a well-established characteristic, which has a particular effect on the trade of developing countries (see Balassa, 1967).

17. The growth in the shares of West Germany and Japan in direct investment in the world as a whole is obvious, even though the share of the United States is still four times greater.

Percentage shares in the world total of direct investment

	USA	UK	W. Germany	Japan	Switzerland	France	Canada	Netherlands
1967	54	17	3	1	5	6	4	2
1973	51	14	6	5	6	4	4	3
1980	40	14	9	8	7	5	4	4

Source: Ehrsam, 1984.

5
The domestic demand for services

The previous chapter showed the limited prospects for using foreign trade in services to offset a relative decline in trade in manufactures. The present chapter will examine the prospects for using a change in domestic demand for services as the basis of a new phase of economic growth. There are two dimensions to this question, according to whether it refers to the intermediate or final demand for services. In the first case, it is necessary to analyse the effects (particularly on competitiveness) of a new way of integrating services into the production process as a whole. In the second, it is necessary to assess the prospects for autonomous development of the final demand for services.

I The different uses of services

Services, produced domestically or imported, can be exported, used in other production processes or utilized by households (or by those non-commercial sectors in which the consumption of services is considered to be part of final demand). Exports of services, which have just been analysed in relation to imports, account for only a small proportion of total uses. Intermediate and final consumption in the home market accounts for more than 90 per cent of services sold (except in the case of transport, in which exports account for 20 or 30 per cent of the total).

Moreover, it is clear from the distribution of the uses of services presented in Table 5.1 that a particular type of use (intermediate or final) is predominant in each category of service. Almost 60 per cent of sales come from final transactions; this proportion of final use rises to 70 per cent for those services classified under the heading 'personal, entertainment and various'. On the other hand, 60 per cent of the income from communications services is accounted for by intermediate expenditure. Similarly, about 50 per cent of expenditure on transport is linked to productive activities. As far as financial activities and services to firms are concerned, this percentage rises to an average of 75 to 80 per cent.

Table 5.1 Utilization of services (as % of total output), year 1975 (except USA, 1977)

Nomenclatures SOEC	SIC E.U.	Sectors	Countries	Exports	Intermediate consumption	Final consumption	Prod. % total output
57	69	Distribution	FRG	1.2	5.1	18.4	15.2
			FR	0.3	2.7	12.2	15.9
			IT	1.0	4.5	11.8	18.0
			NL	2.8	3.7	9.8	17.1
			BEL	2.6	3.8	9.7	16.5
			UK	1.5	4.9	9.7	16.2
			USA	0.6	5.9	11.9	20.3
61	65	Transport	FRG	1.4	3.6	1.7	6.8
+			FR	1.7	5.1	1.3	8.0
63			IT	1.7	3.8	2.1	7.8
+			NL	4.0	3.5	0.8	8.4
65			BEL	4.2	3.0	1.8	9.1
			UK	3.5	6.4	2.1	12.2
			USA	0.5	3.9	2.1	6.8
67	66	Communications	FRG	—	1.6	1.0	2.6
	+		FR	0.02	1.4	0.5	1.8
	67		IT	0.03	1.2	0.6	1.8
			NL	0.07	1.3	0.7	2.1
			BEL	0.1	1.2	0.5	1.7
			UK	0.11	2.1	0.8	3.4
			USA	0.03	1.2	1.4	2.8
69	70	Banking and Insurance	FRG	0.08	4.9	1.3	6.2
			FR	0.08	4.1	0.8	5.0
			IT	0.16	6.6	0.3	7.0
			NL	0.3	4.6	1.2	6.0
			BEL	0.09	3.9	1.2	5.1
			UK	0.7	5.4	1.2	7.3
			USA	0.03	3.1	3.6	6.8
71	73	Services to firms	FRG[†]	0.3	9.5	2.1	11.9
			FR	0.9	7.1	0.7	9.4
			IT	0.5	3.1	0.5	4.1
			NL	0.6	3.1	0.3	4.8
			BEL[‡]	1.5	5.1	3.3	10.6
			UK[§]	1.3	10.2	4.1	16.0
			USA	0.2	6.9	1.2	8.5
55	72	Various personal, recreational and leisure services	FRG[†]	0.2	3.0	4.1	6.9
+	+		FR	0.2	3.0	7.1	10.2
59	74		IT	—	3.8	9.4	13.4
+	+		NL	0.9	3.1	3.7	7.7
79	75		BEL[‡]	0.3	1.7	6.8	8.6
	+		UK[§]	0.02	0.6	6.0	6.6
	76		USA	0.03	3.0	7.5	10.6

Sources: European countries, SOEC (1983), SEC National Accounts Input–Output tables, 1975; USA, Survey of Current Business, May 1984, Input/Output Table 1, 1977.

* Services imported or produced locally. The services listed in this table include all market services except renting services (SOEC 73 to 77, SIC 77). The disparity between the sum of the three uses listed and total demand corresponds to services recorded as investments or stock fluctuations.

† For West Germany, SOEC sector 79, recreational and cultural services, is included with sector 71 (services to firms).

‡ In Belgium, SOEC sectors 75 (market education) and 79 (recreational, personal and various services) are included with sector 71 (services to firms).

§ For the UK, the SOEC sectors 55 (recovery and recuperation) and 71 (services to firms) are included in SOEC sectors 75, 77 (market education and health) and 79 (recreational, personal and various services).

Services to producers and services to consumers

Economists tend to make extensive use of the distinction between services to producers and services to consumers by dividing all service activities in this way. The relative proportions of intermediate and final demand given above make it possible, according to Greenfield (1966), actually to distinguish between services that are mainly directed towards producers and those aimed mainly at consumers. This dichotomy is also the basis for the distinction between 'integrating services' and 'distribution services' used by Brender *et al.* (1980). 'Integrating services' are defined as those whose main function is to facilitate external divisions in productive activities. According to these authors, they include transport, communications, the wholesale trade, financial services and specialized services to firms. Browning and Singleman (1978) suggest that services should be classified into four main categories: distribution services (commerce, transport and communications), services to producers (financial activities, services of renting of immovable goods, and services to firms), social services and personal services.[1] These divisions are rarely satisfactory, since the boundaries between the intermediate and final uses are particularly hazy. This is true of commerce, financial intermediation, transport and communications. The price of these services in fact varies with the type of use for services linked to production. A good example of this is financial activities, where many banking services are free, which means that they are classified, from the point of view of expenditure, as being mainly a service to producers. The differences between countries in final or intermediate use confirm the limitations of a strict a priori division between services to producers and services to consumers. It would be more accurate to say that within the service sector there are two poles, around one of which are grouped services used for the most part by firms, while around the other are services used for the most part by consumers. Between these two poles is a whole series of services that combine in a structured and well-established way services to producers and services to consumers. By analogy with financial intermediation services, which mediate between borrowers and lenders, the general term 'intermediation services' will be used to describe these activities.

Our examination of the dynamics of the demand for services will concentrate mainly on the two poles of services to firms and services to consumers. Firstly, however, it is necessary to describe some of the characteristics of these intermediation services.

Intermediation services: the differences in use between countries

A quick analysis of the use of these intermediation services by country (Table 5.1) reveals a wide diversity in the average distribution between intermediate and final uses.

This diversity, which concerns activities such as distribution, transport, communications and financial services, arises out of such major characteristics of the supply of services as size (United States), the degree of involvement with the world trade system (as in the case of Belgium and Holland), concentration (West Germany and the United Kingdom) and pricing policies (France).

In the distribution sector, if the importance of export activities in Holland and Belgium, which is a result of their high level of involvement in the world trade system, is ignored, final distribution is very important in France, whereas the wholesale trade is relatively small; this is the opposite of what is observed in West Germany and, to a lesser extent, in the United Kingdom.

In the transport sector, the large share taken by exports and demand from firms in the United Kingdom partly explains why there is a significantly higher volume of activity relative to total output than in the other countries. In the United States, on the other hand, economies of scale and a low level of exports of transport services help to reduce the share of this type of expenditure in total output. The low level of final expenditure on transport in France and Holland seems to be the result of a pricing policy for public transport that is favourable to households and of a marked use of private transport.

The same relatively low level of final uses in the French economy is found in the financial and communications sector. Here again, pricing policies (cheap rates in the communications sector and free banking services) in these largely nationalized sectors account to a large extent for the relatively low level of final expenditure. This is not offset by a higher level of intermediate expenditure, as is the case in the United Kingdom.

The unusual nature of the fairly similar distribution between intermediate and final uses of these services in the United States is worthy of attention. More than 50 per cent of financial and communications services are accounted for by households and public administration, whereas the comparable figure for the other countries studied is only 30 per cent. The low level of concentration in the banking sector and the well-established diffusion of the telecommunications network partly explain this situation.

Moreover, it should be noted that the United States and France, where the distribution between intermediate and final uses in the communications and financial sectors is very different, are both countries that devote a relatively low share of their total output to these activities. The few physical indicators available give only incomplete anwers: it is true that the number of telephones is twice as high in the United States (80 telephones per 100 inhabitants in 1980) as in France (41 per 100 inhabitants in 1980, which was the European average) and that the number of telex lines per 1,000 inhabitants is twice as high in France (1.5) and in Europe as a whole (1.6) as in the United States (0.7).[2] Similarly, there seem to be more free banking services in France, although a similar proportion of households hold bank accounts. All this helps to explain the higher proportion of final uses in the United States, but not the relatively low level of expenditure relative to total output in both countries.

When all is said and done, there does not seem to be any single factor common to the industrialized countries that determines the extent and form of these intermediation services. The size of the country, its level of involvement with the system of world trade, the maturity of certain service sectors and the level of state intervention in those sectors contribute to the retention of specific national characteristics in the organization of these services. The resulting differences in the cost of these intermediation services are reflected in differences in production costs. It is difficult to assess the impact of this. However, the pressure of competition does not seem to give rise to any norm for the costs of these intermediation services in the industrialized countries. Each country seems to have retained networks of these services adapted to its own geography and the history of its economic activities. A survey of the determinants of the intermediate demand for these intermediation services will make it possible to clarify their specificity relative to the two poles of the service sector.

Intermediation: the choices made by producers

The development in each country of intermediation services relative to total output between 1970 and 1975 (Table 5.2) shows firstly that expenditure on communications and (with a few exceptions) transport remained stable, and secondly that there was a general increase in expenditure on financial intermediation. Expenditure on distribution, on the other hand, appears very variable. The broad characteristics of the supply of these services partly explain these sectoral differences.

Table 5.2 The development of intermediate demand for certain services, 1970–1975 (intermediate use of these services relative to total output, in percentage)

	West Germany		France		Italy		Netherlands		Belgium		UK		USA	
	1970	1975	1970	1975	1970	1975	1970	1975	1970	1975	1970	1975	1972	1977
Distribution	7.7	5.1	3.8	2.7	3.3	4.5	5.5	3.7	3.5	3.8	2.9	4.9	4.8	5.9
Transport	3.8	3.6	5.8	5.1	2.8	3.8	5.4	3.5	3.1	3.0	4.1	6.4	3.9	3.9
Communications	1.6	1.6	1.3	1.4	1.2	1.2	1.3	1.3	1.1	1.2	2.0	2.1	1.1	1.2
Financial institutions	3.4	4.9	3.7	4.1	3.9	6.6	3.8	5.8	3.3	3.9	–	—	3.0	3.1

Sources: SOEC. Input–Output tables, 1970, 1975.
Survey of Current Business, Input–Output data 1972, 1977.

The use by firms of distributors reflects their decisions on the externalization of purchasing and sales functions. The conditions under which these decisions are made are similar to those under which decisions on specialized services to firms are made; these will be analysed later. Nevertheless, the existence of long-established distribution networks limits the alternatives. But this does not preclude all new opportunities, as is shown by the development of direct purchasing and selling consortia and international trading companies. The contrasting developments shown in Table 5.2 underline the diverse ways in which distribution networks are being reorganized. The use of financial services would answer the same criteria were it not for the fact that these activities are strictly regulated. The externalization or internalization of financial activities is not the sole responsibility of firms. Nevertheless, the general liberalization of regulations, which has to a large extent been encouraged by the internationalization of the movements of industrial and finance capital and by the technological changes in the banking sector brought about by computerization, has extended the scope of financial activities. These general developments offer new opportunities for the externalization of financial management functions. The growth of firms' expenditure on financial intermediation may thus follow the same pattern as that on services to firms.

Existing infrastructures and government supervision are even more important factors in the transport and communications sectors, which are both more concentrated and often under more or less direct state control. The relative stability of intermediate expenditure on transport and communications (Table 5.2) is also explained in part by significant productivity gains and a higher capital/labour ratio than in other services.

The comparison with the dynamics of the intermediate demand for services to firms, the limits of which have already been underlined as far as distribution and financial services are concerned, is of little relevance here because of the dominant role played by the existing structure of supply. Transport and communications functions are already in fact to a large extent externalized. Moreover, supply is very concentrated and has until now been able to integrate major technical changes. At the beginning of the 1980s, none of the countries studied was suffering from obvious underdevelopment of its communications or transport networks.

Technological developments often cause the installation of a 'modern' communications network to be presented as a major challenge. Although the strategic importance of these networks should not be ignored, it should be pointed out that the telecommunications sector in a reasonably large country is capable of financing this modernization itself. This was the conclusion of an OECD study (1983), which pointed out that large investment programmes[3] in West Germany, the United States, Japan and Canada were very largely self-financing. Only France, because of the scope of its projects, and Italy, where pricing policies in public services are very constrained, have had to have recourse to a significant degree of external finance. It must be concluded from this that the installation of a new communications network need not involve the structural upheavals in the economy caused by the building of canals, railways, roads and the national grid for the supply of electricity. It is significant in this respect that none of the programmes for economic revival drawn up since 1975 has made such transformations of the transport and communications networks a fundamental priority. It is true that every Keynesian programme for revival has seen such investment as a potential means of relaunching economic growth. But there has also been concern about the increased mobility of capital made possible by such investment. Only the Scandinavian countries have made it clear that they consider the development of communications networks within Europe as essential to economic revival.

However, note should be taken of this capacity of the transport and communications sectors to carry out the required modernization of the communications network on an autonomous basis, both from a financial and employment point of view (the above-mentioned OECD report predicts that numbers employed will at best stabilize).

In conclusion, the intermediation services have, to varying extents, their own patterns of development, in which existing structures of supply pay a major part. Their specificity should be noted, but the demand for services will be analysed essentially through the two poles of the service sector represented by services to firms and personal services, in the widest sense of the term.

II Services to firms and changes in the productive system

As a result of their importance in the total demand for services and their potential effect on industrial growth, services to firms may contribute indirectly to a transformation of the conditions of production in manufacturing industry and thus open up new opportunities for development. The starting point for this analysis of the nature and determinants of this intermediate demand for services will be an examination of the sectors using these services.

In view of the difficulties of measuring even the value of services to firms (see Appendix VIII) the following analysis by sector will be restricted to the American and French experiences.

In an economy like that of the United States, which is already heavily orientated towards the tertiary sector, services to firms account for 8.2 per cent of total output ($161,016 million in 1977), 81 per cent of which is intermediate consumption (equal to 6.6 per cent of total output).

This intermediate demand for services is relatively lower in manufacturing industry than in the other sectors. The demand for services to firms represents 57 per cent of the total (whereas these services produce only 52 per cent of value added). This concentration is even greater in other service sectors. Trading activities use 22 per cent of these intermediate services (14 per cent of value added) and financial activities 6.6 per cent (4 per cent of total value added). Apart from the service sector, the rest of this intermediate demand for services to firms is concentrated in a small number of other sectors: the construction industry accounts for 10.8 per cent (3.7 per cent of total value added). As far as the remaining 32 per cent of this intermediate demand is concerned (44 per cent of value added), only a few manufacturing activities have a level of demand higher than the average; these industries are characterized either by high expenditure on advertising (food products, pharmaceuticals, tobacco) or by their low level of concentration (textiles, leather, furniture). On the other hand, the capital goods sector and most of the industries producing intermediate goods are not among the heaviest users. The office machine sectors and aeronautical engineering, where the use of services to firms is slightly higher than the national average, are notable exceptions.[4]

This is not an orientation specific to the American economy. A similar analysis of the sectors that use services to firms, carried out on the basis of input/output data for 1975 (SOEC, 1984), leads to similar conclusions in the case of France. The service sector and the construction industry account for 66 per cent of services to firms and produce 61 per cent of value added. These figures conceal wide disparities between non-market activities, where the use of these services is significantly lower than the average, and activities where the demand for these services is very high; these include financial activities, and especially the insurance sector (10 per cent of demand and 1.7 per cent of total value added) and the construction industry (20 per cent of intermediate demand for services and 8 per cent of value added). One significant difference between France and the United States is the structure of the intermediate consumption of services; in France, the distribution sector spends the equivalent of only 3.4 per cent of its value added on services to firms, whereas the national average of 7.9 per cent is more than double this figure.[5] As in the United States, the manufacturing sector as a whole makes less use of services to firms, and those industries that do make greater use of these services have the characteristics mentioned above:

1. consumer goods industries with low levels of concentration (furniture, plastics etc.);
2. industries with a high level of expenditure on advertising (the food and drink industry, chemical products);[6]
3. two capital goods industries, office equipment and aeronautical engineering, which spend the equivalent of 20 per cent of their value added on services.

The similarity in the distribution by sector of users of services to firms in two economies as different as those of the United States and France[7] gives a certain degree of generality to a description of the demand for services to firms that can be summarized as follows.

There are two categories of activities in which the use of services to firms appears to be higher than the average:

(1) Sectors in which the productive or commercial activity is specifically linked to a service activity which has been externalized for a long time. These include construction and architecture, insurance, brokerage and legal services, banking and security services, certain consumer goods (food and chemical products) and advertising and the manufacture of complex machinery and research and development services (aeronautical engineering and office equipment).
(2) Sectors which include many small firms. The organization of work in these sectors with a low level of concentration may reflect the subcontracting of such functions as distribution, accountancy and research.

This characterization of the sectors that use services to firms shows firstly that the proportion of value added transferred to the purchase of services is generally relatively low. This is particularly true of the oligopolistic sectors.

These observations cast some doubt on the theories linking the development of services to firms to a major transformation of the dynamics of industrial growth. In particular, the relatively low transfers of value added do not enable a direct link to be made between the development of productivity in manufacturing industry and the use of services to firms. However, this restriction applies only to transfers of value added and is only an accounting identity. It is conceivable that certain services have a strategic importance as far as firms' competitiveness is concerned, although the oligopolistic sectors make relative use of these services, while at the same time being major exporters. The heterogeneous nature of services to firms would be sufficient to explain this paradox.

From this point of view, the role of these services is largely qualitative and strategic in character. Thus, for example, the services of computer consultancy firms seem to be used much more by manufacturing industry than by the tertiary sector.[8] That being the case, such services, to the extent that they do not require large transfers of value added, act as catalysts in the process of industrial development. But if these components are freely available on the world market, their strategic importance as far as competitiveness is concerned is lessened. These points can be clarified by an analysis of the factors determining the use made by firms of external services.

Two factors combine, to varying degrees, to create the demand for intermediate services: the appearance of new tasks in the organization of production and the opportunities for using production processes external to the firm in order to perform these new tasks. This duality does not mean that services to firms necessarily always fulfil new functions. It is possible for innovation to concern only the organization of production. This is the case, for example, with the agencies providing contract labour.

There are four types of change that lead to the creation of new tasks:

— changes in product markets;
— changes in labour and commercial law;
— the development of computer technology;
— the spread of new forms of management.

The gradual formation of a world market that both exposes national industries to competition from countries with very different production costs and also opens up new opportunities for foreign markets means that firms must have greater awareness of markets and rates of innovation. This continuous transformation of the markets encourages the development of a whole range of services such as market research, promotion and research and development. This is a long-term trend aimed at reducing uncertainty about demand and the conditions of competition.

The complexity of the national and international division of labour that accompanies the development of economies leads to similar complexity in the regulatory frameworks. It is perhaps in the sphere of trade and commerce that this development is most recent, due to the double effect of international trade agreements (enforcement of the conditions of free trade, defence of patents, import and export formalities, conditions for international payments) and the new opportunities for consumer protection (standardization of products for health and safety reasons, legal proceedings to establish liability). These changes encourage the development of legal advice services.

The new data processing and information storage technologies also contribute to the appearance of new tertiary tasks forming part of the production process. It is true that they have given a new dimension to research and consultancy functions; however, it is difficult to assess their final impact on the demand for and use of these functions (cf. Chapter 6). More directly, however, the new information technologies have created new needs for computer expertise and consultancy (methods of computerization, management and programming of data processing equipment).

Moreover, by freeing some tertiary activities from the constraints of fixed location, the new computer technologies have facilitated the development of techniques for carrying out management tasks at a distance. This has tended to accelerate the diffusion of new management practices, which is a fourth change to be added to the list of those leading to the development of 'tertiary' tasks. The economic rationalization of the various stages of the production process is not predetermined but is a function of the intensity of competition in the product and factor markets. In the industrial economies under consideration, standard management practices are largely the result of practices in large firms, where management techniques are developed; these include the differentiation of functions, analytical accounting methods and cost benefit analysis for new projects.

These practices encourage the definition of new jobs in management and the use of external management and consultancy centres in small and medium-sized firms, since they enable a supply of services to firms to be built up.

These new functions can thus be carried out either within or outside the firm. The prevailing pattern in large modern firms, as shown in studies by Chandler (1977 and 1981)[9] is one in which functions are internalized in order to bring into play the synergies inherent in a hierarchical organization. The externalization of functions, on the other hand, is an attempt to maximize the advantages of the economies of scale made possible by the extension of external markets (cf. Stigler, 1951 and 1965).

Further examination of these two analyses of the division of labour will show that they can be used in a complementary way to explain the distribution of demand by sector for services to firms.

Stigler's analysis of the externalization of functions

The principle of the extension of markets put forward by Stigler (1951) as an explanation of the externalization of certain functions accounts, a priori, for the recent development of the intermediate demand for services. A firm's activity comprises several functions. An increase in the scale of production means that these various functions offer different economies of scale. According to Stigler, at a certain level of production, it becomes preferable to turn to the external market and to externalize those functions that offer the greatest economies of scale. Stanback *et al*. (1981) rightly stress that it is less a question of economies of scale than of specialization of tasks. Firstly, economies of scale at the level of functions are difficult to spot. On the other hand, the specialization of tasks in a given function reveals opportunities for externalization. The development of services to firms is based precisely on the ability of entrepreneurs to spot which of the specializations within a firm offer opportunities for externalization. However, these specializations are more closely linked to organization than to scale of production. Thus, a certain way of organizing personnel management or a firm's accountancy department will make it possible for part of the process of paying wages or auditing to be carried out externally. Appendix IX is a general survey of the diversity of functions concerned in the case of the French economy; it also shows the frequency with which firms use these services.

Once this distinction between specialization (which is a question of organization)[10] and economies of scale (which is a question of volume of production) is made, the criterion of the size of firm no longer operates in the same way. An initial reading of Stigler's principle might well lead to the conclusion that an increase in the size of the firm in terms of volume of production results in an increased use of external services or even in the establishment of an external production process (open to external users). A second reading of Stigler's proposition suggests, on the contrary, that a firm of any size may use external services as soon as a certain pattern of organization is sufficiently widespread. In this context, the scale of production in a large firm may make it possible to consider the complete internalization of a given function, and not the opposite. This different way of looking at Stigler's principle alters the conclusions that can be drawn on the development of the demand for services to firms. Since the 1950s (Stigler's first article dates from 1951), the situation has changed, both from the point of view of standard management practices and from that of the supply of services to firms. The growth of services to firms is thus the result of a cumulative process in which the diffusion of new organizational practices facilitates the extension of services to firms and in which, in return, the development of this supply of services accelerates the diffusion of standard management practices. Under these conditions, the distribution by sector of the users of services is due to a large extent to the level of development of the supply of services and to the diffusion of modern management practices (in particular those made possible by computer technology). Thus, the frequent use within the tertiary sector of services to firms is not only linked to the importance of small or medium-sized firms but also to the development of the supply of services and to the diffusion of modern management practices, which in these sectors are particularly susceptible to externalization. Seen in this light, the arguments put forward by Chandler and Stigler become largely complementary.

The internalization of new functions according to Chandler

Chandler (1977) stresses the development of different forms of hierarchical organization which created and are still creating the power of large firms. This throws light both on the development of the demand from large firms for external services and the gradual structuring of the supply of services to firms. In an early form of organization, which developed in the United States at the beginning of this century, the large firm was divided into departments according to the major functions within the firm (personnel, research and methods, production and general management). This early form of centralized organization—the U-shaped structure in Williamson's formulation (Williamson, 1975)—led to most of the firm's requirements being met internally (vertical integration). The rigidity of this very centralized organization tended to increase with the size of the firm. It was largely this rigidity that gave rise during the 1930s to criticisms of the separation between the ownership and control of firms, expressed particularly by Berle and Means in their book *The Modern Corporation and Private Property* (1932) (cf. Williamson, 1983). A more recent form of organization, which appeared during the inter-war period, integrated the diversification of production processes by setting up product divisions (the M-shaped structure). These divisions, which reproduced on their own level the unitary functional division of the U-shaped structure, had greater autonomy as far as product management was concerned; it was thus easier for them to use external production processes. The same was true of central management, whose task was to assess the results of each division and to draw up an overall strategy for the firm. This positive correlation between a structured internal division of tasks and the use of external services seems to have been extended to small and medium-sized firms. Barcet and Bonamy (1983) found that the use by French firms of services to firms increased with the development of the functional division of tasks (for firms with U-shaped management structures). From this point of view, the demand for services to firms is more a complement to than a substitute for a reorganization of a firm's internal activities.

This sharp multiplication in the use of these services to firms can be dated. The studies by Williamson (1981) and Chandler (1981), as well as the survey carried out by Caves (1980) on firms' strategies, all agree that the widespread establishment of a multidivisional organizational structure in large firms took place in the immediate post-war period in the United States and at the end of the 1960s in Europe. This makes it virtually impossible to extend the earlier increase in the externalization of tertiary functions in the oligopolistic sectors beyond 1975. Nevertheless, the slower pace of reorganization in small and medium-sized firms may contribute to the retention of a sustained growth in the demand for services to firms. The development of the supply of services is in itself a factor that encourages this evolution. Indeed, the emergence of conglomerates producing a wide diversity of products also leads to a structuring of the supply of services capable of accelerating the diffusion of new standard management practices. The large chains that are already widespread in the distribution, hotel, catering and car hire sectors are also found in activities such as consultancy, data management, research and agencies supplying contract labour. The standardization of the production of services which is a determining factor in the development of such chains makes it easier for small and medium-sized firms to gain access to intermediate services. This structuring of the supply of services therefore explains to a large extent the relatively high level of the demand for services to firms in those service and consumer goods sectors with a low level of concentration.

In this way a combination of the principles of industrial organization put forward by Chandler and Stigler explains to a large extent the sectoral structure of the demand for services to firms. The growth of this demand is both the cause and the consequence of three successive changes in the production process:

(1) changes in the organization of large firms;
(2) a particular structuring of the supply of services to producers and
(3) the reorganization on a functional basis of the management of small and medium-sized firms.

It is possible to draw several conclusions from this as to the prospects for the development of this demand and its effect on the dynamics of the economy as a whole. However, it is none the less true that certain important aspects of the intermediate demand for services are not accounted for at all by the organizational principles discussed above.

The duality of the demand for producer services

The analyses presented above in terms of economies of scale or complementarities are more or less linked to the purely technical aspects of production. There is no explicit mention of the interactions between the social and technical aspects of the organization of production. However, the nature of industrial relations plays a decisive role in decisions on whether to internalize production processes or to use external services. This criticism, made by Williamson (1981) of Chandler's studies of American firms, is even more justified in the case of the European economies, in which collective agreements and labour law are more constraining. According to sector, size of firm and the extent to which the work-force is organized, conditions of employment and pay can respond more or less quickly to variations in the general level of economic activity or to changes in the nature of products. The use of external specialized services thus avoids the need to develop expertise within the firm that is little used or which does not fit in with the existing structure of skilled jobs in the firm. On the other hand, the use of external services for tasks with a low skill level makes it possible to limit the extension of an advantageous internal labour market. The development of external services such as caretaking and cleaning can be partly attributed to this segmentation of the labour market. Thus, firms in which the organization of the internal labour market is fairly rigid can benefit from conditions in the external labour market. For production processes that are particularly sensitive to cyclical variations in economic activity or which are subject to strict timetables, it is advantageous to use contract labour as a means of adapting the numbers of people employed to changes in production rates. This factor helps to explain the high level of demand for services in the building industry.

From this point of view, the externalization of certain tasks is aimed mainly at increasing flexibility in the use of the labour-force. This brings us back to the problems of adjustment costs (the costs of adjusting conditions of production to variations in markets). The use of leasing services is a response to this same concern. These multiple aspects of the adaptation of productive systems mean that decisions on the externalization or internalization of productive activities are not wholly dependent on purely technical considerations.

In the final analysis, the use of services to firms concerns a wide range of diverse functions within the firm. It is thus difficult to establish a direct link between this demand and changes in the performance of firms. There are several reasons for thinking that the externalization of tertiary functions is less important for manufacturing industry than is often assumed.

Firstly, the transfers of value added represented by this externalization are still moderate. Even if it is assumed that all the intermediate demand for services corresponds to value added (i.e. that its production requires no intermediate consumption), the statistics for the United States and France quoted above show a transfer of approximately 6 per cent of the value added of manufacturing industry to the service sector. Even this is an average figure that is unevenly distributed among the various sectors of manufacturing industry. Moreover, the hypothesis that the intermediate consumption of services is equivalent to a pure transfer of value added overestimates the actual transfer. The opposite hypothesis, according to which the transfer of value added taken into account is reduced to the value added immediately created in the services to firms, is certainly a better estimate of the direct effect on balance sheets in manufacturing industry of the use of external services. This effect can be roughly estimated for each country by means of the ratio of production to value added for services to firms as a whole. This ratio makes it possible to assess the level of value added that corresponds to the intermediate demand for services in each country.

Table 5.3 shows approximate estimations of these transfers of value added for the manufacturing sectors of the countries studied. On

Table 5.3 Estimates of the relative level of the intermediate demand for services to firms, 1975

	West Germany	France	Italy	Nether-lands	Belgium	UK	USA
Intermediate use of services to firms as % of total output* (a)	8.4	7.2	3.2	3.1	4.2	7.1	7.0
Share of value added in the total resources of the sector 'services to firms'[†] (b)	0.53	0.58	0.65	0.53	0.68	0.55	0.61
Corresponding transfers of value added to the sector 'services to firms'* as % of total output ($c = a \times b$)	4.4	4.2	2.1	1.6	2.9	3.9	4.2
Transfers of value added to services—the example of three manufacturing sectors (as % of value added in the manufacturing sector):							
(27) motor industry	5.3	3.7	3.4	1.6	3.6	3.4	3.2
(45) timber, furniture	2.7	4.7	0.9	1.4	2.5	4.2	5.8
(23) office machines	2.6	11.5	4.9	1.1	2.4	7.4	5.0

Sources: SOEC Input–Output data, 1975
Survey of Current Business, 1977, Input–Output data, May 1984

* In order to compensate approximately for the differences in the sectors covered by the statistics available for the various countries (cf. Table 5.1), the data for West Germany, Belgium and the United Kingdom have been calculated with reference to the structure of intermediate consumption in France. The correction coefficients for intermediate consumption in these three countries were, respectively, 0.87, 0.84 and 0.70.
† Without correction for differences in the sectors covered by the statistics available.

average, they represent only 4 per cent of value added in manufacturing industry.

The relatively low level of these transfers of value added rather invalidates the theories that see a change in the relationship between manufacturing industry and the service sector as a means of transferring a large part of the value added produced in the manufacturing sector to the tertiary sector. There is thus no hope of explaining the phenomenon of de-industrialization by reconstructing a fictitious manufacturing sector that has somehow managed to incorporate the intermediate demand for services.

It is true that the data used refers only to the year 1975; however, there has been very little more growth in services to firms since 1975 than in the manufacturing sector; this contrasts with the rapid growth in the decade prior to 1975. Statistics on inter-industry exchanges in France in 1980 confirm the hypothesis that the demand for services has been stable, with the notable exception of those manufacturing sectors characterized in 1975 by a high intermediate demand for services (the consumer goods sector, aeronautical engineering and shipbuilding).[11] This slower rate of growth could be predicted from the structural changes in manufacturing industry. On the other hand, the figures used only took into account the demand for services that came directly from manufacturing industry to the service sector. Other figures that take into account all the service activities set in motion by the growth of final demand in manufacturing industry (cf. for example Momigliano and Siniscalco, 1982) include in their estimations the effects of the reorganization of tertiary activities themselves. This overall view of the 'tertiarization of the productive system' is interesting, but it is important to make a distinction between those services that are a direct substitute for industrial tasks (services to manufacturing firms directly ordered by the firms themselves) and those that restructure traditional services (distribution, transport, communications, accommodation agencies).

A decisive catalyst in the reorganization of manufacturing industry

The above observations on the modest level of the transfers of value added should not, however, lead us to minimize the importance of the use of external services for manufacturing firms. Firstly, in certain manufacturing sectors, the demand for services to firms represents a not insignificant proportion of value added. Table 5.3 shows the very different examples of a 'new' industry, office machines, and a traditional industry, furniture. In both cases, services may facilitate innovation and the organization of the distribution networks of industries that are exposed to strong foreign competition. Moreover, it is significant that the intermediate demand for services in these sectors has continued to increase in the recession. Nevertheless, the situations in the two industries are still very different. In the first, the market is expanding and there is a continuous process of technical innovation; in the second, the market is stagnating and foreign competition has rapidly transformed the profitability of the industry. These different contexts hardly make it possible to establish direct relationships between the intermediate consumption of services and productivity gains and market shares.

Nor is it possible to conclude that there is a systematic difference in the kinds of services used. The use of contract labour represents only a small proportion of the demand for intermediate services (6 per cent in the United States in 1972 and less than 15 per cent in France in 1980)[12] and its distribution within the manufacturing sector does not reveal any great differences in the frequency of use. Moreover, some temporary work contracts of this kind involve highly skilled personnel; in this case, the use of contract labour is equivalent to the use of other research and consultancy services of a technical nature.

The strategic value to firms of such expert services lies precisely in the highly skilled nature of those services. The services of highly skilled specialists are of assistance to the decision-making centres of the modern firm in many different areas. Stanback (1980) points out that in matters of commercial strategy, engineering, financial management and international law, specialist firms perform better than the corresponding internal services of the various divisions of the modern firm.[13] This reorganization of the function of the entrepreneur facilitates the diversification of products and markets, which is one of the aims of the management of large firms. The recent desire of many multinational firms to create international trading companies is part of this strategy. At the same time, this external expertise offers opportunities for adaptation to small and medium-sized firms subject to strong foreign competition in their domestic markets.

In the final analysis, the importance of this intermediate demand lies in the capacity of service firms to solve temporary strategical problems or to assist manufacturing firms in processes of structural adaptation. This being the case, it might legitimately be wondered whether this externalization of 'strategic functions' might not be largely temporary in nature. Although in a crisis the need to adapt the productive structures is obvious, it is far from easy to see what direction such changes should take. The use of external specialized services concentrates expertise and thus reduces this uncertainty. If this level of uncertainty is subsequently reduced as the world economy stabilizes, the effect of competition may well lead to these strategic functions being re-internalized within the framework of a new type of hierarchical organization of the firm at the world level. The question is not without validity. The evolution of foreign trade in services shows the relative fragility of established positions. The fluctuations in markets for engineering services are a good example. The difficulties experienced by firms offering information or advice in controlling their cash flows are indications that a certain degree of caution should be exercised in assessing their prospects for development.[14]

In the current phase, the information required as a result of the reorganization of productive activities is diffused mainly through the working of the market. In the future, new hierarchical relationships within multinational firms may reduce this use of the market, as Chandler (1981) and Williamson (1981) suggest in their studies. Nevertheless, services to firms would still be the key factor in the structural organization of small and medium-sized firms. Their importance would then be dependent on the role that these smaller firms might be able to play in international trade. These hypotheses show that the permanent or transitory changes in manufacturing industry that accompany the development of services to firms is still uncertain.

III Final domestic demand for services

The questions that underlie the analysis of the final domestic demand for services are different from those examined above. It is no longer a matter of competitiveness or of the internal reorganization of productive activities but of the prospects for autonomous growth in the demand for services from households and government departments.

In fact, analysis of this final demand for services does give rise to questions of social organization, but this time a distinction must be made between market activities involving direct money payments and public or private non-market activities without direct money payment. These private non-market activities can be divided into two fairly distinct categories: domestic activities on the one hand, and non-profitmaking activities on the other. The boundaries between these activities differ according to period and country. Education and health services provide a good example of this: over and above purely family activities, all the various combinations of marketed and non-marketed services are to be found. Examination of this distribution and of the way in which it has evolved lies at the heart of an analysis of the final demand for services. The usual examination of consumption by chief category (food, housing, clothing and leisure) is not sufficient, since it does not show the distribution of this demand between goods and services. A particular category may be made up of various combinations of goods and services. Food requirements, for example, may be satisfied by going to a restaurant or by purchasing and preparing food. Thus, an analysis of the final demand for services must also be concerned with the substitutions within each purpose between goods and services. In this distribution between market and domestic activities, the institutional provision of services (public sector and private institutions) is decisive in various ways. It is both the producer of services used in domestic and market activities and the supervisory authority that defines the institutional framwork of this social division of labour. Thus the question of the autonomous growth of the final demand for services becomes that of a 'new' shift in the distribution between market activities, public and private non-market activities and domestic activities.

'New' is a fundamental concept here. There is a tendency to assume that past substitutions of institutional marketed or non-marketed for private domestic services are irreversible. Inherent in this assumption is the belief that this type of substitution means that needs will be better satisfied, and so this shift in the boundaries between activities is interpreted as social progress. Our initial analysis will be made from this point of view. It is known that this socialization of domestic services may be a short-term process. This is the paradox raised by those such as Illich (1975) who have attempted to weigh up the longer-term advantages and disadvantages of the extension of market and institutional activities. This critique of social organization is distinct from that put forward by Meadows *et al*. (1972), which is based on the possibility that an excessively high rate of growth may lead to the exhaustion of natural resources. This latter critique, far from questioning the extension of tertiary activities, recommends that they should be developed as a means of slowing down the exhaustion of the resources used in purely material production.

The recession has reduced the influence of this questioning of material well-being and growth. The damage to employment prospects and social justice caused by the stagnation of the developed economies has strengthened the arguments in favour of growth (cf. for example Thurow, 1980; Beckerman, 1979). It remains to be seen whether the emergence of new marketed or non-marketed services (whether private or public) can help to regain this momentum.

The first point to be made is that the extension of the tertiary sectors has not been able to prevent more than ten years of slow growth in the main developed economies. If the dynamics of the final demand for services are to play a new role capable of restoring the bases of a kind of economic growth that is socially acceptable in terms of employment and social justice, then the effects will be felt only in the long term. The characteristics of a transformation of this kind are hardly to be seen in the evolution of the main objects of consumption. Of greater significance are the changes in the determinants of the distribution between goods and services. In order to understand the conditions for the emergence of these new forms of services, an attempt will be made to bring out the internal coherence of consumption patterns.

The extent of the formal economy: the dilemmas of national accounting

The common conception of the economy has been determined largely by the development over the past forty years of national accounting. These studies have institutionalized the scope of the formal economy. However, the boundaries of the formal economy are somewhat hazy, and the areas of contention are precisely those in question here, which lie at the boundary between market and non-market activities, whether public or private.

The countries with a centrally planned economy have strictly limited the definition of production to that which contributes to material output. This includes, in addition to goods, those services, such as distribution and transport, that contribute to the circulation and exchange of these material goods. Other countries, such as France until 1975 (cf. Vanoli, 1983), are more concerned with monetary exchanges and exclude non-market activities from the definition of productive activities. Most countries with a market economy now use systems similar to the United Nations' National Accounting System, in which the sphere of production includes all institutional services, both public and private. This consensus in the countries with market economies to extend the sphere of production to public services can be explained by the mixed nature of these services. The national product would lose much of its meaning if it were to be altered by marginal transfers between the public and private parts of the same education or health system, for example. In the case of these activities in which public and private provision are mixed, the UN System of National Accounting

(SNA) includes in the sphere of production those services which are public goods, the so-called 'regrettable necessities' such as general administration, the police force, the armed services and the legal system. The beneficiaries of these 'public goods' are by their very nature not identifiable. Accounting convention includes them in government consumption expenditure.

This is obviously an extension of straightforward notions of production. The value of these public services is measured simply by their direct cost. The social validation given by the market to the production of goods and services is here replaced by a social contract between officials who authorize expenditure and their electors. This extension of the sphere of production to strictly non-market activities has its counterpart in the sphere of domestic activities in production for private consumption. The UN SNA recommends that production for private consumption, both by firms and households, should be taken into account. The fictitious value accorded to this kind of production is the same as that of the corresponding market activity. In accordance with the logic of his definition of goods and services (that we have largely retained), Hill (1979) points out that all services carried out by households for themselves should be included under the heading of production for private consumption. This would include in particular all do-it-yourself tasks. A number of studies have estimated the total value of domestic labour either on the basis of the wages forgone by those involved in domestic labour or on the basis of the expenditure avoided by not employing a person from outside the household. In view of the numbers of people involved, these estimates represent considerable proportions of total output: of the order of one-third for the first method and two-thirds for the second (cf. the survey by Hawrylyshyn, 1976, and that by Jugand and Lemennicier, 1982).

The sphere of productive activities as thus defined is vast and excludes only a few personal needs that cannot be carried out by anyone else. Indeed, it is extended so far that it vanishes among the interactions of life in a society in which all our actions have effects on others and on ourselves. In any case, accounting convention only includes housing services under the heading of production of services for private consumption. This heading records both rent paid to landlords and an estimate of the rent that would be paid by owners of property if they were tenants. This convention has a certain logic. The choice between being an owner or a tenant is a direct function of the financial capacity of each person and the alternative opportunities for financial investment. The exclusion of housing rental services for private consumption would reintroduce the possibility of arbitrary fluctuations in the national product (paradoxically, a loss of interest in home ownership and a corresponding increase in the number of tenants would lead to a growth in the national product).

The scale of this 'fictitious' production and the arbitrary nature of its measurement introduces a significant element of uncertainty into the assessment of the level of economic activity. Thus Table 5.4 shows that there are considerable differences in expenditure on housing rental services for countries with physically comparable housing stocks:[15] from 4.2 per cent of total output in the Netherlands to 6.3 per cent in Italy for a housing stock of similar volume (320 to 330 units per 1,000 inhabitants) or from 5.4% in Belgium to 7.1% in West Germany for a housing stock of 390 units per 1,000 inhabitants. It remains difficult to separate differences in accounting practices from real differences in the relative values of housing stocks. The fictitious nature of these services, which is more akin to a capital investment, distinguishes them from the rest of the consumption of services by households. And, to the extent that they are concerned with assets of the existing house stock, these services are located upstream of the demand for building services. This position is similar to that of the services imputed to durable goods, which are not taken into account by national accounting systems, although numerous attempts have been made to assess their value (for a survey of these attempts see Katz, 1983).[16] This argument could be extended to impute a service to all goods that are not consumed when first used.[17]

In some ways, an extensive approach to the notion of production like that outlined above calls into question the usual concept of growth. Moreover, there are no limits to the scope of such fictitious accounting.[18]

Our analysis, on the other hand, will attempt to take account of the differences in the nature of services, according to whether they are the result of market or non-market activities or of production for private consumption. This restrictive approach responds to a concern which is prevalent in the recession, for the development of wage employment.[19]

Final demand is largely predetermined

The services 'consumed' by households are of various kinds, according to their mode of production (marketed, non-marketed, production for private consumption). Market consumption by households is generally

Table 5.4 Final demand for services by households, 1975 (as % of total output)

	West Germany	France	Italy	Nether-lands	Belgium	UK	USA
Renting services SOEC: 73; SIC 71	7.1	5.8	6.3	4.2	5.4	5.9	9.6
Integrating services* (distribution, finance, communications, transport)	14.5	15.4	15.2	12.7	16.5	17.9	20.2
Personal and various market services†	4.1	7.1	9.4	3.7	6.8	6.0	7.5
'Mixed' education and health services‡ SOEC: 75, 77, 85, 89; SIC: 77	9.9	10.3	9.4	14.0	10.8	10.9	11.7
Total	35.6	38.6	40.4	34.6	39.5	40.8	49.0

Source: Input–Output data, 1975, Eurostat
Input–Output, 1977, Survey of Current Business.

* This group includes the first five categories of services in Table 5.1, i.e. SOEC headings: 57, 61, 63, 65, 67, 69 and 71 and USA SIC: 69, 65, 66 + 67, 70 and 73. The same warning about the differences in the sectors covered by the statistics given in Table 5.1 thus applies.

† The sixth category in Table 5.1 is used here, i.e. SOEC: 55, 59 and 79 and USA SIC: 72 + 74 + 75 + 76.

‡ In the case of the United States, education expenditure by the individual states and local communities has been added to SIC heading 77: health, education, social services and non-profit organizations.

analysed by purpose. These purposes refer to certain broad categories of needs felt by households, which are listed as food, housing, clothing, leisure, health and education. The way in which these needs are fulfilled is largely determined for each individual by a set of social practices. This is recognized in the everyday classification of individuals according to their way of dressing, the food they eat and where they live. Thus, reference groups for the study of consumption patterns are built up according to historical period and country. These groups are distinguished by such characteristics as income, age, sex and geographical area.

In establishing patterns or norms of consumption, cars and housing play a central role. According to the conditions specific to each country, the place of residence (rural or urban), the type of car and the kind of housing give a fairly precise definition of the pattern of consumption. This structuring makes it possible to speak of models of consumption. The reference to the American model is explained by the early development in the United States of a model of mass consumption based on cars and housing (cf. Aglietta, 1979).

During the 1960s and 1970s, the higher rate of economic growth in the European countries brought consumption patterns in these countries closer to the American model. The relative shares of the various households' expenditures by object in the European countries tended to catch up with the relative shares in America (cf. Table 5.5).

The final demand for services operates at various levels in this strong convergence in the way in which needs are satisfied. A distinction can be made between four types of services characterized by their relationship to the consumption norm.

(1) Some consumption of services is directly linked to the infra-structures of the consumption model (location, supply of products and means of exchange to the consumption unit). For households, the intermediate aspect of these services predominates. Retail and financial services are the most typical components of this category. The term 'integrating services', already used in the discussion of services to firms, will be used to describe these services as well. Moreover, there is a link between the production of services to producers and of those to consumers, which raises the problem of how these different uses are to be priced. Because of this mix between the intermediate and final aspects of demand, transport and communications services can be considered to be mainly integrating services.

Table 5.5 Some indicators of the change in market consumption patterns (excluding education and health) in certain European countries* and the United States, between 1960 and 1978

	Budgetary coefficients[†] (%)				Annual rate of variation of budgetary coefficients (%)	
	EUR4		USA		EUR4	USA
	1960	1978	1960	1978	1960–1978	1960–1978
Food	36.6	26.2	24.0	18.9	−1.83	−1.32
Clothing	12.6	9.0	9.8	7.9	−1.77	−1.16
Housing costs	13.5	18.0	20.6	23.2	1.63	0.67
Household maintenance and equipment	11.9	10.5	8.7	8.4	−0.68	−0.22
Personal transport	2.2	4.4	5.9	7.1	5.29[§]	1.01
Other transport and communications	6.6	10.3	10.4	11.9	2.70	0.74
Leisure activities	6.7[‡]	8.5[‡]	6.0	7.7	1.35	1.40
Various goods and services	9.9	13.1	14.6	14.9	1.74	0.13

Source: Taken from Lévy-Garbona, 1983, p. 6, UN Statistical Yearbooks (extract from Chap. 1, Tables 5 and 6, pp. 14–15).

* West Germany, France, the Netherlands and the United Kingdom. The European indicator EUR4 is the arithmetic average of the four corresponding national indicators.

[†] The value of consumption in each category is compared to total consumption expenditure, excluding expenditure on private education and health services.

[‡] Including expenditure on private education in Holland in 1960 and in Germany in 1960 and 1978.

[§] This high value is due in part to the very rapid growth of this budgetary coefficient in the Netherlands. The average for the other three countries is only 2.38 per cent.

(2) A second category of services is made up of all the services produced for private consumption. House rental services are the main component of this category, in national accounting systems. We could also include in this category the services rendered by durable and immovable goods—the amount of expenditure involved means that they cannot be discounted. Moreover, the fact that the services imputed to these durable goods could possibly be included in national accounts makes it necessary to note the distinctive nature of these services.

(3) This third category includes a range of personal and leisure services. There is a direct link in these services between price and

quality, which can be a source of subtle social differentiation. They appear to be, even if only formally, substitutes for domestic activities. This last characteristic has played a major part in making this category the natural reference point for any examination of the final demand for services (cf. the examples of the hairdresser and the opera singer quoted above).

(4) Finally, the so-called 'mixed' services, health and education, will be discussed separately. Their mixed nature is directly due to the combination of market and non-market services that they represent. National health and education systems are administered by the state, and there is thus little room within them for the operation of market forces.

This typology takes commonly used distinctions in order to differentiate between the various factors that determine the consumption of services by households. This makes it possible to assess the relative importance of each component in the hypothesis of autonomous growth of the demand for services. Thus, in addition to the importance of the demand for services by households (between 35 and 50 per cent of total output), Table 5.4 shows the large share taken by the 'integrating services' (from 15 to 20 per cent of total output). In contrast, the services open to individual choice account for only slightly more expenditure than housing services (from 5 to 10 per cent of total output). The table also shows that expenditure on education and health services represents almost 10 per cent of total output in all the countries (with the exception of Holland). On the basis of this distribution of relative shares, the prospects for autonomous growth in the final demand for services can be examined. This in turn raises two basic questions: one on the dynamics of the 'personal' services sector, and the other on the prospects for the development of health and education services.

Choosing between goods and services

The growth in the final demand for personal services, which represents at most 25 per cent of total demand, occupies a central position in an analysis of the development of the tertiary economy. The first statistical studies of consumption (surveyed with precision by Stigler, 1951) highlighted the fact that, as income grows, so too does the proportion of consumption expenditure by households allocated to certain goods and services, which led to various types of consumption being associated with different degrees of necessity. This effect is known as Engel's law and helped to give to the consumption of services an aura of affluence distinguishing it from the notion of necessity attached to the consumption of certain goods.

Studies of services written in the past two decades have strongly qualified this initial assessment in two ways. Fuchs (1969) showed that the long-term evolution of the relative shares of the various elements of consumption in the United States were to a large extent linked to a more rapid growth in the price of services. The studies by Gershuny and Miles (1983) showed, moreover, that the growth in expenditure in services in line with the growth in income, as observed at a given point in time, overestimated the evolution over time of expenditure on services.[20] In other words, the income effect on the expenditure on services by households became weaker between the 1960s and 1980s. These qualifications made to the analysis of the final demand for services rather undermine the notion that significant changes can be made to life styles as the consumption of services increases. Indeed, they lead to the following redefinition of the process by which expenditure on services increases over time:

(1) the growth of national income raises the price of labour;
(2) this increases in turn the relative price of services;
(3) this variation in prices has the effect of substituting goods for services, thus limiting the effect of a rise in income on the consumption of services.

The negative effect of the price elasticity of the demand for services reduces the positive effect of income elasticity.

This interpretation depends to a certain extent on the significance that can be given to the measurement of prices, which basically restricts its validity to the 'personal' services in the third category. In fact, it can be observed that the long-term growth of the volume of personal services has been very moderate. The evolution of employment (in a sector in which productivity gains are very low) provides the first indicator. According to Singelmann (1979), the share of personal services in total employment between 1930 and 1974 fell in both the United Kingdom and Germany, from 14 to 7 per cent and from 8 to 4 per cent respectively, and increased only slightly in France (from 6.5 to 7.5 per cent) and Italy (from 5 to 6 per cent). Another indicator of the moderate long-term growth rate for personal services is to be found under the heading 'Goods and various services', which includes a large proportion of personal services.[21] Table 5.6 shows that for the period

Table 5.6 *Per capita consumption*: (1) average annual growth in constant prices for the period 1960–1978; (2) annual rates of variation of relative prices in percentage

	West Germany		France		UK		Netherlands		USA	
	1	2	1	2	1	2	1	2	1	2
Various goods and services*	3.0	1.02	6.6	0.09	0.9	0.25	4.1	1.27	1.8	0.56
Health	2.6	1.88	7.4	0.31	3.2	1.04	2.1	6.21	5.0	1.25
Education	3.8	−0.12	5.4	0.24	2.4	2.18	4.6	2.89	4.1	1.27
Final consumption by households	3.4		4.3		1.8		3.4		2.9	
Total output	3.8		4.9		2.4		4.4		3.8	

Source: Gardes, 1983.
* Heading 10 of the UN nomenclature includes personal services, restaurants, cafés, hotels, financial services and other services.

1960–78 the volume of personal services did not grow faster than total output, while their price increased more than average.

France, which appears to be a notable exception, with a particularly high growth rate in the consumption of these services (+6.6 per cent), is also the country in which price differentials are lowest. Nevertheless, rapidly increasing prices and a moderate growth rate for the volume of consumption should not make the overall picture in this sector too static. The interaction of a favourable income effect and an unfavourable price effect conceals a process by which new services are created and goods are substituted for obsolete services.

Innovation and the substitution of goods for services

Although the share of personal services in total employment has remained stable for more than half a century, there have been profound changes in the types of jobs. The diffusion of durable goods such as cars, televisions, washing machines, refrigerators and other household goods has led to the disappearance or transformation of certain services to households and the creation of new ones. Studies by Gershuny (1978 and 1983) and by Gershuny and Miles (1983) have stressed this aspect of the growth in consumption by households. The increase in the relative price of services makes it easier for a long-established service to be replaced by a durable good. This substitution may cause the service activity to disappear or contribute to a change in its status. Gershuny (1978) links the emergence of a self-service economy to the diffusion of durable goods that characterized the growth of the 1960s and 1970s. However, if a very long-term view is taken, this same relationship between substitution and innovation is found to be the basis of the use value of all goods. All goods provide a service. Thus, the new element in the post-war mode of consumption lies more in the network of services to which the diffusion of new durable goods gives rise (maintenance, insurance, financial and consultancy services, etc.). Paradoxically, the diffusion of durable goods among households can be said to have increased the predetermined nature of a large part of the consumption of personal services, i.e. of those services linked to the possession, acquisition, maintenance and transfer of durable goods. The growth observed in the relative shares of service activities in total consumption expenditure is, therefore, largely correlated to that of durable goods. This correlation, together with the very average growth in the volume of personal services (cf. Table 5.6), underlines the narrow margin that exists for the consumption of new services on which many analyses of the development of the tertiary sector are based. It is true that the supply of services may respond flexibly to a new need, as Lévy-Garboua (1983) suggests, but this kind of flexibility seems during the 1960s and 1970s to have played only a minor role in the personal services category, which is precisely where its impact should have been most striking.

Was the crisis that began in 1974 accompanied by a re-evaluation of the prospects for growth in this demand for services by households? This is rather what Aglietta (1984) suggests in his hypothesis of a new tendency towards differentiation in consumption habits. The earlier phase of homogenization that accompanied the diffusion of a pattern of consumption based on motor cars and on houses indicated 'the greater status of durable goods compared to current consumption.' The crisis, on the other hand, gave rise to a new trend towards differentiation as far as personal and leisure, health and education were concerned.

Nevertheless, the conditions under which the past expansion of health and education services took place, and the reasons for the present stagnation of demand, highlight precisely the limits of the purely market development of personal services.

A particular type of growth: expenditure on health and education

There has obviously been a sharp rise in expenditure in real terms on education and health. Table 5.6 shows clearly that during a long period of economic expansion expenditure on education increased a little more quickly than total output, without being affected by the various increases in relative prices. During the same period, health services grew at an even faster rate, except in West Germany and Holland, where the increases in relative prices were particularly high.

Governments were largely responsible for this expansion of health and education services. This is self-evident in the case of the European countries, where the public sector already played a dominant role, either in the production of health and education services or in subsidies to the consumption of these services.[22] It is also true of the United States, where the expansion of the 1960s and 1970s was accompanied by a continuous extension of the role of local or federal government. O'Connor (1973) stresses this constant use of public funds to finance the development of education and health services in the 1960s; there is an indication of this in Table 5.7 in the astonishingly high growth in public expenditure in the United States in these areas for the whole of the period between 1960 and 1975: 10.3 per cent per annum in real terms for expenditure on health and 6.1 per cent per annum in the case of education.

An analysis of public expenditure on education and health reveals both the nature of the past growth in these services and the extent of the reduction in growth since 1975. It is clear that growth in the past was based principally on the increase in real terms of the average level of services rather than on demographic changes or an increase in those covered by the services. An OECD study (Table 5.7) made it possible to assess the relative importance of demographic factors, rates of cover and the average level of services in the growth of health and education services. Demographic factors and rates of cover usually account for less than a third of the increases in real terms (education in Italy and health in the United States are the only exceptions).

The slowing down of the growth of the average level of services since 1975 has been as spectacular as the sharp rise in growth rates during the period of expansion. Between 1975 and 1981, the average levels of services in health and education grew less rapidly than total output, with the notable exception of expenditure on health in France and the United Kingdom.[23] This reduction was largely due to tight financial policies brought about by the fall in tax income in a period of slow growth and the growth of expenditure on transfer payments. In contrast to what might be expected, it was not the share of expenditure on unemployment benefit in the social security budget that increased but expenditure on pensions that increased much more rapidly than total output.[24] It was thus the net reduction in expenditure on health and education that made it possible to limit the growth of social expenditure between 1975 and 1981 to 2 per cent of total output (average of seven large OECD countries), in contrast to the increase of 10 per cent in most countries between 1960 and 1975.

This reduction was not simply the consequence of temporary financial restrictions. It was accompanied by a general reconsideration of the role of the state as the main force in the extension of social services. The stated intentions of governments to limit the growth in expenditure on social services (OECD, 1981b) gave rise to talk of a crisis in the welfare state.

This sudden halting of a process of growth that had characterized the development of the market economies in the thirty years after the War has two dimensions as far as education and health are concerned: one concerns the nature of the services provided, and the other the conditions under which they are financed.

Table 5.7 Development of public expenditure on education and health (average annual growth rates in percentage)

		Education				Health				Total output
		Real expenditure	Demo-graphic factors	Relative prices	Average real services	Real expenditure	Demo-graphic factors	Relative prices	Average real services	
USA	1960–75	6.1	1.1	0.9	4.0	10.3	1.2	4.1	4.7	3.4
	1975–81	0.4	-0.2*	-1.3*	1.9	3.8	1.0	0.0	2.8	3.2
West Germany	1960–75	7.2	0.6	1.9	4.6	6.6	1.0	0.5	5.0	3.8
	1975–81	1.6	-0.9*	0.0*	2.5	2.1	0.0	0.0	2.1	3.0
France	1960–75	—	1.2	0.7	—	10.9	1.0	1.0	8.7	5.0
	1975–81	1.0	-0.6*	-0.1*	1.7	6.3	0.4	0.3	5.6	2.8
UK	1960–75	5.0	0.6	1.1	3.2	3.4	0.4	0.0	3.0	2.6
	1975–81	-2.0	-0.4*	-0.5	-1.1	2.0	0.0	0.0	2.0	1.0
Italy	1960–75	4.6	0.3	3.0	1.2	6.7	0.6	0.9	5.1	4.6
	1975–81	3.9	-0.2*	1.3*	2.8	0.1	0.2	0.2	-0.5	3.2
Netherlands	1960–75	4.3	0.7	1.2	2.3	11.4	1.2	1.3	8.7	4.5
	1975–81	1.1	-0.5*	0.3*	1.3	4.4	0.6	2.5	1.2	2.0

Source: SOEC, Social expenditure, 1960–90, 1985

* 1975–80.

The crisis in the welfare state and health and education services

The crisis in the welfare state is a term often used, in a very general way, to describe the difficulties encountered by a form of 'modern capital- ism', in which the development of state intervention in the social services after the Second World War seemed to be a way of avoiding a return to the economic crises and mass unemployment of the 1930s. There are many aspects to these difficulties and mention has already been made of the limits of traditional Keynesian policies of stimulating demand in an open economy. Our concern here is with the present conditions of state intervention in social security services as well as in health and education.

Education and health systems still reflect the history of social struggles: a long sequence of conflicts and agreements accompanied the development of the wage-earning class (on the conflicts leading to the establishment of the Welfare State cf. Gough, 1979). In the course of these struggles, new and durable forms of social security emerged; according to the severity of economic crises and the degree of political change, these new systems were either grafted on to existing services or else they transformed them. In the case of France, Delorme and André (1983) speak of 'institutionalized compromises' in order to describe the widely accepted basic principles that lie at the heart of the organization of particular areas of the social security system.[25] Education systems often bear the mark of national 'compromises': of political unification in the case of Germany and Italy, of racial integration in the United States, of the secular and Republican character of the nation in France and even, in the United Kingdom, of the communal and religious bases of nationalism. These tendencies towards institutionalization on the national level seem to be less typical of the development of health systems. But the progress made in medicine in the first half of this century (in particular the discovery of antibiotics), the struggles fought by trade unions to improve working conditions and the experience of unemployment in the 1930s laid the foundations for the institutional- ization of health systems in the post-war period, which gave a formal structure to these compromises, the general orientation of which is reflected in the Beveridge Report.[26]

The forms and rate of state intervention in the social sphere are not subject to a strict determinism, even though the long-term tendency is towards the widespread development of a publicly financed social security system. State intervention in health and education has neither followed a single model nor been pursued with the same vigour in countries with markedly different social histories. The present period of crisis, on the other hand, seems to be characterized by a general desire to reduce the level of state intervention in the social sphere. Moreover, there seems to be a greater concern to reduce public expenditure on health and education (cf. Table 5.7) at a time when unemployment and the rising costs of the state pension systems established in the post-war period are putting increasing burdens on state resources.

This reduction is attributed either to the fact that obligatory contributions have already reached the level generally considered to be acceptable or to growing dissatisfaction with the services offered by existing health and education systems. It should be noted first of all that the hypothesis of an acceptable level of compulsory contributions seems to have little real foundation. Tax revolts have been decisive factors in the social movements that led ultimately to the development of modern states. There is thus a common thread linking the 1381 Rebellion and the Glorious Revolution of 1688 in England, the French Revolution of 1789, the American Revolution of 1776 and the Revolutions of 1848 in Germany and Italy. However, this historical perspective of political change is not called into question here. The hypothesis that there is a limit to the level of compulsory contributions is concerned with an economic irrationality within the political system which is said to give rise to effects different from those that might be expected. An increase in tax rates is said, through disincentives and inflation, to lead to a reduction in national output and thus to a reduction in tax receipts.

But the perception of this acceptable level of compulsory contributions is an historically contingent observation: Colin Clark fixed this level at 25 per cent; however, the share of tax income in total output in 1982 was more than 45 per cent in West Germany (45.3 per cent), France (46.9 per cent) and Holland (55.8 per cent); it was nearly as high in Italy (41.5 per cent) and the United Kingdom (43.7 per cent), but was only 32 per cent in the United States (OECD, 1985b).

Moreover, the negative effects of an excessively high level of taxation, which is said to lead to a reduction in income from taxation because of the reduction in activity brought about by an increase in the burden of contributions, have never been precisely and irrefutably measured. This is the conclusion reached by an OECD survey (OECD, 1985b) that considered the effect of tax levels on the supply of labour, the supply of jobs, the demand for investment and savings. The tax system is too vast for it to be possible to identify with any certainty the impact of an increase in the tax burden on the behaviour of economic agents. Assessing the effect of tax levels on the supply of female labour illustrates these difficulties: the impact seems to be more easily explicable than in many other cases, but the multitude of alternative explanations for the behaviour of economically active women, linked to the opportunities for child care, the school system and geographical locality, require more comprehensive behaviour models than those most commonly used. Even at a very general level, no negative links have been found between direct tax constraints (assumed to be more sensitive) and the rapidity of economic growth.

It is particularly difficult, therefore, to assess the moment at which any given country might reach the acceptable minimum level of taxation. The use of opinion polls to offset the absence of evidence is of little help, since the opinions do not account for the effective dysfunctioning of market incentives. The perception of the social security system reflected in such polls is important political evidence, but it cannot be interpeted directly in terms of institutional reform. The organization by Californian taxpayers in 1978 of a referendum on limiting compulsory contributions (the famous vote on Proposition 13) is a good illustration of the ambiguity of such tax protests. This wave of protest, which reached the seat of power with the election of Reagan, has had the effect of shifting expenditure rather than reducing it. In the final analysis, it is not possible to distinguish tax protests from the challenge to the quality of services concerned.

An opinion poll carried out in 1978 in the United Kingdom, which contained a question based on the Proposition 13 argument, but mentioning also the reduction of services, is very revealing. Fifty-nine per cent of the people questioned favoured a limit on compulsory contributions (22 per cent were against and 19 per cent had no opinion), but this figure fell to 33 per cent when the question contained a reference to the possible consequences on services of such restrictions (27 per cent were against and 40 per cent did not reply) (cf. Harris and Seldon, 1979, Chap. 2).

Thus, it would appear that the concept of the welfare state has not been rejected outright, but rather that commitment to the principle of an extensive system of social security now exists alongside a questioning of the nature of the services provided. It might be possible to explain this paradox as the result both of the erosion of the hopes that sustained the development of the services for forty years and of the pressures caused by recurrent financial problems. The great majority of people now have educational and health care opportunities that until forty years ago were reserved for a small minority. This extension of opportunity has been accompanied by a certain disillusionment. The massive expansion of the education system has neither made it possible to avoid a return to mass unemployment nor reduced to any significant extent the unequal distribution of pay; nor has much progress been made in solving problems of social integration. As far as health services are concerned, there is no obvious link between the services supplied and the state of the population's health defined in terms of functional capacities. Life styles and environment have an obvious influence on the state of the nations's health, but one that is almost impossible to define. Over and above the very general criterion of an increase in life expectancy, changes in life styles and medical progress have shifted the focus of attention to, among other things, the care of old people, and long-term degenerative diseases.[27]

The development of medical technology and the improvement of the education system, by widening the scope of those covered by the system, for example, seem to play little part in the discussions to which current developments have given rise. On the other hand, continuously increasing costs constantly raise the problem of financing systems whose development, at least as far as health care is concerned, is to a large extent autonomous. Attempts to make savings in the management of services, in the absence of coherent strategies for the development of health and education systems, has led to deteriorations in local services. This in turn leads to a cumulative cycle of mistrust that bears little relation to the actual merits of the services themselves. As a result, attempts are made to find new methods of financing that are more directly linked to the services offered. As far as health care is concerned, the increase in expenditure by households on market health services tends to offset the reduction in expenditure by the State. Between 1975 and 1982, expenditure on health services increased each year by an average of 2.8 per cent in West Germany, 6.6 per cent in France, 3.9 per cent in the United Kingdom, 3.6 per cent in Italy and 2.4 per cent in Holland. But this substitution does not usually make up the gap between current spending and the level of expenditure reached before the recession (cf. Table 5.7). It may thus not only prove insufficient to maintain services at current levels, let alone to provide for growth, but it is also very likely to increase still further inequality of access to health care.

In this respect, the interest aroused by the development in America of Health Maintenance Organizations (HMOs) is revealing. These private health centres, which offer general health care cover in return for an annual subscription, have made it possible to reduce costs by between 20 and 40 per cent (Launois *et al*., 1985; Rodwin, 1984), but discrimination against high-risk populations is one of the conditions for the efficiency of these new organizations. Similar problems of discrimination would be found with education vouchers, advocated by Milton Friedman as early as 1955.

This discrimination is a major factor in the current phase of the differentiation of demand (in contrast to the previous phase of homogenization). Unless the demand for health and education services can be renewed in such a way as to make these services accessible to all households, this differentiation of demand will be nothing more than an indication of social and economic regression.

Chapter 6 will show that the opportunities for such renewal are still directly dependent on the evolution of the wage relationship. This also applies to the total demand for services by households, which showed on the whole very little autonomy.

Notes

1. The so-called transformation and extraction industries (agriculture and mining) are the two other headings in the classification suggested by these authors.
2. Source: *Eurostat Revue*, 1972–81.
3. Investment in the communication sector is given in billions of dollars per year. The figures for 1980 are: 19 in the United States, 5 in France (1979), 4 in Japan (1979), 0.6 in Belgium, 0.4 in Holland, 1.7 in Italy, 2.1 in West Germany (1978) and 3.4 in the United Kingdom (figures for these last four countries refer only to investment in the telephone system).
4. The industries included under the heading 'various' (miscellaneous machinery, except electrical) make greater than average use of services to firms, but this may well be due to the low level of concentration in the sector rather than to the level of technology.
5. The situation in the United States is almost completely the reverse: this ratio reaches 10.7 per cent in the distribution sector, which is almost double the national average of 6.6 per cent.
6. Pharmaceutical and detergent products are the subject of considerable advertising expenditure. But other factors must be included in an explanation of the fact that the use of services to firms in France is equivalent to 20 per cent of the value added for the sector. One of these factors is the share of expenditure on research. But patent fees and payments for services are indications of the links with foreign firms: 23 per cent of intermediate expenditure on services is accounted for by imports.
7. Estimates of the intermediate demand for services in a few industrial sectors (given in Table 5.3) reveal that the structure of the intermediate

demand for services to firms is fairly similar in the United Kingdom but different in West Germany, as it is in other European countries (where the demand for services to firms as a whole is less high).

8. According to an INSEE (French Government Statistical Service) survey quoted by the Commissariat général du Plan (1983), a third of the demand for services and computer consultancy comes from manufacturing industry, which produces only a quarter of value added.

9. The intense debate of the 1930s on the monopolistic structure of the economy and its effects emerged again in the 1960s in studies by, among other people, Chandler (1977), Marris (1964), Baran and Sweezy (1966), Houssiaux (1967) and Galbraith (1968).

10. Marglin (1973), in his critique of the famous example of the manufacture of needles, criticizes Adam Smith in a similar way for confusing economies of scale and the organization of production.

11. The ratio of the intermediate demand for services to actual production increased from 4.82 per cent in 1975 to 5.79 per cent in 1980 in the consumer goods industries (the figure was 3.74 per cent in 1960). By way of comparison, this ratio remained stable at 3.09 per cent for marketed services and fell from 28.5 per cent to 23.15 per cent in the insurance sector.

12. The increase in the use of contract labour has been very rapid in France: the sector employed 23,000 people in 1968, 71,000 in 1974 and 150,000 in 1981. The legal restrictions on the use of contract labour introduced in 1982 have stabilized the growth rate.

13. The specificity of these highly skilled services is also evident in the typology of services put forward by Buttner and Mouriaux (1983).

14. According to the *Financial Times* (10 April 1985), the challenging in courts of expert reports by auditing companies is threatening the conditions under which the profession operates. The British Government, for example, is claiming $270 million damages against A. Andersen after their involvement in the De Lorean affair. In the United States, Peat Marwick Mitchell face ten claims for damages, amounting to $400 million.

15. According to the *Eurostat Review*, 1972–81, the number of housing units per 1,000 people in 1975 was 383 in West Germany, 339 in France, 328 in Italy, 320 in Holland, 396 in Belgium, 364 in the United Kingdom and 384 in the United States.

16. To give some order of magnitude to these services imputed to durable goods, Katz and Peskin (1980) estimated that the figure for 1977 was $226.1 billion, or 12 per cent of total output in the United States.

17. Fisher (1906) put forward this extension by pushing his definition of capital to extremes. The existence of hire services for most goods, including consumer goods such as clothes, crockery, tools, furniture, books, etc. makes it possible a priori to assess the extent of the services that can be imputed to capital in this extended sense.

18. For this reason, it is possible to add to the valorization of services produced for private consumption that of the private services constituted by the effects on the environment of productive or domestic activities.

19. The extension of the notion of production to the services imputed to assets, including durable goods, does not put an end to the debate on the measurement of growth. In particular, there remains the question of illegal activities. The development of the black economy during the recession, for example, means that the reduction in economic activity may be overestimated. It is known that the black economy may represent up to 10 per cent of total output (cf. for the OECD countries, Blades, 1982).

20. It remains to be discovered which services are concerned. In the case of all services consumed by households, the growth in the relative share of services as income rises is observed only above a certain income level. For low-income households, taking into account the absolute necessity of house rental services, for example, and state subsidies to health and education services, the share of services begins to fall when income rises (cf. Gardes, 1983).

21. The data that break down consumption expenditure by households between durable and non-durable goods and services (cf. UNO Yearbooks) do not provide a satisfactory indicator, since they combine under one heading and impute the same value to a wide range of very diverse services.

22. According to Abel-Smith and Maynard (1978), quoted by Gershuny and Miles (1983, p. 218), the share of the public sector in the financing of expenditure on health was 78 per cent in West Germany, 77 per cent in France, 88 per cent in the United Kingdom, 87 per cent in Italy, 70 per cent in Holland and 84 per cent in Belgium.

23. Nevertheless, it is difficult to compare the 2 per cent annual growth in the United Kingdom with the sustained rate of increase (5.6 per cent) in health expenditure in France. It should also be noted that demographic changes in the United States and changes in the rates of cover in Holland and Italy led, during the period between 1975 and 1981, to slightly more rapid growth in health expenditure (and in education expenditure in the case of Italy) than that in total output.

24. Expenditure on unemployment benefit in the OECD countries first increased between 1960 and 1975 mainly because of improved levels of benefit. After 1975, a reduction in the number of those covered by unemployment insurance led to the fall in this increase in the total amounts of benefits, despite the increase in unemployment. For all OECD countries, unemployment benefits as a proportion of total output increased from 0.5 per cent in 1960 to 1.1 per cent in 1975 and 1.2 per cent in 1981. At the same time, the share of pensions increased from 4.8 per cent in 1960 to 7.3 per cent in 1975 and to 8.8 per cent in 1980.

25. Indications that such compromises are widespread emerge as soon as others appear that call them into question. Harris and Seldon (1979) recall

the unanimous opinion that their challenge to the British social security system was 'politically impossible'.

26. In such processes of institutionalization, the personnel involved are rather like priests safeguarding the dogmas of knowledge and their utilization. The more recent nature of the development of health care systems has helped to make the power of the medical profession more obvious. The most important dates in the organization of the profession are in the 1930s (restricted entry to the medical profession in the United States was established at the same time as the passing of the 1935 Social Security Act) and the 1940s (establishment of the French Medical Association and of the French social security system, and nationalism and the division of tasks in the United Kingdom).

27. On the disillusion with health and education services, cf. the studies quoted by the OECD (1985b, Chap. 4).

6
Developments in the production of services

This final chapter will be concerned directly with the conditions of production in the tertiary sector. Their development is a crucial factor in the future of the industrial economies, which are characterized more by the extent of the production of services than by the dynamism of demand for them. The analysis of the demand for services in Chapters 4 and 5 highlighted the constraints restricting the expansion of foreign trade in services, of services to firms and of final domestic demand for services. These constraints are specific to each type of demand.

In the case of foreign trade in services, a slowly increasing tendency towards de-specialization within the developed economies seems to be calling into question the dominant positions inherited from the past, without new markets in the developing countries being opened up. There are still many restrictions on trade in services and the prospects for liberalization are not good.

There are two reasons for thinking that the extension of services to firms is simply a stage in the organization of productive activities. Firstly, it enables forms of the division of labour already implemented in large firms to be extended to small and medium-sized firms. Secondly, it makes possible a broad restructuring of specific service activities that are strictly complementary to certain production processes. It is difficult to see how these adjustments in the national division of labour will be able to change the relative competitiveness of the developed countries in the world market to such an extent that their manufacturing industries will be able to regain their former dynamism

The evolution by major category of the final demand for services by households brings to light two types of constraints. The relative stagnation in the very long term of the demand for personal services is evidence of the lack of incentive for households to increase the volume of their consumption of services. The constant process of innovation in the service sector and the substitution of goods for services that characterizes our industrial societies does not alter this observation. The development after the Second World War of social security systems enabled this first constraint to be lifted, at least to a certain extent. The crisis in the welfare state has tended to put a halt to this process. The era of rapid growth in health and education services seems to be past.

The above observations do not mean that the slow growth rates experienced for the last ten years in the developed countries constitute a stable pattern of stagnation. Transformations in the conditions of production may either set in motion a cumulative cycle leading to even worse recession or, in the longer term, establish the foundations for more sustained growth in demand. In the transitional phase of the 1980s, the bases for possible virtuous (or vicious) circles of development can be seen in the evolution of production processes.

The purpose of this final chapter is to extend in both these directions this direct questioning of the conditions of production in the tertiary sector. The first line of argument is concerned with the conditions of employment and the social division of labour, while the second concentrates on the technological changes brought about by computerization in the service sector.

One of the risks of the present economic stagnation is that it encourages a cumulative process in which pay and employment conditions gradually worsen. The desire to create new jobs may lead to industrial policies that underestimate these risks by relaxing minimum wage regulations and guarantees on the working conditions that distinguish wage employment in the developed economies from the chronic underemployment in the poor countries with a plentiful supply of labour.

In the final analysis, the outcome of decisions on new production technologies in the tertiary sector depends on the development of these industrial relations. There would appear, a priori, to be a clear choice between a reorganization of tertiary activities in which computerization accelerates the deskilling of jobs and a reorganization leading to an extension of the services supplied. In the first case, the substitution of machines for labour is dominant (innovation in the production process), while in the other, computerization also leads to product innovation. It is difficult to judge whether this product innovation will be able to increase employment in the economy as a whole. This chapter will develop these two lines of questioning on the evolution of employment conditions and the forms taken by the computerization of tertiary activities.

I The determinants of employment in the tertiary sector

Mention was made as early as Chapter 1 of the rapid growth in employment in the tertiary sector in the thirty years after the Second World War and of the slowing down in this growth after 1975, which was more or less marked according to the country. These contrasting patterns of development raise the problem of the determinants of employment: in what way is employment in the tertiary sector linked to changes in the general economic situation and why are there such great differences in this area between countries with similar growth rates? A large part of the answer to this question can be found in the relationships between employment in the tertiary sector and movements in the labour market.

The impact of the state of the labour market

The relationship between production and employment in the service sector is particularly difficult to specify. Firstly, activity in the service sector is less subject to variations in the business cycle than manufacturing industry; secondly, employment levels in the tertiary sector seem to be less sensitive to variations in the rate of activity than is the case in manufacturing industry.

In their initial studies, Fuchs (1965) and Lengelle (1966) stressed the reality of cyclical variations in the service sector (although these are less marked than in manufacturing industry). In view of the remarkable inertia of employment in the tertiary sector, this implies that there is an appreciable productivity cycle.

The fact that productivity in the service sector increases rapidly when demand picks up and that it falls equally rapidly when demand falls off is due partly to the rather particular way in which the volume of activity in the tertiary sector is measured. The distribution sector is the classic example (highlighted by Fuchs, 1965) of an activity in which there is little short-term connection between the volume of production and the volume of labour. Levels of activity are measured on the basis of turnover, which explains to a large extent why productivity in the distribution sector (analogous to the level of sales per capita) is more sensitive to the general economic situation than it is in manufacturing industry.[1] Lengelle (1966a and b) highlights the cyclical variations in another service activity, banking and insurance, in which the measurement of the volume of value added is particularly problematic. Cyclical changes in the volume of activity in the service sector are in fact poorly defined. Analyses of productivity cycles are thus based on fragile foundations.

The essential element in the above observations is the stability of employment in the tertiary sector during periods of expansion and of recession. The maintenance in the 1930s and the present crisis of growth in tertiary employment, even at a reduced rate, reveals a capacity for softening the effects of economic fluctuations, the beneficial effects of which are felt in periods of unemployment. A comparison of the fluctuations (relative to the long-term trends) in employment in manufacturing industry and in the service sector in periods of expansion and contraction during the years from 1948 to 1980 in the United States is very revealing: during the periods of economic growth, employment in manufacturing industry increased on average by 3.8 per cent, while employment in the service sector increased by 4.8 per cent; during the periods of recession, employment in manufacturing industry fell on average by 8.6 per cent, whereas employment in the service sector increased by 2.1 per cent (cf. Urquhart, 1981).

This ability to resist the effects of recession (and of expansion) can be explained by the nature of the relationships between employment in the tertiary sector and local labour markets. Studies of the distribution sector at the local level have shown how 'productivity' in the distribution sector increases as the situation in the local labour market becomes tighter (cf. the study by George (1966) of the wholesale trade in the United Kingdom). According to these studies, service activities have a 'sponge effect' on local labour markets, absorbing surpluses in times of underemployment and reducing their employment needs when labour is scarce. This behaviour is reminiscent of the overemployment in the agricultural and service sectors in developing countries, where there is a plentiful supply of labour (this dualism in the labour market was formalized by Lewis, 1954). It was on the basis of this approach to the determinants of employment in the service sector that Kaldor proposed a tax on tertiary employment in the 1960s in the United Kingdom, in order to free labour for the expansion of manufacturing industry (cf. Kaldor, 1980). It has proved impossible to determine whether this Selective Employment Tax was effective.[2] However, the analysis of the labour market on which it was based has retained some of its relevance.

The specific character of the relationship between employment in the tertiary sector and the labour market is due to two factors: work organization in the service sector and the determination of prices.

Service activities lend themselves more easily to changes in the division of labour, as is shown by the greater increase than in manufacturing industry of part-time and self-employed work. In the United States in 1980, for example, 19.2 per cent of jobs in the service sector (excluding distribution) were part-time[3] compared with 3.2 per cent in manufacturing industry; 10 per cent of jobs in the service sector were taken by self-employed people, compared with 1.6 per cent in manufacturing industry. Table 6.1 shows that the figures are similar for the European countries. This latitude within the organization of labour provides greater opportunities for adapting the production of services to the local availability of labour. In fact, the evolution of product and of product are concomitant.

Market conditions, price determination and employment

This interdependence between the nature of the product and the nature of the conditions of production, which gives rise to the specificity of the service sector, means that service activities can be described as 'local monopolies', in the words of Wright Mills (1951). Because of this, the way in which prices are determined tends to distinguish them from manufacturing activities. To use the hypothesis put forward by Kalecki (1971), prices are determined by applying a margin to current expenditure per unit of production. The margin is used to cover fixed produc-

Table 6.1 Part-time employment: more widespread in services, chiefly in distribution; part-time mainly concerns women's jobs (% of total employment in 1981)

Industries	USA	FRG	France	UK	Italy	Netherlands	Belgium
Manufacturing	3	6.7	0.9	6.6	5.1	5.9	1.0
Wholesale distribution	5	15.5	1.8	10.4	2.7	10.5	3.4
Retail distribution	23	36.9	12.9	39.2	8.2	46.0	29.5
Credit institutions	5	14.3	4.5	7.7	0.2	11.1	7.9
Insurance	5	8.5	5.0	7.9	0.4	11.1	5.1
Women's share of part-time employment (%)	70	94	85	94	64	68	86

Sources: Eurostat (1984), 1981 Labour Costs Survey; OECD Employment Outlook, September 1983.

Notes: The scope of the Eurostat survey is limited to firms with ten or more employees. No correction is made for full-time equivalent units in assessing part-time employment.

ɔn costs and to provide for profits, but the level of this margin is still dependent on the market conditions in which the firm operates, without fixed costs being directly and systematically passed on in prices.⁴ For tertiary activities, these market conditions are characterized by the local monopoly situation and the relative assimilation of labour costs into fixed costs. It follows from this that employment and wages in the tertiary sector do not have such a direct effect in the short term on pricing as they do in manufacturing industry. In the short to medium term, the total wages bill appears as a fixed cost determined by conditions in the local labour market and the regulation of employment levels is determined by the optimal use in the local labour market of the firms' wages fund. From this point of view, the 'sponge effect' has a theoretical foundation based on the adaptability of modes of production (or at least that part corresponding to fixed costs) to changes in market conditions. If there is underemployment in the local labour market, this adaptability forces wages down and increases the number of jobs in the tertiary sector, regardless of all other institutional constraints.

At a very general level, there is indeed a clear correlation between a growth in tertiary employment and a growth in the economically active population (cf. CEPII, 1983), as is shown in the contrast between the reduction in the growth of tertiary employment in West Germany and the sustained growth in this area in France and the United States. Moreover, it is in the United States that the particular characteristics that may be taken by the growth in tertiary employment are at their most obvious. Table 6.2 shows, through the evolution of employment by occupation, the composite reality that lies behind the rapid increase in tertiary employment in the past ten years. The kind of employment created includes both highly skilled jobs in the health care professions and in services to firms as well as a larger number of low-skilled and low-paid jobs with poor prospects. This dualism is not as obvious in the European countries, where the institutions regulating employment conditions leave less scope for an unrestricted reorganization of tertiary employment. It is also true that employment has grown at a lower rate in Europe.

Dualism in wage determination

The determination of tertiary employment, in which local factors play a significant role, implies that the process of wage determination will be potentially unstable and that there will be differences in this respect

Table 6.2 Employment growth in the United States, 1969–1995

By industries (in 000s)	Actual		Projected	Employment increase
	1969	1982	1995*	1982–1995*
Total	82,401	102,315	127,563	25,248
Government	12,195	15,803	17,230	1,427
Manufacturing	20,469	19,234	23,491	4,257
Transport & public utilities	4,718	5,543	6,637	1,094
Trade	16,704	22,536	28,545	6,009
Finance, insurance	3,864	5,899	7,685	1,786
Private services	13,747	22,617	31,290	8,673

Ten occupations with largest job growth

1972–1980			1982–1995*		
Total increase (000s)	15,568	(%)	Total increase (000s)	25,248	(%)
Secretaries	927	6.0	Building custodians	779	3.0
Cashiers	556	3.6	Cashiers	744	2.9
Nurses, registered	501	3.2	Secretaries	719	2.8
Cooks	465	3.0	General clerks	696	2.7
Truck drivers	403	2.6	Sales clerks	685	2.7
Accountants	333	2.1	Nurses, registered	642	2.5
Engineers	331	2.1	Waiters, waitresses	562	2.2
Computer operators	326	2.1	Teachers, kinder-		
Bookkeepers	320	2.1	garten, elementary	511	2.0
Computer specialists	311	2.0	Truck drivers	425	1.7
			Nursing aides	423	1.7

Sources: *Monthly Labor Review*, June 1982, November 1983.
* Projection for 1995 corresponds to the medium growth rate assumption.

between the manufacturing and tertiary sectors, as there are within the service sector itself. In countries where the *rapport salarial* is fairly strictly codified, this diversity in employment conditions and pay is significantly reduced. The establishment of minimum wages, the evenness of wage deductions and the regulation of employment conditions, particularly of hiring, dismissal and part-time work are all factors that limit the degree of divergence in wage conditions between sectors. By way of example, the relative evolution of average wages in manufacturing industry and certain tertiary activities before and after the sharp rise in unemployment in the mid-1970s (cf. Table 6.3) leads to a distinction between countries like the United States, the United Kingdom and France, in which underemployment gave rise to a tendency towards divergence between wages in manufacturing industry and those in the tertiary sector as a whole, and countries like West

Table 6.3 Changes in real worker compensation—by activity (yearly growth rates on two periods—1970–1973 and 1973–1979). Compensations are less affected by the economic slowdown in manufacturing

	USA		FRG		France		UK		Italy		Netherlands		Belgium	
	1970–3	1973–9	1970–3	1973–9	1970–3	1973–9	1970–3	1973–9	1970–3	1973–9	1970–3	1973–9	1970–3	1973–9
Market services	1.9	−0.9	6.8	2.1	6.7	2.4	5.7	1.0	9.9	2.9	7.6	3.1	9.0	3.9
of which:														
Trade	1.7	−1.7	6.2	3.9	7.6	0.8	7.5	−0.1	10.6	5.5	7.7	4.0	9.1	5.2
Miscellaneous*	1.7	−0.6	6.4	3.5	6.4	3.2	na	na	10.8	3.4	7.9	3.3	4.9	3.9
Non-marketed services	3.4	−1.1	7.7	0.6	7.0	3.8	7.5	0.5	7.8	2.4	7.2	2.2	8.9	3.6
Manufacturing	2.7	+0.6	7.0	3.4	6.3	5.8	8.0	3.3	11.0	4.0	7.8	2.9	10.7	3.9
Consumer price index	5.0	8.5	4.6	4.7	6.1	10.7	7.5	15.6	5.8	16.1	6.9	7.2	4.9	8.4

Source: SOEC, Structural Data Bank, US National Accounts.

Note: Worker compensation is the average cost of labour per person employed; it thus encompasses, with wage rate, the effect of part-timing, shifts in working hours and changes in social security expenditure.

* From SOEC Data Bank Classification, mixes personal and business services.

Germany, Italy, Belgium and Holland, in which an incomes policy (in the case of Holland), the widespread indexation of wages (in Italy and Belgium) and even collective consultations on wage increases (in West Germany) has led to a strengthening of the wages hierarchy since 1974.

These differences in employment conditions and wages are not simply the result of a polarity between the service and manufacturing sectors, but are also to be found within the tertiary sector itself. An analysis of the determinants of tertiary employment obviously cannot be applied in the same way to all service activities. An examination of employment trends in periods of expansion and recession (cf. Urquhart, 1981) shows, for example, that there is a fairly clear difference between health care services (7.3 per cent in periods of growth, 6.3 per cent in recession) and services to firms (10.1 per cent and 2.5 per cent respectively). Moreover, certain service activities, such as communications and transport, are highly unionized, and work is organized on a hierarchical basis that is hardly affected by conditions of underemployment in the local markets. In this case, there is little basis for the close relationship between the local labour market and tertiary employment proposed above; dualism is thus to be found within the tertiary sector itself.

It is necessary to make a distinction within the service sector between those activities dominated by large firms, in which the work organization is already highly institutionalized, and those activities dominated by small firms. This common distinction between competitive and monopolistic sectors (used, for example, by O'Connor, 1973) is a complement to but not a substitute for the distinction between services and manufacturing industry. All service activities are to a certain extent local monopolies, but this specificity has few implications for the organization of work within each activity, which may be particularly sensitive to fluctuations in the local labour market; this is a general characteristic of activities within the competitive sector. It thus becomes necessary to distinguish between activities according to the nature of their market (size and local monopoly distinguishing services from manufacturing industry) and according to the way in which employment levels are regulated (the traditional competitive system or the hierarchical system usually attributed to large organizations in general and monopolistic firms in particular). It should be pointed out that the tertiary sector includes both these activities best able to benefit from fluctuations in local labour markets (greater opportunities than in manufacturing industry for reorganizing tasks) and those in which the hierarchical systems of work organization make them most closely comparable to government services (absence of competition at the local and national level, whereas monopolies in manufacturing industry have to take account of their competitiveness in world markets).

The very characteristics of tertiary activities, therefore, make them open to a marked degree of dualism in methods of labour force utilization. As a result, it might well be feared that the increase in service activities will be accompanied by an even more marked difference between good and bad jobs on the level of the economy as a whole. This dualism within the service sector itself actually hides strong divergences between activities, as is shown in the wages hierarchy for the service sector as a whole (cf. Table 6.4): there are many insecure and badly paid jobs in the retail trade and personal services; on the other hand, the majority of jobs in banking, insurance and telecommunications are good ones. These generalizations conceal differences between the wage hierarchies for different activities in different countries. In the United States, for example, average pay in the banking sector is lower than in manufacturing industry (cf. Table 6.4).

In a country like the United States, where, on the one hand, the *rapport salarial* is less institutionalized than in Europe and, on the other hand, the organization of this relationship is still based on the major industrial sectors,[5] the increase in service activities may lead to the development of a marked division between good and bad jobs, as was pointed out by Ginsberg (1979). This concern was taken up by

Table 6.4 Monthly earnings in industry and services: manual and non-manual workers (in purchasing power standards, PPS*), 1981

Industries	USA[†]	FRG	France	UK	Italy	Netherlands	Belgium
Manufacturing industries	1,189	861	790	766	759	834	925
Wholesale distribution	1,087	856	842	867	912	1,077	1,225
Retail distribution	591	649	678	648	804	806	945
Credit institutions	856	880	927	983	1,429	1,031	1,667
Insurance		953	874	967	1,373	1,130	1,374

Sources: Eurostat, Labour Costs Survey, 1981; *Monthly Labor Review*.
* One Purchasing Power Standard equals, in 1981, respectively, 2.6 DM; 6.20 frs; £0.577; 945.1 L.; 2.82 Gld; 40.8 Bfrs.; US$ 1.07.
† Non-supervisory workers only.

Thurow (1980), Stanback *et al.* (1981), Bluestone and Harrison (1982) and Kuttner (1983), who stressed the consequences that the development of this dualism might have on the distribution of income. Thus, the development of the service sector might indirectly, as a result of the number of 'bad jobs' created during periods of recession, become one of the main factors in the weakening of the middle income class. Depending on its scope, such a development could destroy the mass market on which economic growth has in the past depended. That there has been a decline in the middle class income is fairly clear:[6] Steinberg (1983) notes that between 1973 and 1982 the percentage of American families with an income 15,000 and $30,000 (at 1982 values) fell from 51 to 44 per cent. There are other obvious signs that the consumer market is splitting up: on the one hand, the markets for the new electronic goods, which can be afforded only by a small section of society typified by the so-called young urban professionals, are expanding; on the other, the continuous increase since 1974 in the number of households living below the poverty line (from 23 million in 1974 to 35 million in 1984) has reduced the demand for ordinary consumer goods. These developments in the United States show the great changes in the bases of economic growth that can be caused by zero growth in a tertiary economy in which the *rapport salarial* is not highly institutionalized.

Fluctuations in employment conditions in some tertiary activities are sometimes attributed to the extension of the black economy encouraged by economic stagnation and unemployment. However, the effect of such activities on the service sector is uncertain, according to the various studies of the black or underground economy that have been published.

Only a part of the black economy is a substitute for or an extension of the formal service sector. The black economy is by its nature difficult to measure; most estimates of the volume of activity in the informal economy use indirect methods of measurement.[7] Starting from the hypothesis that payments in the black economy are made in cash, Gutmann (1977, 1979) and Feige (1979, 1981) used the relationship between money in circulation, bank deposits and total output. If it is further assumed that in the period just before the Second World War there was no black economy, these authors conclude from changes in the composition of the money supply that the black economy has increased considerably. According to Gutmann, it represented more than 10 per cent of total output in the United States in 1976, and 19% according to Feige.[8] These methods have given substance to the idea that the black economy has grown rapidly during the years of stagnation (Feige's estimate rises to 27 per cent of total output in 1978). However, as Blades (1982) points out in his critical survey of these studies, these methods do not take sufficient account of the role of the dollar as an international currency. Between 1970 and 1979, the amount of money in circulation increases less rapidly than bank deposits in the four major EEC countries. The growth of the black economy in the recession is not as obvious as the estimates quoted above suggest. Moreover, this black economy is made up of a wide range of different activities: Blades distinguishes between undeclared legal activities, illegal activities (drug trafficking, fraud, theft, etc.), and undeclared sources of income in kind (basically theft of raw materials by employees). Only the first category can be directly related to declared service activities. Nevertheless, it is difficult to measure the impact on each type of activity: among the activities most affected, the only service activities mentioned in the national accounts of the various OECD countries (cf. Blades, 1982, p. 34) are distribution (United States, France, Belgium), financial activities (Belgium and the United Kingdom) and legal and medical services (France and Belgium).

Although estimates of the impact of the black economy on sectors such as the construction industry and clothing can be found, such estimates hardly exist in the case of tertiary activities such as personal services, street selling, advisory services, private lessons and child care. Nor is it all obvious that economic stagnation and unemployment have helped to expand the black economy. The lack of increase in household incomes may have reduced demand to a greater extent than the supply of services has been increased by underemployment. Surveys of the black economy activities of unemployed people provide contradictory results which seem to bring into play the existence of a network of social relationships within which the black economy may increase in scale (cf. Archambault, 1985, p. 197).

Taken as a whole, the studies of the black economy highlight in particular the specific nature of the organization of the wage relationship in each economy. This is especially what comes out of the very diverse estimates of the extent of the black economy, which appear to have no correlation with the level of development nor to be arranged in any stable order when the method of measurement varies (cf. Table 6.5). Since no general trend emerges, it is impossible to decide whether the black economy actually operates as a sort of expansion chamber, capable of absorbing tensions in the labour market. Underemployment leads to an increase in activity in the black economy only to the extent that this is made possible by social organization. The persistence within social relationships of some of the solidarity typical of essentially agricultural societies or those based on craft industries is obviously a favourable condition. However, little is known of the reversibility of the processes that have contributed to the spread of wage labour. Moreover, any shift in the boundaries of the black economy are certainly still very dependent on the extent of the wage society; this involves not only the total amount of wage labour in a given economy, but also the level of participation rates, particularly for women, and the degree of protection afforded by the security system. These changes in the wage society, to use the words of Aglietta and Brender (1984), themselves have an influence on the black economy, in which tax avoidance, the non-payment of social security contributions and the illegal claiming of benefits are increasing in scale.[9]

It would be tempting to conclude that the development of the tertiary sector is no more affected than other activities by these shifts in the boundaries of the black economy (which is not the case in the construction industry, for example). Activities such as domestic services and the catering and hotel trade are still very much affected by the black economy, although it is not possible to confirm whether such informal activities have increased or diminished during the present period. Studies of the black economy make no mention of the significant emergence of new service activities in the black economy relating to leisure and consultancy (computers, tax, research). Thus, there is no a priori reason to make a link between these shifts in the boundaries of the black economy and any possible prospects for the future expansion of the service sector.[10]

The growth in female participation rates and the extension of new needs

In the final analysis, the black economy does not seem likely to lead to much expansion in other service activities. On the other hand, the increase in female participation rates which has accompanied the trend towards the service economy would appear on first sight much more likely to lead to an extension of the service sector. The assumed sequence of events is quite simple. The increased participation of women in economic activity necessitates the development of a certain number of 'formal' services in order to lighten the burden of domestic tasks. This substitution facilitates the development of predominantly female jobs within the personal services sector, which in turn stimulates an increase in the participation of women in formal activities.

Table 6.5 The underground economy—measurement: some methods and results

Countries	Years	Authors	Method	Results	Comments
USA	1976 1979 1981	Internal Revenue Service*	Audits for misreporting legal source of income	$78.3 bn in 1976, e.g. 6% of all income	Persons who do not file income tax returns are covered in the following study
USA	1972 1977	Internal Revenue Service*	Matching income data from current Population Survey and Social Security Administration to pick up non-filers	$53.2 bn in 1976, e.g. 4.1% of all income	Persons who do not file Federal individual income tax returns are likely to under-assess their income in a survey
USA	1981	J. D. Smith T. E. Moyer E. Trzcinski*	Household survey on purchases from informal suppliers	$25 bn in 1981 of undeclared income, 1% of GDP	Direct approach, purchaser may not be able to recognize informal suppliers
USA	1977 1983	P. M. Gutmann[8]	Setting a norm for the ratio of currency to bank deposits	$176 bn in 1976, 10% GDP. $420 bn in 1981, 14–15% GDP	Assumes no hidden economy in the immediate post-World War II period
USA	1939–79	E. L. Feige*	Setting a norm for the ratio of transactions to income	Over $600 bn in 1979, 27% of GDP	Benchmark year arbitrary, unrelated factors may explain shifts in ratios
USA	1930–80	V. Tanzi*	Based on an econometric equation of demand for currency	4.5 or 6.1% of GDP in 1980	Uncertain assumptions on tax behaviour
Italy	1977	B. Contini*	Based on assumption of labour-force participation in the irregular workforce	14–20% of GDP	Other factors than underground can influence participation in the labour-force

Country	Year	Author	Description	Estimate	Comments
UK	1977	A. Dilnot C. N. Morris*	Comparing, in the Family Expenditures Survey, reported expenditures with reported income	2–3% of GDP	Bias, as non participation in survey is likely to be linked with underground activities
UK	1960–78	K. Macafee*	Comparing macro-economic estimates of consumption and income	3.5% of GDP	Omits what is concealed on both sides
UK		E. L. Feige‡	As done in US case	15% of GDP	As for US case
FRG	1960–78	B. S. Frey*‡	Econometric procedure based on incentives to contribute to the hidden economy	8% of GDP	Indicates rising trend only, estimation from later work for 17 OECD countries
Netherlands	1979	Broesterhiuzen*	On sources and methods used to estimate GDP	4.8% of GDP	Comes after the trade-off done by national accountants
France	1979	P. Barthélémy†‡	Based on an econometric equation of demand for currency	6.3–6.7% of GDP	As for V. Tanzi
France	1971	H. Roze†	Comparisons between income and expenditure estimates	23% of GDP	As for Broesterhiuzen and Macafee

* Study surveyed in Carson (1984).
† Study surveyed in Gaudin and Schiray (1984).
‡ Study survey in Heertje and Barthélémy (1984).
§ Study surveyed in Blades (1982).

A cumulative process is thus set in motion, leading both to an increase in formal service activities and female participation rates. However, there are many factors that act as a brake on this process of self-generated growth, even in the long term.

Firstly, there is no uniform tendency across age groups and countries for female participation rates to increase. According to the most widely used model, participation rates fall for the younger and older age groups but increase for women aged between 25 and 45.[11] There is a simple explanation for these movements. The raising of the school leaving age and the difficulty of obtaining a first job tend to delay the start of economic activity. Similarly, the lowering of retiring age and the difficulties of finding employment lead to a fall in participation rates above a certain age. On the other hand, the continued growth in participation rates for women between 25 and 45 can be explained by the fall in the birth-rate, the increase in service sector jobs and part-time work and the decline in discriminatory practices, to say nothing of changes in attitudes. Nevertheless, Table 6.6 shows that movements in female participation rates are different from one country to the next (in particular, in the United States, participation rates increase for the under-25s[12]) and that there are significant differences in employment levels (77.3 per cent of the 20–25 age group work in the United States, compared to only 62 per cent in Italy).

As a result of this lack of uniformity in female participation rates, overall participation rates (for all age groups and both sexes) decrease rather than increase, as was initially assumed, in all the countries studied except the United States. Because of this, if there really is a substitution effect between formal services and domestic activities, this substitution between formal and informal activities operates in both directions. Thus it must be concluded that there will not be an increase in service activities but, at most, changes within the service sector.

A second factor, the high level of unemployment among women, limits still further the scope for an increase in female employment. In four countries out of seven, it is significantly more difficult for women to enter the labour market than it is for men: between 1973 and 1983, unemployment rates for women, although initially higher than those for men,[13] increased at the same rate (Table 6.7); the exceptions to this are the Netherlands, the United States and the United Kingdom. This significant degre of underemployment has restricted the effect that the growth of the tertiary sector has been able to have on any increase in female participation rates. From this point of view, the evolution of women's behaviour in the labour market would appear to be a largely

Table 6.6 Labour force participation by sex and age in 1975 and 1981, percentages

Age		USA		FRG		France		UK		Italy		Netherlands		Belgium	
		Male	Female	Male	Female	Male	Female	Male	Female	Male	Female	Male	Female	Male	Female
Teenagers	1975	59	49	37	33	25	20	33	29	23	18	18	22	20	18
	1981	59	52	37	33	28	25	50	46	31	27	24	28	22	19
20 to 24	1975	85	64	78	68	81	67	90	66	67	43	72	59	73	62
	1981	86	70	79	71	85	73	90	69	76	57	76	72	78	72
25 to 54	1975	94	55	95	49	96	55	97	60	93	30	95	22	95	43
	1981	94	65	95	53	97	65	96	64	96	43	94	39	94	51
54 to 64	1975	76	41	75	27	69	35	89	42	60	12	73	11	70	15
	1981	71	41	64	26	56	34	79	38	58	16	59	13	52	12
15 to 65	1975	85	53	82	47	81	51	86	56	75	29	77	26	76	43
	1981	85	60	81	50	81	56	86	57	79	38	77	38	78	40

Source: EUROSTAT, Labour Force Sample Surveys 1975, 1981; US Bureau of Labor Statistics, Employment and Earnings, monthly.

Table 6.7 Male and female unemployment, 1973–1983, percentage of labour force: an increasing differential in four countries

	USA		FRG		France		UK		Italy		Netherlands		Belgium	
	Male	Female	Male	Female	Male	Female	Male	Female	Male	Female	Male	Female	Male	Female
1973	4.0	6.0	0.9	1.2	1.5	4.6	2.9	0.9	4.1	11.4	2.4	1.8	1.8	3.1
1983	9.7	9.2	7.5	9.3	5.9	11.3	13.3	7.9	6.4	16.1	14.0	13.5	9.2	17.1

Source: OECD, *Employment Outlook*, September 1984.

exogenous social phenomenon. Its effect on the labour market is rather to put pressure on conditions of employment and pay in the service sector.

The nature of the jobs in question facilitates such developments. For the most part, the growth of female employment is linked to a growth in the activities in which women have traditionally been strongly represented rather than to a general opening up of jobs to women. Table 6.8 shows that the percentage of female employment is relatively large and stable in those service activities that are expanding rapidly.

This phenomenon is particularly marked in health care services and marketed social services, in which the number of jobs, more than two-thirds of which are held by women, has continued to grow in the 1970s and 1980s.[14]

As a result, the majority of these 'new' jobs are held by women; however, these jobs, which have traditionally been done by women, are also very often low-skilled and low-paid.

If the increased participation rates for women are due to the increase of poorly-paid jobs, this could be a new explanation for the decline of the middle income classes. But this financial situation makes the substitution of formal activities for domestic tasks even more difficult. The low purchasing power to be gained from paid employment leads us to look for other, less onerous, solutions. The central role of non-market education and health care services has already been stressed, as have the limits to their development. Other forms of collective financing may lead to a growth in personal services, as the growth in collective catering has shown. But, to a very large extent, the development of female participation in the labour market has been based on changes in the nature of household tasks. The widespread use of household machines, the introduction of convenience foods and the increased ease with which modern building materials can be maintained have helped to simplify domestic tasks. This change in the nature of domestic tasks goes hand in hand with a relative distribution of tasks within households.

Changes in the social role of women and in household tasks have led to a questioning of the division of domestic tasks. It is true that the use of external services is encouraged by the rigidity of a division of labour within households in which the man is responsible for all do-it-yourself jobs, which are themselves increasing in volume (between 1972 and 1980 the percentage of households carrying out such tasks in France increased from 25 per cent to 60 per cent, according to Stoclet, 1983). But this effect seems to be particularly reflected in a change in the demand for services. The dominant phenomenon of the increase in

Table 6.8 Female employment by economic activity (percentage of total unemployment, 1963, 1973, 1983)

	USA			FRG			France			UK			Italy			Netherlands			Belgium		
	63	73	83	63	73	83	63	75	83	63	73	83	63	73	83	63	77	83	63	73	83
Agriculture, Forestry Fishing	19	18	20	56	53	49	–	15	17	16	21	18	34	33	35	–	8	14	28	21	21
Industry (including building and utilities)	21	23	26	27	26	26	–	25	25	25	25	23	25	22	24	–	13	13	20	21	19
Services of which	44	48	52	46	47	49	–	48	51	44	49	52	33	33	39	–	38	40	43	45	47
Distributive trades, catering, repairs	42	44	48	57	55	55	–	43	45	51	51	52	–	–	–	–	34	37	48	44	46
Transport and communications	20	23	27	17	20	22	–	22	27	14	16	19	–	–	–	–	11	13	7	12	13
Finance, insurance and business services	45	48	54	46	47	47	–	48	50	46	44	46	–	–	–	–	34	35	30	38	39
Other services	56	56	59	48	50	53	–	58	60	49	57	61	–	–	–	–	47	49	54	57	58

Sources: EUROSTAT, *Employment and Unemployment*, Luxembourg 1985 for France and the Netherlands; *OECD, Labour Force Statistics, 1963–1983*, Paris, 1985, for the United States, Germany, the United Kingdom, Italy and Belgium.

female participation in the labour market is still, in a period in which households' earned income is stagnating or falling, the desire to reduce to the minimum any new use of personal services made necessary by the changes in female participation in the labour market.

This at least is the conclusion suggested by the evolution of the demand for services during the recession: the growth in employment in these sectors represents only 6.8 per cent of the growth in employment in marketed services in West Germany in the period 1976–82, 5.5 per cent for the United Kingdom and 4.9 per cent for France (cf. OECD, 1984b for Germany and the United Kingdom, Trogan, 1984 for France).

Our analysis of demand has already revealed this low propensity of households to consume personal services as soon as their cost falls to them directly. It has now been shown that the growth in women's participation in the labour market does not seem to be about to change this situation by laying the foundations for renewed expansion of the demand for personal services.

II Information technology and the future of the service sector

Mention has already been made on several occasions of the effects on demand of technological changes both in the services provided and the mode of production. To judge from the recent evolution of the demand for services, the medium-term impact of these technological changes is in fact much weaker than is usually assumed. The purpose of this section is to consider these questions from a more long-term point of view. Here again, the problem is whether technological changes are capable in the long term of creating a cumulative process of growth in the supply of and demand for services. This question cannot be answered by examining recent trends in the major components of demand. It is necessary to examine the initial stages of these technological changes in order to assess the prospects for extensive changes in the conditions of economic growth. In the highly speculative area of the prospects opened up by technological changes, it is essential to remain cautious about the possibilities and attempt to locate them within a general scheme for economic regeneration. The need for caution is linked partly to the initial decision to focus the present analysis on the dynamics of medium-term growth in a tertiary economy. It is also linked to the intrinsic difficulties of assessing the prospects for change in the economic and social structure as a whole. Never before has technology been as closely intertwined with the various aspects of social organization.

A widespread technological change

It seems to us important to locate the technical innovations that affect the nature of services and their mode of production within the context of general technological change linked to the use of microprocessors to review both product and process. This hypothesis has the advantage of clearly linking the beginnings of the large-scale diffusion of this general transformation of the technical system to the appearance of microprocessors at the beginning of the 1970s.[15] This hypothesis is one of those on the long-term trends in technological change found in the work of writers such as Freeman, Gille, Mandel and Rosenberg.[16] The main effect of this hypothesis is to specify a time horizon of some twenty-five years for such technical changes. On the other hand, it also brings out the original nature of the changes now taking place: they are being diffused throughout the world with unprecedented rapidity. Whereas the pace of previous technological revolutions fairly clearly reflected the unequal capacities for change of economies at different levels of development, the electronic revolution is doubly ubiquitous, both in terms of the wide range of economies simultaneously affected and in terms of the diversity of activities to which it is being applied. The radically different nature of the electronic revolution and the possibilities thus created for all kinds of data processing open the way for all kinds of speculation, from the strictly controlled society of Orwell's *1984* to the convivial electronic society of Toffler, 1979. It remains to be seen what place can be found for these works of fiction within the changes now taking place.

Our line of questioning will be the same as before: in the context of the long-term technological changes now taking place, is it possible that the consequent changes in the conditions of production in the service sector will in the long term lead to the development of a new kind of demand? The example of the financial sector will help to clarify some ideas. In this sector, the computerization of the payments system can lead to the development of new consultancy and management services to both households and firms. Our analysis of demand underlined the relatively modest effect that these innovations have had on households.[17] Will these innovations be better received in the longer term, if computer and telecommunications networks continue to develop?

The technical conditions of the production of services, mentioned in the previous chapters, have been reorganized on three levels:

— the first concerns changes in the nature of production tasks (the introduction of wordprocessing equipment into office jobs is a classic example);
— the second involves a change in relationships to customers, i.e. in relationships with the local market (a commonly used example is the extension of the self-service practices found in the retail trade and also in banking);
— the third concerns the installation of enormous computer and tele-communications networks offering a whole range of services to households.

An attempt will now be made to analyse the possible consequences of the development of new technologies at these three levels.

The transformation of tasks: the organization issues at stake in the 'natural trajectories of innovation'

This is one of the most striking aspects of the new technologies. Data processing of a fairly routine kind is very often a part of tertiary employment in both manufacturing industry and the services sector itself; thus, the appearance at the end of the 1970s of machines offering greater flexibility in data processing gave rise to fears of drastic reductions in the number of secretarial jobs. The International Federation of Employees and Technicians anticipated in 1978 that five million typists' jobs, or 20 per cent of office jobs as a whole (*Intersocial*, 1981), would disappear in ten years as a result of the introduction of new technology. Jenkins and Sherman (1979), in the case of the United Kingdom, and Nora and Minc (1978), in the case of France, predicted job losses on the same scale, particularly in the banking and insurance sectors. These forecasts were based mainly on figures provided by the producers of the new machinery, who claimed that a word processor could do the work of three or four people. The extent of the predicted changes was thus remarkable, even if it was a question of the abolition of certain jobs and not of net employment losses. Some five to seven years later, the diffusion of the new machines seems to have taken place at a slower rate than forecast and to have had less impact on employment; recent studies indicate that the productivity gains attributable to word processors, for example, are ten times less than predicted (of the order of 30 to 50 per cent and not 300 to 500 per cent).[18]

Thus, changes in production techniques have been reflected in a change in the quality of services supplied. In particular, there is no evidence in the tertiary sector of the process found in manufacturing industry by which productivity gains are passed on in the form of price cuts. Research and marketing are classic examples of this change in production norms: the multiple uses to which chips can be put establish new criteria of efficiency, without it being possible to assess either the productivity gains or the qualitative improvements attributable to changes which result rather in the appearance of new products.

In the context of this reorganization of tasks within the firm, the diffusion of the new technologies is similar to that of a general production norm, the use of which spreads rapidly and thus does not afford any comparative advantage. Nelson and Winter (1974, 1977, 1982), on the subject of this evolution of production 'norms', speak of the 'natural trajectory of innovation'. Firms in a given sector seem to follow a fairly similar path in the various stages of the computerization of their production processes. Thus, for example, Barras (1983), in the case of the insurance sector, and Adler (1983), in the case of banking, distinguish three stages in the computerization process: remote processing on punched cards or discs ('batch processing'), direct access to central systems ('on-line systems') and decentralized processing ('distributed processing').[19]

In view of the significantly more moderate than predicted effect of technological change on employment levels in the tertiary sector, it would be tempting to conclude that firms adapt their production techniques at a rate relative to the opportunities for the internal management of the work-force. This capacity to adapt is one of the characteristics of service activities in a monopoly situation, in which there is little relationship between prices and productivity. Thus, there seem to have been significantly higher losses of tertiary jobs in manufacturing industry. At the beginning of the 1980s, Ford-USA reduced its training and supervisory staff by 26 per cent; this example was followed by General Motors, Exxon, Polaroid, Xerox and Honeywell (cf. *Intersocial*, 1981). It is true that the development of services to firms partly explains this decrease in tertiary jobs in manufacturing industry. However, as far as tertiary employment as a whole is concerned, this is perhaps only a respite, since the absorption capacity of these sectors may only have put off the impact of technological changes.

According to this last hypothesis, the future growth in tertiary employment would be slowed down in the long term by this 'reserve of productivity'. This conclusion is often put forward in the case of financial activities (cf. Petit, 1984). But it became especially apparent at the end of the first phase of the computerization of tertiary production that the organizational decisions made at any given stage in the process of technological change were one of the main isues at stake in the changes being made.

The dangers of increased Taylorization in the tertiary sector

The reorganization of tasks arising out of the computerization of production processes in the service sector involves a change in the structure of qualifications. In this case, the organizational choices available are largely dependent on the technical decisions made. Computerization can thus increase the Taylorization of the work process, in which tasks are strictly defined in order that they can be carried out in a strictly routine way and without any special qualifications. In the examples cited above of the banking and insurance sectors, the first phase of centralized computerization increased the number of routine data collection and transmission jobs. Braverman (1974) and Kuttner (1983) give examples of similar changes in the organization of tasks connected with the recording of insurance files: the jobs are repetitive (one minute per file), badly paid ($5 per hour) and use a casual labour-force consisting of sixth form students and housewives. This atomization of office work is a factor in the proletarianization of white-collar work. However, the impact of computerization is not always so unambiguous. Firstly, we must be careful not to have too rosy a view of office work prior to computerization. Since the end of the nineteenth century, office work has been organized on a hierarchical basis, with routine and repetitive jobs. This type of organization is different from that advocated by Taylor: the work process is not broken down into individual operations but divided into strict categories (for Taylor, jobs formed part of a sequence of operations, whereas in Fayol's hierarchical, functional model they are carried out in parallel to each other. See Muldur, 1983). It was with the introduction of mechanical data processing after the Second World War that Taylorism entered the office. The computerization of tertiary production has certainly made it easier to tighten still further the control required by the Taylorian organization of production. But certain forms of computerization can also help to reduce the number of repetitive tasks and make the work process more satisfying.

In the banking and insurance sector (which best lend themselves to computerization and which were the first to go down that path), decentralized computer systems offer opportunities for making tasks more rewarding by giving more responsibility to cashiers and other clerical workers. More generally, two broad categories of computer systems are developing: centralized processing systems, which put fairly strict constraints on work organization, and decentralized, decision-making systems, which offer opportunities for developing skilled work. There are many factors at work in this process. Firstly, there is the problem of the qualifications of existing staff. There is much resistance to a change in the organization of work, even if it reduces the number of routine jobs. This resistance is based either on the fear that this reorganization is a threat to jobs (example from the insurance sector, quoted by Verdier, 1983), or on the fact that it involves upheavals in established hierarchies (example from the banking sector quoted by Boisson, 1984). Another factor that encourages the development of a system of work organization offering greater motivation to the individual is the high degree of vulnerability characteristic of centralized computer systems. This at least is the lesson that can be drawn from the strikes in France (1974) and the United Kingdom (1979) in the computer departments of certain large banks. The acceptance of computerization is thus encouraged by a concerted policy of training and promotion to new jobs.

The technical decisions and choices of work organization made in the tertiary sector have long-term consequences.[20] This issue of decisions on work organization concerns the capacity for innovation in the traditional service sectors. A system of work organization based on a centralized computer system is relatively rigid and restricted to one range of products. On the other hand, a positive system of adapting the labour force and production techniques to the new conditions opens the way to an extension of the range of services offered, whether in the insurance, personal services, retail or banking sectors. This process leads inevitably to a certain breaking down of the boundaries between activities. Depending on the capabilities of the work-force, this may in turn lead to an efficient differentiation between services or to the development of highly standardized services. In some degree, the development of home work might seem to represent the ultimate form of this degradation of work.

Computerization is in fact opening the way to a return to a 'putting-out' system, a form of subcontracting that accompanied the initial stages of industrialization. The isolation of the worker and the absence of guarantees on pay and conditions make this form of employment unstable and badly paid. The paradox is that this marginal form of wage labour can be considered as a positive image of the future of social organization.

In fact, the home work made possible by the new computer and tele-communications systems puts us in mind of a modern work of fiction: the advent of Alvin Toffler's 'electronic cottage', in which the productive and consumer activities of the household are gathered together under the same roof. This notion can hardly be applied in any general way, even though it has been estimated that some 5 to 10 million people might be affected by this development of 'home work'. The segmenta-tion of the labour market that it implies bodes ill for the future. The examples are revealing: Mattera (1983) quotes the case of a woman processing 2,000 insurance files per week in her own home at a rate of 16 cents (1983 value) and 90 seconds per file. This isolated wage labour, open to all kinds of pressure from employers, may, by lowering the status of wage labour, lead to a deflationary cycle in which wages and demand would contract alternatively. Although home work has obvious advantages in that it saves commuting time and enables workers to organize their own working hours, it is important to contrast it with the institutional framework (minimum wages, employment guarantees) that safeguards conditions of pay and guards against the deleterious effects of a worsening in wage earners' ability to negotiate.

In effect, writers like Toffler who have a very positive image of home work implicitly base their ideas on the position of 'professional' workers who have sufficient qualifications to guarantee their income. In this way, the model of the home-centred society reveals its dualistic nature, and can be presented as an acceptable or even desirable change in the life-style of some high earners (principally the young urban professionals). The problems posed by the decline of the middle income class, namely the splitting up of the mass markets on which past economic growth was based, are thus raised once again.

III The advent of the information economy?

In the previous section, the 'electronic cottage' was taken out of its context of a world in which domestic life and consumption habits are completely transformed by the new technologies. Home work is thus only one aspect of a wider transformation of life-styles. This raises some of our criticism, in particular the reference to the isolation and penury of home work in the early stages of industrialization.

Apart from work, the new telecommunications and computer

networks make it possible to shop from home, as well as offering entertainment, information, financial management and advice services. In this vision of the future, the world becomes a village. But even a fuller description of this vision of the future does nothing to resolve the doubts raised by the low pay and routine nature of a large part of the home work made possible by the chip revolution.

Is it possible that the potential opened up by computer and tele-communications networks is leading us towards a dualistic society, in which two extremely unequal ways of life are developing separately from each other?

Those who are enthusiastic about these changes stress their produc-tive efficiency and the opportunities that they present for cutting working time and getting rid of useless activities. The attractions are usually indirect ones: as far as final demand is concerned, these innovations appear less exciting and arouse no more than mild interest in consumers. The television and telephone are already firmly estab-lished, stereo systems and video recorders are agreeable amenities. However, it is difficult to see in them the foundations of any sizeable extension of consumption norms capable of stimulating economic growth and employment. It is indeed from this point of view, linking as it does changes in the conditions of production and of demand, that an attempt can be made to assess the transformation of our industrial societies brought about by the developments in computer and tele-communications technology (Alvin Toffler's 'third wave'). Within the limited framework of the present book, an attempt will be made not to assess the full impact of these transformations but to attract attention to the significant disparity between the opportunities for changes in the conditions of production and the apparent inertia of the structures of final consumption. It is precisely from such an imbalance that a dualistic society could actually emerge.

Let us look firstly at production. Data processing is said to represent the next stage of development after the major phase represented by manufacturing industry. Data processing involves the conception, production and transmission of a signal, whether the signal involved is sound, speech, pictures, text, data or electronic impulses. It pervades the whole of social life; it is found to varying extents in all productive activities. The automation of the production process in manufacturing industry and the service sector is one component, already mentioned above, in this formation and processing of data. Its innovatory aspect lies in the opportunities for the remote dispatch of data on physical or financial operations connected to the production and distribution of goods and services. Difficulties related to the fixed location of activities, the need for transport and the delays thus involved are considerably reduced.

In addition to production functions as such, purchasing and sales, together with stock, personnel and financial management are also affected. All data processing activities inside or outside the firm can, as a result of the new computer and telecommunications network, be moved from any fixed location. This potentially increases every firm's markets by extending its sales networks. In fact, it is competition in the product market that increases.

The same is true of the factors market: data processing linked to the functions discussed above can be carried out anywhere in the world. There are already some impressive examples in the insurance sector: Shelp (1983) cites the case of an American company whose current files are processed, via satellite, in South Korea. In the face of this distant competition, it is easy to understand why the same work done at home in the United States is so badly paid.

It is difficult to assess with any accuracy how many jobs are affected by the growth of data processing on a world scale: probably only a small percentage (mainly routine tasks). The growth in data processing activities has indeed given rise, in the wake of studies by Machlup (1962), to a series of estimates of their scale relative to the economically active population and total output (cf. Porat, 1977; OECD, 1981a).

The methods used in these estimates are very empirical: the list of individual activities is used to find those that can be classified as 'information' activities. Thus, teachers and doctors are part of the 'information' sector, but surgeons are not. Despite the arbitrariness of the distinctions, most studies of the information economy come to similar conclusions: the information sectors accounted in 1975 for 32% of the economically active population in France, for 45% in the United States in 1968, 29% in West Germany in 1968, 35% in the United Kingdom in 1968 and 30% in Japan in 1975 (according to the OECD, 1981a). Thus, at least one-third of the economically active population is involved, in jobs of very different kinds (two-thirds of them routine).

The number of people employed in the information sector has increased continuously since the beginning of the century. Porat (1977) estimates that it rose from 5 per cent to 50 per cent in a century in the United States.[21]

This rapid growth has been and still is going on in France, West Germany and Japan. But in the United States and the United Kingdom, the share of the information sector seems to have stabilized in recent years.

These estimates underline in a fairly crude manner the extent of the activities affected in a general sense by changes in the way that information is handled. The installation and control of telecommunications networks are two of the crucial supply-side aspects of the development of the information economy. It has already been pointed out in Chapter 5 that the telecommunications sectors for the most part have the financial capacity for such installations (OECD, 1983b). The sector includes industries manufacturing telecommunications equipment and the operators of such equipment who sell services provided by the networks. According to Caty and Ungerer (1984), the world market for telecommunications equipment should increase from $59 billion in 1982 to $130 billion (1982 values) in 1992, and the markets for the services provided by the telecommunications systems from $140 billion in 1982 to more than $200 billion in 1992.

At the same time, the strictly monopolistic and state-owned structures of the sector are being liberalized. The shock wave of liberalization was set in motion by the deregulation in 1982 of ATT, which held 80 per cent of the American market. This deregulation was followed by a series of agreements in Europe between ATT, Philips and Olivetti and between IBM and STET, by the privatization of British Telecom in 1984, the cautious liberalization of NTT in Japan and similar measures in West Germany.

Together with this oligopolistic restructuring of the supply side, runs a parallel process of mobilization among the major users: eleven national associations—like the TMA (Telecommunications Managers Association) in the United Kingdom—have joined forces to set up the International Telecommunications Users Group (INTUG).[22]

The extent of the markets for telecommunications services and the large-scale reorganization that has taken place in the supply of equipment and services contrast with the lack of change in final demand. We have alrady seen that people hardly seem in a hurry to conduct their banking business from home.

Moreover, the predicted cost of access to the networks is still high: according to the Institute for the future at Menlo Park in California, the cost would be of the order of $1,000 to $3,000 per year for each household in the United States in the 1990s. (By way of comparison, expenditure on education is of the order of $3,000 per family.)

Cable televsion has spread rapidly, to the point where almost 45 per cent of American homes are connected. However, the sale of teletext services is stagnating. The uncertainities of the home computer market (fluctuations in demand, low use of equipment purchased—39 per cent of those owning home computers stop using them within six months of purchase) clearly illustrate the ambiguities of the demand from households as far as the information economy is concerned.

The new services that may arise out of the development in computer and telecommunications systems[23] increase in particular the opportunities for controlling existing activities, e.g. monitoring of household equipment and telephones, security services for buildings, managing household payments, etc. The availability of increasing amounts of information (sales catalogues, trade directories, various guides, educational services, etc.) which is continuing the increase in advertising and the diffusion of information that has been taking place since the 1960s, is very likely soon to reach saturation point. Therefore there is little possibility of it bringing about radical changes in life styles.

In fact, the changes brought about by the new electronic networks seem rather to affect the conditions under which traditional goods and services are produced than to open up opportunities for new kinds of final consumption. Nevertheless, this effect on the conditions of production has a very general impact on the nature of products by making it easier for them to be differentiated.

Toffler (1984) thus attributes greater product differentiation to this 'third wave'. In his view, the information era should make it possible to put an end to the product homogenization of the industrial era. To the extent that this heterogenization of production is not accompanied by major productivity gains leading to a period of affluence, the end of the era of mass consumption may also signify poverty for some and a wider range of products for others.

The disparity between changes in the conditions of production and the inertia of the structure of final demand is acutely revealing of the threat of the increasing bipolarization of life-styles in the advanced industrial societies.

IV Social changes and recovery from recession in a tertiary economy

The possible undesirable social consequences of an increase in the segmentation of jobs in the tertiary sector have just been discussed. Prior to this, the constraints on the development in the medium term of the various components of demand had been analysed. The conjunction of these uncertainties on the supply side and the slackness on the demand side lends weight to the argument that the development of a service economy will not in itself lead to lasting economic recovery. The development of the demand for services seems unlikely to lead to economic recovery in the short to medium term. The absence of major cumulative sequences, in which changes in the conditions of production and in the formation of demand help to sustain each other, also makes it unlikely that there are any real opportunities in the long term of establishing a stable model of slow growth. The future of the service economies, which is what the developed industrial countries have become as the result of changes in the structure of their productive activities, remains uncertain. The current period of stagnation seems to be a transitional phase, while the predominantly Fordist mode of industrial growth of the past has, at the level of the individual economies, revealed its limits in the face of the rapid internationalization of production.

The main purpose of the introductory paragraph above was to recall the principal issues at stake in the changes currently taking place in the tertiary economies and briefly to mention the policies to which they have given rise. For a century, periods of crisis were accompanied by an increase in the role and methods of state intervention. In the current period, however, more attention is being paid to policies aimed at reducing state intervention, while Keynesian programmes for world economic recovery are now largely ignored. The cause of this abrupt reversal is largely fiscal. It is true that the obvious desire to reduce the level of compulsory deductions can only be realized by a reduced level of socialization of the demand for education and health services in those countries with a significant degree of state intervention in those areas. But there is no evidence that this retreat from state intervention is in any way beneficial. The conditions of state intervention have changed, but the reasons for it have reappeared (long-term underemployment of men and machines).

Although some economists have reached the conclusion that collective forms of intervention have failed, the conclusion of this present book is, on the contrary, that it is necessary to change the forms of state intervention in order to take into account the tertiary nature of the majority of economic activities and the increasing integration of manufacturing industries into the system of world trade.

Low demand and volatile conditions of production in tertiary activities

A large proportion of service activities are closely linked to the circulation of and trade in goods or to the professional activities of individuals.

The only areas in which this complementary relationship is changing to any significant extent are services to firms and social services to households. Developments in these two areas are a good illustration of the limits of the move towards the service economy.

Services to firms have experienced a period of particularly sustained growth. The externalization of tasks not directly linked to the production process in fact represents on two levels a phase in the organization of productive systems. It gives medium-sized firms access to a functional division of labour that has been used for several decades by large firms, and it also enables large firms to diversify their production in accordance with new strategies for multi-product development on a world scale.

The scale of this double change in the division of labour has been made possible by data processing technology, which has facilitated the externalization of tertiary production. Telecommunications and computer systems are thus a major element in this reorganization, but the upheavals that they have caused have contributed, paradoxically, to a reduction in the long-term prospects for growth in the service sector. This at least is what is revealed by an analysis of the reasons for the growth in the intermediate consumption of services by volume of production.

The increased use by firms of these services cannot be directly explained by a desire to improve the quality of products or to make greater productivity gains. In this respect, there is an obvious contrast with the major reorganization represented by Taylorization. The increased use of services to firms is essentially part of a process by which a norm for the management of the fixed-cost activities of a firm is diffused. The new data processing technologies facilitate this trend towards the externalization of tertiary functions, and also allow small firms to benefit from that same trend.

However, the fact that the new technologies enable data to be processed anywhere in the world means that the competition for the performing of certain routine tasks, such as the processing of files, is greatly increased. Similarly, highly skilled service activities can immediately begin to operate in the world market. This is of interest to multinational firms in two ways: it offers scope for new activities and is also a means of organizing trade within the group.

This capability also tends to increase the polarization between good and bad jobs (with the latter coming into direct competition with workers in countries where wages are low). A whole range of other service activities that externalize routine tasks, such as caretaking and cleaning, that are not directly linked to the production process, further reinforces this segmentation.

Over and above this phase in the reorganization of the division of labour, the prospects for the development of services to firms result from a combination of three factors:

(1) the evolution of these intermediate services in accordance with that in the rest of the economy;

(2) a trend towards a reduction in the relative level of these intermediate services as a result of the transfer of production abroad or of the computerization and internalization of certain tasks. There are many factors limiting this tendency: the specificity of many tasks reduces the opportunities for substitution by foreign work forces and the less predetermined relationship between computerized machinery and the organization of work may mean that there is no systematic substitution between capital and labour;

(3) the increase in activities representing fixed costs for firms may also have a positive effect on the intermediate demand for services. Increased competition forces firms to increase their advertising and research and development budgets. The complexity of national regulations within the system of world trade increases the need for legal advice. And personnel management itself may require increasing use of external expertise.

The slow-down in the intermediate consumption of services at the beginning of the 1980s underlines the preponderance of stabilizing and reducing effects.

Considered as a phase in the evolution of the division of labour, this development in the intermediate consumption of services to firms has a significant effect on the evolution of the conditions of production. It leads to a significant increase in the mobility of productive combinations, both in the choice of factors of production and of products. It is not certain whether this mobility makes it easier for each national economy to become integrated into the system of world trade, but there is no doubt that it leads to increased polarization of jobs within each national economy. It can be assumed that this development will contribute to the long-term destabilization of the slow growth models that have been observed in the industrialized countries for about ten years.

In this context, the restrictions on international trade in services seem to be long-lasting. The liberalization of the trade in and setting up of specialized services to firms (including financial services) is in fact caught between two opposing trends:

(1) a desire for a greater degree of liberalization in trade in services, based on a real but widespread specialization within the tertiary sector of the developed economies;

(2) fear of the more extreme opportunities for externalization (tax havens, flags of convenience) and crossing national boundaries available to multinational companies.

The present status quo is, therefore, no accident, and much of the demand for deregulation reflects the obsolescence of the controls (particularly in the case of financial activities) rather than any clear desire to reduce the amount of regulation.

Equally significant obstacles to the growth of final demand largely explain the lack of dynamism in a tertiary economy. A high proportion of this demand is complementary to other household consumption or production activities (distribution, transport, housing, financial inter-mediation).

As far as the rest of the service sector is concerned, personal services seem to be subject both to intense internal movements leading to the substitution of new services for old ones and to relative stagnation in terms of consumption by households. This contrasts with the dynamism of expenditure on socialized health and education services. The socialization of this expenditure encouraged by the welfare state explains this former dynamism. However, the crisis in the welfare state has called into question the prospects for the continued growth of expenditure in these areas, although there is no indication that new forms of validating this social demand are emerging.

The challenging of the welfare state has gone hand in hand with a relative decline in solidarity. The concern to differentiate between various forms of care and to adapt training to needs that will change in the course of a lifetime reflects the well-founded criticisms of Illich and others of the excessive diffusion and use of medicine and of over-specialized education systems. But in the absence of any overall plan for financing social demand, in which the role of collective organizations is clearly defined, this differentiation leads to social discrimination and, at the best, to stagnation in the whole range of health and education services.

This differentiation in consumption modes provides the basis for the development of the model of slow growth in a dual economy already hinted at by changes in the conditions of production. Moreover, this division of consumption modes is also found in the diffusion among households of 'new services'. Information technologies have made it possible to develop new services, but these products have received only a lukewarm response from households. Comparison with earlier social phenomena such as the spread of car ownership, household goods and radio and television reveals that the use of computers for leisure activities, household management and specialized information services has little attraction for most people. Only the consumption patterns of a certain category of households attracted by these products (mainly young urban professionals) are affected to any significant degree. Thus these new services help to widen the gap between different consumption patterns without being sufficiently widespread to provide the basis for economic recovery.

The evolution of consumption by households shows in particular the persistence of the model of consumption that underlay the economic growth of the 1950s and 1960s, in which the possession and use of goods played a central role in the organization of time (both on a personal level and in terms of the use of external services) and in the imagery and symbolism of everyday life.

Changes in consumption patterns brought about by the increased participation of women in the labour market have not altered the validity of this observation. This increased participation, which has accompanied the growth of service activities, seems on the contrary to have played a major part in the diffusion of the consumption pattern on which the growth of the 1950s and 1960s was based.

In a period of slow growth, the ever-increasing participation of women in the labour market has a greater influence on the forms taken by the development of service activities than on consumption patterns. The availability of female labour facilitates the development of part-time or fixed-term employment, and hence the increase in the number of 'bad' jobs.

All these factors seem to combine with the development of the service economy to encourage the emergence of a dual economy in a state of relative stagnation. This is a very general description of developed economies, in which the social content of economic growth depends on institutional factors that vary considerably from one country to another, with the greatest differences being those between the United States and the European countries.

The United States: a barely transposable example of a service economy

The development of the service economy has advanced further in the United States than in most of the European countries, but the example of the United States alone is not sufficient to characterize the model of a slow-growth dual economy, which in many ways is emerging as one of the directions most likely to be taken by the service economies. There are two reasons for this. Firstly, the American model of dualism and stagnation is still badly defined: is it the cause or the consequence of the development of service activities, is it a recent phenomenon, contemporaneous with the present slow-down in the world economy, or the final phase in the long-term evolution of the conditions of production? Secondly, a distinction must be made between those elements of the model specific to the American experience and those that can be transferred to the development of service economies in the European countries. Only this last question can be answered by a description of dualism in the American economy.

There are many dualist approaches to the American economy, beginning with the studies written during the 1970s on labour market segmentation. The arguments to which we have referred reflect a more recent and wider debate, in which the evolution of employment, of the distribution of income and of consumption patterns is seen as the break-up of the productive system and mass market that underlay the 'Fordist' growth of the 1950s and 1960s.

The relative decline of manufacturing industry and the parallel development of service activities are said to have played a major role in these changes. This is the macroeconomic context of the debate on the decline of the middle-income classes in the United States. Several studies have helped to clarify the ways in which this decline has taken place.

It seems that the process has been going on since the 1960s; Stanback and Noyelle (1982) show its effects on the distribution of individual incomes between 1960 and 1975 (which coincides with the beginning of the decline of manufacturing industry at the end of the 1960s). Studies by the Bureau of Labor Statistics (Rosenthal, 1985) suggest either that this development reached its conclusion at the end of the 1970s (which is contradicted by other sections on household income) or, more importantly, that this decline in the middle-income classes has been brought about mainly, at least since 1973, by the development of part-time employment. This raises the question of the composition of family incomes. Taken in their macroeconomic context, the theories on the decline of the middle-income classes encourage in particular consideration of the incomes of the units of consumption that households in fact constitute. Thus the increase in the number of families living below the poverty line in the 1980s is a recent expression of the phenomenon under consideration. Nevertheless, there are many causes for this decline in the number of families belonging to the middle-income classes. The distribution of unemployment and of inherited wealth and the cuts in welfare benefits have played their part in the process, which reflects the cumulative effects of a period of slow growth in which the poor have grown poorer and the rich richer. Even though the development of service activities has played a less central role, its part in the process is none the less real. The greater flexibility of the division of labour in service activities, the lower levels of unionization and the radical nature of technological developments, together with the immaterial nature of production in the tertiary sector, are all factors that encourage the segmentation of jobs and life styles.

The extent of these developments, particularly as far as jobs are concerned, depends on the degree to which employment is institutionally regulated. Each of the economies under consideration has established its own practices in this respect; they can be distinguished from each other according to the role played by the state, by collective bargaining and by the free working of the power relationships prevailing at any given time. The United States is characterized by the low level of institutionalization in many activities.

The extremely extensive nature of growth in the United States over a long period explains why neither the regulations of the 1930s nor the procedures for collective bargaining established after the Second World War led to the widespread institutionalization of conditions of employment similar to the conditions to be found in most of the European countries. This 'flexibility' is reflected in the wide fluctuations in employment levels in accordance with the cycles of economic activity; moreover, it facilitates the establishment of 'secondary-type' jobs. This explains to a large extent the great difference in employment levels in low growth economies observed in the United States and in Europe. It is necessary to take account of these different modes of growth in any assessment of the desire of the European countries to make employment conditions more flexible as part of the fight against unemployment. It is true that is paradoxical that the United States has one of the lowest rates of unemployment (although high unemployment has traditionally been an element in a mode of extensive growth in which there has always been a great deal of movement in the labour market), whereas those in Europe are very high, despite the fact that full employment formed the basis for consensus policies in the post-war period. It is still an illusion for the European countries to believe that they can alleviate unemployment by making employment conditions more flexible, since the flexibility in the United States is the consequence rather than the cause of the mode of extensive growth in that economy.

Adaptation without dualism

In a world in which economic relationships develop rapidly, a national economy must be able to adapt its productive potential equally rapidly. This argument underlies both industrial policies, with marked sectoral characteristics, and general macroeconomic policies for adapting to world market forces. General policies for making employment conditions more flexible belong in this latter category. However, these policies of 'positive adjustment' are extremely paradoxical. By their very nature, their effects are felt in the tertiary activities that represent more than two-thirds of total employment, lending themselves for the most part to large-scale reorganizations of tasks which are, however, those jobs that are the least directly susceptible to foreign competition. On the other hand, a greater degree of flexibility in tertiary employment may, through the extent of its effects and their deflationary consequences, reduce the ability of a national economy to participate in world trade in a way that will contribute to its own growth. There is thus a risk that such policies may lead to a cycle of depressions in which production and demand adjust at increasing low levels. There is no guarantee that this model of slow growth in a flexible economy will be a stable one. Reference is made spontaneously to the American experience, using the criterion of job creation and evolution of unemployment that is not really adapted to the European experience, whereas there is little mention of the experience of the developing countries where there is both relatively low institutionalization of employment conditions and the coexistence of very different consumption patterns. The participation in world trade of economies with very different *rapports salariaux* does not imply that these relationships should be homogenized. As a result of their increasing interdependence, the market economies should certainly adapt their modes of growth and their methods of regulating the *rapport salarial*. But any process of adaptation must itself take into account these initial differences in the social organization of the economies concerned. To disregard these differences will mean that excessively uniform and general policies for adjusting to the market forces of the moment will turn out to be unrealistic and hazardous. Industrial policies, in the usual sense of the term, avoid this pitfall through a more sectoral and pragmatic approach. This empiricism, which often makes the measures taken dependent on local or conjunctural uncertainties, is frequently, and justifiably, a target for criticism. The absence of any overall perspective is in no way inherent to a differentiated industrial policy; on the contrary, such a perspective is a guarantee that decisions taken with regard to manufacturing industry, which by their very nature involve risks, will not lead to disastrous changes of policy. In particular, this more general perspective would result from a clearly defined policy on the *rapport salarial*.

This implies that it is necessary to clarify the ways in which a unitary principle for the regulation of the *rapport salarial* would be applied to sectors subject to different conditions of competition. Wage determination is a key area in these policies. Minimum wages and guarantees on the distribution of the results of growth, however small they may be, help to maintain unity among wage earners. Suitable adjustments to the tax system in each economy should make it possible to offset the effects of these homogenizing measures on manufacturing costs.

This same principle of homogenization and compensation should also govern the orientation of changes in general employment conditions. Taking into account employment conditions in the service sector will make it possible to assess the opportunities available for a socially progressive policy on wage determination and the status of wage employment. In other words, taking into account the specificity of service activities in terms of employment will help to make industrial policies more coherent.

There is no point in hoping for a miraculous solution to the difficulties experienced by the industrial economies in adjusting to the new state of the world economy, but only a programme involving all activities would appear to offer any chance of escaping from the long-term decline that would be the certain outcome of a drift towards increasingly divided societies.

Notes

1. In this way a shift in purchasing habits towards less costly products in a period of recession is reflected in a fairly fictitious fall in activity.
2. A study carried out in the 1970s came to no decision on the efficacy of the Selective Employment Tax. It is true, however, that the low growth rate in British manufacturing industry was incorrectly diagnosed as being attributable to a shortage of labour.
3. In the distribution sector the percentage of part-time jobs is even higher, at 25 per cent.

4. On Kalecki's notion of monopoly in the analysis of price formation, see Reynolds, 1983.

5. Gordon (1982) correctly points out the central role in the organization of the wage nexus in the United States played by long-term wage agreements, which developed after 1948 mainly in the major industrial sectors, following the recognition of union rights in 1935 (Wagner Act).

6. Lawrence (1984, p. 80), assessing only the direct composition effects of the increase of tertiary activities, concludes that the total disappearance of the manufacturing sector would reduce the middle income class by only 3.7 per cent. But studies of the decline of the middle income class also points out that economic stagnation causes a reduction of middle income earners even within the tertiary sector.

7. Carson (1984) provides a recent synthesis of the methods for measuring the black economy.

8. Feige (1981), using the same method, found that in the United Kingdom the black economy represented 15 per cent of total output.

9. Heertje and Barthélémy (1984, Chap. 4) quote an English study by A. L. Ilerssic, in which it was estimated that for 1976/77 tax fraud on the income of non-wage earners amounted to £2.7 billion, that on wage income to £2 billion and that on illegally claimed unemployment benefit to £1.3 billion. The 1979 report of the Conseil des Impôts in France, quoted by the same authors, estimated income tax fraud to be lower than this in France (4.4 billion frs. 1971), which may be partly explained by the differences in the tax structure in the two countries; but the most significant difference in the results is in the distribution of income tax fraud, more than three-quarters of which in France is attributable to non-wage earners, who represent only 13.7 per cent of income tax declarations.

10. Archambault and Greffe (1984) attribute only a minor role to the black economy in the stagnation being experienced by the industrial economies.

11. This model presupposes that the exodus from the land, which led to a marked downward trend in female participation rates, has now come to an end.

12. This increase is attributed to the fact that American students tend more and more to do paid work while studying. In this case, the diversity of statistical developments does not conceal a similar diversity in the underlying realities.

13. Which might be attributed to the fact that women enter and leave the labour market and change jobs more frequently.

14. Thus, in France between 1975 and 1980, employment in market services increased by 864,000 jobs, 435,000 of which were in the health and welfare services sector in which women accounted for 70 and 83 per cent of total employment respectively; women accounted for only 51 per cent of total employment in market services (cf. Trogan, 1984).

15. The take-off of the process of computerization as a world-wide change in the technical system was brought about not so much by electronics, which

was already well established, but by miniaturization and its multiple applications. The rapidity of the miniaturization process underlines its extent: in less than twenty years, the density of integrated circuits will have increased by a factor of 1,000 (5,000 transitors to the cm^2 in 1970, 500,000 in 1980 and 5,000,000 before 1990).

16. For a survey of the debate on the relationships between long-term economy changes and long-term technical changes see the studies edited by Freeman (1982).

17. According to a report by the Bank Administration Institute (1982), only 10 per cent of American households would wish in 1990 to be able to carry out banking operations from home.

18. This estimate is given both by Alter (1985) in the case of France and by Karon (1982) and Murphree (1982) in the case of the United States (studies quoted by Leontieff and Dutchin, 1983).

19. These stages in the process of computerization can also be dated fairly precisely: batch processing developed in the 1960s, on-line systems appeared in the mid-1970s, and distributed processing in the 1980s. It should be noted that this last phase would appear to be complementary to on-line systems, whereas the first two involved total substitution.

20. Bertrand and Noyelle (1985) stress the long-term effects of production decisions on labour markets and the organization of work.

21. Porat (1977) estimates the changes over a century in the distribution of the economically active population among four activities: agriculture, manufacturing industry, material services and information.

    Thus, until 1905, the economy was predominantly agricultural; the era of the industrial economy followed, to be succeeded about 1959 by the information economy. It is interesting to note that 'material services' declined continuously until the end of the 1950s and then began to grow at the same rate as activities connected with data processing.

22. Thirty multinationals have observer status on the general council of INTUG. These include Shell, Citybank, Rank Xerox, American Express, IBM, among others. (cf. *Le Monde*, 12 January 1984, J. M. Quatrepoint).

23. This is what stems from a list of sixty-four new services predicted for the year 2000 by the long-term planning group of the French Post Office (see Glowinski *et al.*, 1980).

Appendix I: employment in services: long-term and recent trends

1. Employment in services in the long term

The growth in tertiary employment between 1920 and 1980 is unevenly distributed between categories of services, as is shown in Table 1.2. Shares in total employment indicate these differences: rapid growth in social services and producer services, slow growth in distributive services and stagnation or decline in personal services.

These changes, at least those in the last two service categories (Table 1.2),stem from the combination of strongly declining and strongly expanding activities. The decline in domestic services after the First World War is often quoted; the post-1945 period has also seen a marked decline in some personal and distributive services.

Employment in laundries, dry cleaning, cinemas and repairs (except car repairs) was halved between the 1950s and 1980s (from 312,000 in the United Kingdom in 1969 to 185,000 in 1976, according to Robertson, Briggs and Goodchild, 1982, and from 176,000 in France in 1954 to 100,000 in 1980, according to Braibant, 1983). In the meantime, other personal services increased significantly, especially miscellaneous services (from 227,000 in the United Kingdom in 1959 to 534,000 in 1976, and from 48,000 in France in 1954 to 134,000 in 1980). This emphasizes the innovative quality of these expanding activities. More traditional activities, such as automotive repairs, were also buoyant: employment increased from 347,000 in the United Kingdom in 1959 to 439,000 in 1976, and from 180,000 in France in 1954 to 419,000 in 1980. Within the distribution sector there was a mixture of declining and expanding activities. The decline in railways should also be noted: employment fell from 430,000 in the United Kingdom in 1959 to 230,000 in 1976, and from 368,000 in France in 1954 to 254,000 in 1980.

2. Service employment and slow growth

Until the late 1970s, employment in the service sector maintained its upward trend, but in the early 1980s a clear slow-down began to emerge (see Table A.1).

In Europe, over half the jobs (57.5 per cent in the European OECD countries between 1976 and 1982) were created in social services (mainly public employ-

Table A.1   Recent trends in employment in services (average annual growth rates)

	USA	FRG	France	UK	Italy	Netherlands	Belgium
1960–1973	2.8	1.3	1.4	1.4	1.4	2.0	2.1
1973–1983	2.6	0.8	1.7	1.0	2.8	2.3*	1.5*
1973–79/1979–83	3.2 1.8	1.1 0.4	2.1 1.2	1.4 0.4	2.9 2.6	1.8 3.3[†]	2.0 0.6[†]
1976–1982 Percentage of jobs created in services:							
Social, personal services	41.4	59.9	56.3	29.4	51.5	49.5	83.2
Producer services	24.4	21.6	19.7	40.9	13.9	31.1	13.5

Source: OECD documents 1984d, 1985.
  * 1973–82.
[†] 1979–82.

ment or under public supervision) and personal services (this latter category being rather static).

Small countries such as Belgium and the Netherlands are characterized, respectively, by the importance of social services (83 per cent of service jobs created in Belgium) and by a revival of tertiary employment in the early 1980s. This emphasizes the development of the service economy in those countries (service employment accounts for 66.3 per cent of total employment in the Netherlands and 64.7 per cent in Belgium), a feature common to all small North European countries.

Appendix II: manufacturing industry as an engine of growth

The dynamic of productivity gains

The relationship which can be used to explain, for the period 1960–73, the different patterns of development of demand and productivity in the European countries and the United States loses its validity for the period after 1973 (cf. Table A.2: R^2 falls from 0.79 to 0.13, the standard error increases). The term indicative of exogenous technical progress increases, while the elasticity of productivity to demand falls slightly.

However, Figures A1 and A2 show how these developments affected the various countries in very different ways. In the case of West Germany, France and Italy, the relationship observed for the period 1960–73 maintained its validity during the periods of slow growth (cf. regression 8). In the United States, on the other hand, the reduction in the growth of productivity in period II (1973–79) appears to be greater than might have been predicted from the previous relationship between productivity and growth. In the case of the United Kingdom in the third period (1979–84), productivity gains are, on the contrary, too high (relative to the low rate of growth). But it is particularly in Belgium, and to a lesser extent in Holland—both small countries and thus more open to foreign trade—that the period since 1973 has been characterized by an increased rate of growth for productivity relative to a given level of demand.

Thus, the weakening of the Verdoorn relationship from one period to another is largely the result of the marked divergence of certain countries for the whole or part of the period since 1973.

The influence of manufacturing industry on the rest of the economy

We have attempted to show the influence of manufacturing industry by means of the correlations between growth in manufacturing industry and growth in the rest of the economy. Here again, the relationship observed before 1973 between growth rates in the two parts of the economy have tended to disappear completely in the final two periods, although this weakening of the correlations is still linked to the experience of a few countries (cf. regression 8); although there are differences between the divergent countries (cf. Table A.2). These correlations do not establish any chain of causation (which could just as well be

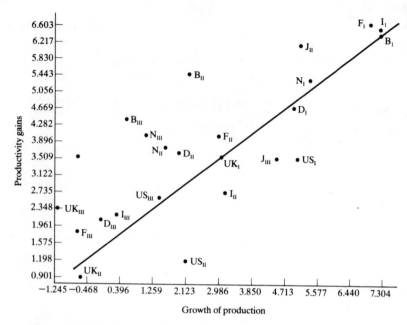

Figure A.1 the dynamic of productivity gains in manufacturing industry

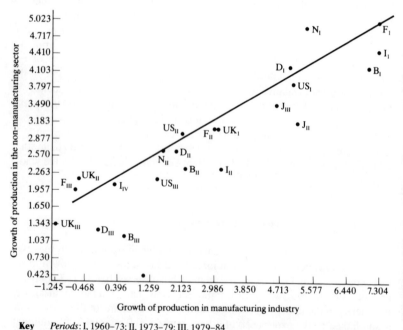

Key   *Periods*: I, 1960–73; II, 1973–79; III, 1979–84

   Countries: US: USA, J: Japan, D: West Germany, F: France, UK: United Kingdom, I: Italy, N: Netherlands, B: Belgium.

Figure A.2 The influence of manufacturing industry on the rest of the economy

Table A.2 The dynamic of manufacturing industry

Countries	Periods	Dynamic of productivity gains in manufacturing industry $\dot{\pi} = a\dot{Q} + b$				Influence of manufacturing industry on the rest of the economy $\bar{Q} = cQ + d$			
		a	b	R^2	SE	c	d	R^2	SE
8 countries $n = 24$	I, II, III	0.53 (8.0)	2.4 (8.0)	0.73	1.0	0.48 (11.5)	1.59 (8.4)	0.85	0.7
7 countries* $n = 21$	I, II, III	0.51 (5.8)	2.5 (7.6)	0.62	1.1	0.42 (8.3)	1.73 (9.2)	0.77	0.6
7 countries $n = 14$	I, II	0.61 (4.8)	1.9 (3.4)	0.66	1.1	0.36 (7.1)	2.1 (9.4)	0.79	0.4
7 countries $n = 7$	I	0.76 (4.9)	0.95 (1.0)	0.79	0.6	0.31 (2.6)	2.5 (3.6)	0.59	0.5
7 countries $n = 7$	II	0.70 (1.4)	1.85 (1.7)	0.13	1.6	0.13 (1.2)	2.4 (10.0)	0.07	0.3
7 countries $n = 7$	III	0.57 (1.4)	2.75 (7.5)	0.13	1.0	−0.03 (−1.6)	1.5 (5.7)	0.0	0.7
7 countries $n = 14$	II, III	0.46 (1.9)	2.53 (6.1)	0.16	1.2	0.31 (2.3)	1.78 (7.9)	0.27	0.7
6 countries† $n = 9$	II, III	0.59 (3.4)	2.1 (7.0)	0.58	0.7	0.25 (2.6)	2.0 (12.0)	0.41	0.4

Notes: Countries: West Germany, France, United Kingdom, Italy, Netherlands, Belgium, United States, Japan.
Periods: I, 1960–73; II, 1973–79; III, 1979–84.
* Japan is excluded from the following regressions in order that its experience does not weight too heavily in determining the relationships. Nevertheless, the graphs show that the changes in demand and productivity in Japanese manufacturing industry since 1973 are close to the general trend.
† Belgium and Japan are excluded, as are US_{II}, UK_{III}, N_{III}.

the converse of the one presented here); nevertheless, the simultaneity and the similarity of the changes in the two relationships would appear to lend greater weight to those arguments which see the origin of the crisis in manufacturing industry.

Appendix III: the interrelationship between the markets for goods and the markets for services

The model

The interrelationships between an extension of the market for goods, the growth in manufacturing yield and the development of the markets for services can be explained by means of a simple model of a closed economy with two sectors ($i = 1$ for goods, $i = 2$ for services), in which the technology for the production of services is fixed and requires no intermediate consumption, while the production of goods uses services and creates productivity gains when demand increases.

We are going to attempt to specify the effects on the prices of and final demand for goods and services of an extension of the market for goods. Let us define first of all the variables used by means of two 'accounting' relationships:

(i) $\begin{cases} X_1 = D_1 \\ X_2 - cX_1 = D_2 \end{cases}$ equalities between employment and resources in goods and services in which X_i and D_i are respectively the production and final consumption of the product i.

$\begin{cases} p_2 X_2 = N_2 w(1 + r) \\ (p_1 - cp_2)X_1 = N_1 w(1 + r) \end{cases}$ relationships specifying the distribution between wages $N_i w$ and profits $N_i wr$, in which p_i, N_i, w and r represent respectively prices, numbers employed, wage rate and the mark-up that determines profits.

If π_i is used to represent productivity in each sector (the relationship between the volume of value added to the number of people employed), the above relationships can be written thus:

(ii) $\begin{cases} \pi_2 = \dfrac{w}{p_2}(1 + r) \\ \pi_1 = \dfrac{w(1 + r)(1 - c)}{(p_1 - cp_2)} \end{cases}$

The hypothesis of the model on the medium-term evolution of the variables can now be expressed:

(1) $\dot{\pi}_2 = 0$ productivity in the service sector is constant

(2) $\dot{\pi}_1 = a\dot{X}_1 + b$ productivity in manufacturing industry increases with the extension of markets

(3) $[p_2 \,^{\cdot} D_2] = v[p_1 D_1 + p_2 D_2]$ the value of the final consumption of services increases more rapidly than household income ($v > 1$ according to Engel's law)

To these relationships can be added those derived from the identities (i) and (ii) if w and r remain constant:

(4) $\dot{X}_1 = \dot{D}_1$

(5) $\dot{X}_2 = \dot{D}_2 \times \dfrac{D_2}{X_2} + \dot{X}_1 \times \dfrac{cX_1}{X_2}$

(6) $\dot{\pi}_2 = -p_2$

(7) $\dot{\pi}_1 = -\dot{p}_1 \times \dfrac{p_1}{p_1 - cp_2} + \dot{p}_2 \times \dfrac{cp_2}{p_1 - cp_2}$

in which a, b, c, d, v are positive and $a < 1$.

The solution of the model

This system of seven relationships with 8 unknowns ($\dot{D}_i, \ddot{X}_i, \dot{\pi}_i, \dot{p}_i$) leads to the following relationships:

$$
\begin{cases}
\dot{x}_1 = \dot{D}_1, \ \dot{\pi}_2 = 0, \ \dot{p}_2 = 0, \ \dot{\pi}_1 = a\dot{D}_1 + b, \ \dot{p}_1 = -\left(a\dot{D}_1 + b\right)(1 - ck) \\[2mm]
\dot{D}_2 = \dfrac{v(1 - a)}{1 - va} \times [\dot{D}_1\,(1 - a + ack) + b(ck - 1)] \\[2mm]
\dot{X}_2 = \dfrac{D_2}{X_2}\dot{D}_2 + c\dfrac{X_1}{X_2}\dot{D}_1
\end{cases}
$$

with $k = \dfrac{p_2}{p_1}$ and $a = \dfrac{p_2 D_2}{p_1 D_1 + p_2 D_2}$

in which the exogenous variable of the growth of the final demand for goods, $\dot{D}_1$, or that of services, $\dot{D}_2$, determines all the other variables.

It can thus be observed that an exogenous extension of the market for manufactured goods, $\dot{D}_1 = d$, has the expected effects (reduction in the prices of goods, growth in the demand for services), provided that the initial price ratio, $k = p_1/p_2$, or the share of services in the volume of final consumption, $a = (p_2 D_2)/(p_1 D_1 + p_2 D_2)$, respect the initial conditions set out below:

— *The extension of the market for manufactured goods leads to a reduction in the prices of manufactured goods* if the price ratio p_1/p_2 is not smaller than c. If the price ratio is smaller than the coefficient of the inputs of services in the production of goods, then the extension of the market for industrial goods will have the effect of reducing the difference between the prices p_1 and p_2 by increasing the prices p_1.
— *The extension of the market for industrial goods leads to an increase in the final consumption of services* as soon as $\alpha < (1/v)$; i.e. as soon as the share of the final consumption of services [α] does not exceed the inverse of the income elasticity of the final consumption of services (e.g. 80 per cent if $v = 1.25$).

But a more obvious indication of the influence of manufacturing industry is the case in which an extension of the markets for manufactured goods is accompanied by an even greater extension of the market for services. Thus we shall be concerned here with the area in which the elasticity of the demand for services relative to that for goods

$$e(D_2, D_1) = \frac{v(1 - \alpha)}{1 - v\alpha} \times (1 - a + ack)$$

is greater than unity. Hence, the relationship between the initial conditions k (price relationship) and α (relationship of final demands) relative to the parameters a and v can be written thus:

$$e(D_2, D_1) > 1 \text{ if } k > \frac{(1/v) - a\alpha + a - 1}{ac(1 - \alpha)}$$

The figures below show that the area in which $\{e(D_2, D_1) > 1\}$ depends to a large extent on the value of v, the income elasticity of the consumption of services. Engel's law ($v > 1$) thus ensures that the area in which $e(D_2, D_1) > 1$ corresponds to perfectly conceivable values for the price relationship (k) and consumption relationship (α) (see Figure A.3c).

Extension of the market for goods or of the market for services?

It might be wondered whether, on the contrary, an extension of the demand for services might not lead, for example, to a higher rate of growth for total consumption, $D = D_1 + D_2$.

In order to answer this question, it is not enough to compare the inverse elasticities, $e(D_1/D_2)$ and $e(D_2/D_1)$

$$\left\{ e(D_1/D_2) = 1/e(D_2/D_1) = \frac{1 - av}{(1 - \alpha)v(1 - a(1 - ck))} \right\}$$

It is necessary first of all to make the two extensions of markets comparable by assuming that they both involve equivalent purchasing powers, i.e.

$d \times p_1 \times D_1 = \acute{d} \times p_2 \times D_2$. In the case of an extension of the market for goods, the following is obtained:

$$\dot{D}_d = \dot{D}_1 \frac{D_1}{D} + \dot{D}_2 \frac{D_2}{D} = \frac{d}{D}(D_1 + eD_2) \text{ with } e = e(D_2/D_1)$$

If the extension takes place in the market for services:

$$\dot{D}_{\acute{d}} = \frac{d}{D}\left(\frac{D_1}{e} + D_2\right)$$

The extension of the market for goods will thus be more advantageous if $\dot{D}_d >$ $\dot{D}_{\acute{d}}$, i.e. (taking account of the relationship linking d and $\acute{d}$ and using only the cases $d < 1/v$ in which the elasticity e is positive) if:

$$e > \frac{1 - \alpha}{\alpha} = \frac{p_1\, D_1}{p_2 D_2}$$

If e is replaced by its expression, it is possible to identify, in terms of the price relationship, $p_2/p_1 = k$ and of the distribution of final expenditure

$$\frac{p_2 D_2}{p_1 D_1 + p_2 D_2} = \alpha,$$

the initial conditions in which the extension of markets for manufactured goods proves to be more advantageous in the sense defined above:

$$\dot{D}_d > \dot{D}_{\acute{d}} \text{ if } k > \frac{1}{\alpha a c v} - \frac{1 + ac(1 - \alpha)}{ac}$$

The continued growth of k and α suggests that the condition $\dot{D}_d > \dot{D}_{\acute{d}}$ is fulfilled in the developed countries (cf. Figure A.3d).

The hypotheses used make it possible to define in a precise but restrictive way the role as an engine of growth of one sector relative to another. In particular, foreign trade (and a growth in exports is the implicit form of the extension of the market for goods) and changes in the conditions of production (sectoral differences in wage levels and intermediate consumption) are not specified. It is necessary to take them into account in order to assess any possible weakening in the crisis of the role of manufacturing industry as an engine of growth.

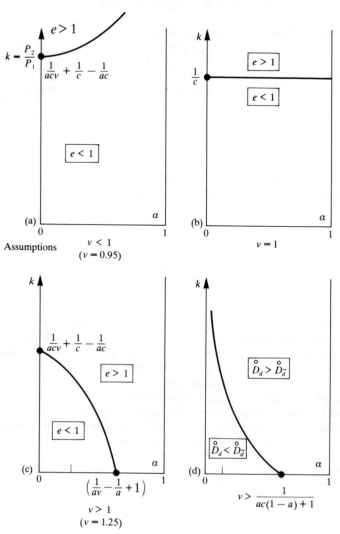

Figure A.3 Elasticities of demand for services under various assumptions

Appendix IV: modes of 'régulation' and accumulation regimes: an example of periodization

Mode of régulation. This is the conjunction of institutions and customs which, in a given society, ensure the reproduction of a given economic system by means of the articulation between production and consumption.

Accumulation regime is the type of growth characterized by the dynamics of the systems of production and consumption.

Expressed simply, the mode of *régulation* analyses the economy more from the point of view of distribution, whereas the notion of accumulation regime is concerned rather with production.

We shall use by way of example the division into four periods suggested by Boyer (1979, p. 12) in order to characterize the dominant modes of *régulation* in the growth of the French economy over the last two centuries.

First half of the nineteenth century. This was a period of transition between an older form of *régulation* governed by the cycles of agricultural production and a competitive *régulation* associated with the beginnings of industrialization.

Second half of the nineteenth century. There was a strengthening of the competitive *régulation* until the First World War.

The inter-war period. This was a transitional period, in which the features of monopoly began to emerge without really disrupting the mechanisms of the competitive *régulation*.

After 1945 was a period of profound social and political change, dominated by a monopolistic *régulation* leading to the concerted development of mass production and consumption.

These changes in the type of *régulation* were accompanied by changes in the accumulation regime.

Table A.3 Some indicators of the nature of the accumulation process (average annual rates for each period, in percentage)

Dominant type of regulation	Indicators Periods	Industrial employment	Working hours	Industrial activity	Productivity per capita	Real weekly wages	Dominant accumulation regime
Competitive	1856–70	-1.0%	-0.8%	-1.8%	2.4%	1.4%	Intensive
	1870–95	0.8%	-1.0%	-0.2%	2.3%	2.0%	Intensive and collapse
	1895–1913	0.8%	-0.3%	0.5%	0.3%	+0.0%	Extensive
Transitional	1913–20	0.3%	1.2%	1.5%	-1.8%	-3.0%	Extensive
	1920–30	1.2%	-2.8%	-1.6%	+5.8%	2.2%	Intensive
	1930–37	3.1%	-2.8%	-6.0%	+2.8%	1.5%	Intensive without disruption of consumption norm
Monopolistic	1937–49	1.0%	0.9%	1.9%	-0.3%	-0.5%	Extensive
	1949–59	1.1%	0.2%	1.3%	4.9%	3.9%	Intensive
	1959–73	0.8%	-0.4%	0.4%	4.8%	4.1%	based on mass consumption

Source: Boyer (1979, p. 25).

Appendix V: the evolution of average productivity and the redistribution of resources by sector

The increase in service activities has been presented as a factor in the reduced growth of productivity in the economy as a whole. And it is true that the more rapid development of activities in which the level and growth rate of productivity is low may lead, by means of a simple composition effect, to a reduction in the growth rate of average productivity.

It is simple to show that the increase in average productivity, $\dot{P}_T$, can be broken down into two amounts, relating respectively to intra- and inter-sectoral effects:

$$\dot{P}_T = \underbrace{\sum_{i=1}^{k} \dot{P}_i \times X_i}_{\text{intra-sectoral effect}} + \underbrace{\sum_{i=1}^{k} \frac{P_i}{P_T} \times dE_i}_{\text{inter-sectoral effect}}$$

in which $\dot{P}_i$ = the rate of growth of productivity in sector i
   X_i = the share of value added in sector i in total value added.
   E_i = the share of employment in sector i in total employment

The intra-sectoral effect is presented as a weighted sum of the changes in productivity in each sector. The inter-sectoral brings out the impact on average productivity of a redistribution of employment by sector. The transfer of a job from sector i to sector j, all other things being equal and with a constant level of employment in the economy as a whole, is reflected in an algebraic increase $(P_j - P_i)/P_T$ in the rate of growth of average productivity, $\dot{P}_T$. These are purely accounting effects that do not take into account the more directly economic effects of such labour flows. Nevertheless, even these calculations have made it possible to attribute a significant proportion of the high productivity gains in the post-war period to the reduction in the number of agricultural workers.

Both the smaller scale of the exodus from the land and the development of employment in the tertiary sector might suggest a slowing down in the growth of average productivity. This is the hypothesis put foward by Denison in 1973, even before the reduction in productivity gains in manufacturing industry had been fully revealed.

In fact, recent estimates show the relatively weak impact of the sectoral redistribution of resources on the growth of per capita GNP. Denison (1983) estimates that these movements between sectors are responsible for only 0.13 per cent in a total reduction of 2.32 per cent in the rate of growth of per capita GNP in the United States between the periods 1948–73 and 1973–83. Baily (1982) produces similar results, again for the United States: movements between sectors accounted for only 0.24 per cent in a 2 per cent reduction in productivity gains between the periods 1948–73 and 1973–81.

For this sectoral redistribution effect to be significant in comparison with the intrasectoral dynamic of productivity gains, it is necessary for there to be massive inter-sectoral employment flows on the one hand and, on the other, large differences in productivity between the sectors losing jobs and those gaining them. These conditions, which were present in post-war periods of reconstruction and crisis, do not seem to be present in the current period. The transfers of labour are continuous rather than sudden and large-scale. Moreover, the levels of productivity in the tertiary activities locate them either above or below manufacturing activities.

Thus, only about 10 per cent of the reduction in the growth of average productivity can be attributed to the development of the service economy. This overall result does not overestimate the impact at a less general level of the redistribution of labour between firms. Lindbeck (1983) attributes a third of the reduction in average productivity to a reduction in the redistribution of labour between more and less efficient firms.

Appendix VI: external constraint and trade surplus

By virtue of its definition in accounting terms, the balance of payments, which records all the transactions of each economy with the rest of the world, is in equilibrium. Thus, what is important is the way in which this equilibrium is achieved. The balance of payments records current transactions in goods and services and movements of capital of various kinds: private and official unrequited transfers, long-term investments, short-term capital and reserves. The current balance of payments is the balance of current transactions in goods and services plus unrequited transfers (which, since they are connected with the presence of foreign workers or payments to international institutions, are permanent in nature). A deficit or surplus in this current balance is reflected in a change in the overall position of the country as a debtor or creditor nation. This change may in turn lead to measures aimed at constraining current transactions if the limits of the capacity for indebtedness (and to a lesser extent those of the capacity for credit) are reached.

These are the conditions which make it *relatively* necessary *to bring the current balance into equilibrium* in the medium to long term. A persistent deficit quickly leads to a level of indebtedness that is virtually intolerable unless an increase in foreign investment is used to finance the deficit, but the possession of assets by foreigners is also limited.

A prolonged surplus in the current balance of payments leads, in the longer term it is true, to protectionist pressures that tend to reduce the increase in indebtedness and the transfer of assets in the rest of the world. Under certain conditions, the achievement in the medium to long term of this equilibrium in the current balance of payments tends to determine the rate of growth in an economy. If:

(1) the evolution of imports is linked with that of GNP;
(2) the evolution of exports is linked with that of demand in the world as a whole;
(3) the evolution of exchange rates does not make it possible in the medium to long term to change the growth rates of exports and imports then (according to Harrod), the rate of growth in an economy $\dot{Y}$ is a direct function of the growth rate of world demand $\dot{W}$:

$$\dot{Y} = \frac{x}{m} \dot{W},$$

in which x and m are, respectively, the export and import elasticities of world demand and GNP.

Thirlwall (1979) thus estimated the growth rates that would be compatible with a situation of equilibrium in the balance of payments and verified that these rates usually turn out to be upper limits. A recent estimate (*European Economy*, July 1983) of the income elasticities x and m of exports and imports make it possible to assess for each country the *upper constraints* placed on its economic growth by the characteristics of its foreign trade.

Table A.4   Income elasticities to total world output*

	Total	Manufactured goods
Japan	2.55	2.43
Netherlands	1.49	1.25
Italy	1.28	1.15
France	1.21	1.03
Belgium	1.14	0.87
FRG	1.00	0.76
USA	0.88	0.64
UK	0.78	0.51

* *Note*: estimated as the ratio between income elasticities of exports (x) and imports (m)

Nevertheless, it should be noted that the hierarchy of constraints presented in Table A4 only gives a picture of the external constraint in the medium to long term. The initial positions of each country (whether they have a surplus or deficit in their transactions in goods and services) and the opportunities for the appreciation or devaluing of currencies relax or strengthen the external constraint in the short to medium term. One of the principal hypotheses in these analyses in terms of external constraint refers to the assumed lack of effect of changes in parities on *the growth rates* for imports and exports.

We shall return rather to the respective roles in the determination of import and export flows of trade flows (transactions in goods, particularly manufactured goods) and of trade in services. Table A4 shows that the hierarchy of 'maximum growth rates' made possible by a situation of equilibrium in the current balance of payments is identical to the hierarchy of the ratios between the income elasticities of imports and exports of manufactured goods. This observation lends weight to the hypothesis that trade in manufactured goods acts as an engine of growth. It is none the less true that balances for manufactured goods and other balances for goods and services play very different roles in the developed economies. Table 3.3 is an indication of these varied 'specializations', the bases of which are analysed in Chapter 4.

Appendix VII: the fall in the profitability of capital in the manufacturing sector

There is a general long-term trend towards a reduction in the profitability of capital. This tendency, which has been in operation at least since the 1950s, seems to be more pronounced in the manufacturing sector than in the rest of the economy. Moreover, this downward trend differs in scale according to country and conceals a variety of fluctuations. The indicators of a weakening of the manufacturing sector (cf. Table 3.2) seem to be largely correlated with the periods during which there was a fall in the profitability of capital in manufacturing industry in the various countries.

Table A.5 Rates of return for the period 1960–1982

	The economy as a whole			Percentage change	Manufacturing industry			Percentage change
	1960	1973	1982		1955	1973	1982	
USA	16.2	14.5	10.9	−2.1**	23.9	18.5	10.6	−2.7**
					1965		1981	
Japan					33.3	32.4	20.7	−4.5**
			1981		1955		1982	
W. Germany	24.3	17.2	14.5	−2.0**	28.9	16.5	11.7	−3.0**
	1967		1979		1967		1979	
France	21.7	22.9	19.3	−1.9**	15.6	18.2	13.8	−1.4*
					1955		1982	
UK	13.3	11.0	10.1	−1.9**	16.9	9.5	5.5	−5.3**
					1970		1980	
Italy					17.7	16.9	15.2	−1.0*
	1970		1981		1970		1981	
Belgium	28.4	27.5	22.9	−1.4**	17.1	17.2	10.7	−3.7**

Source Holtham: 'Profit and Rates of Return', OECD roneo, September 1984.
Notes: * The estimate is significant to 5 per cent.
       ** The estimate is significant to 1 per cent.

Appendix VIII: services to firms: an initial measurement problem

Simply breaking down the value of expenditure on producer services by sector poses some problems. Input–output statistics are in theory collected at the level of the homogeneous unit of production. By their very nature, however, the types of expenditure in question (computer management, management consultancy, research, advertising, communications, insurance, management of movable or immovable property) can usually be identified only at the level of the firm as a whole.

Postner (1982) refers to three sources of inaccuracies:

(1) The first is linked to the problem of the distribution among separate establishments of services ordered by head office. In the United States accounting system, expenditure by head office is attributed to the largest factory or establishment (in terms of value added) in the company. For highly diversified large companies, this practice sharply reduces the significance of the statistics on the intermediate consumption of services by sector. The head offices of highly diversified companies appear in fact as real producers of services.

(2) The second source of error concerns research and development activities. When they are carried out in a research centre owned by the firm, the process of breaking them down among the various other establishments within the firm raises the same problem as in (1) above. The purchase of patents and other rights presents a specific problem, since they sometimes do not correspond to any real service and are more akin to a capital payment.

(3) The third source of difficulties is connected with the 'fictitious' trade in services within multinational companies which use this trade in order to exploit their relationships with their subsidiaries. The example cited by Postner of the imports of services to firms in Canada is revealing. In 1976, 83 per cent of the $1,850 million worth of imports of services to firms (5 per cent of total imports) were attributable to foreign companies (which own only 30 per cent of the capital in Canadian manufacturing industry), and virtually all this international trade in services was connected with the links between American multinationals and their subsidiaries.

As a result of these difficulties in measuring services to firms, it is difficult to distinguish between activities that are internal or external to the firm or even between activities and income from capital.

Appendix IX: the use of external services

The nature of the externalized function and the size of the firm are the main determinants of the intermediate demand for services. A survey of services to firms in France showed the importance of a threshold effect: demand initially increases with size, then stabilizes and then decreases for large firms.

Effect of size on externalization	Percentage of firms using external services for the functions named		
	less than 25%	25–50%	more than 25%
No effect	Pay Analytical accounting	Maintenance Management control	Transport of goods Foreign trade
Frequency of use increases with size	Security Warehouses Staff Transport Non-managerial recruitment	Managerial recruitment Caretaking Catering	Cleaning
Frequency of use decreases with size	Sales representation Managerial computer services	General accounts Translation	
Frequency of use grows until a threshold is reached and then decreases	Hire services Computerized research Handling Prototypes and moulds Software Work organization Research Infrastructures Financial management Methods	Computer maintenance Research Marketing Specialized tooling Trials	Legal problems Managerial training Taxation Advertising Non-managerial training Legal services Patents and trade marks

Source: Taken from Barcet and Bonamy, 1983.

Bibliography

Between brackets are given, after each reference, an indication of its location in the text: chapter, then section, note (n), or Appendix (App).

Abel-Smith, B. and Maynard A., 1978, *The Organisation, Financing and Cost of Health Care in the European Community*, Brussels, EEC (5 n. 22).
Abernathy, W. J., Clark, K. B. and Kantrow, A. M., 1983, *Industrial Renaissance*, New York, Basic Books (3 V).
Adler, P., 1983, 'Trente ans d'automatisation et coûts opératoires dans les banques françaises', *Revue Économique* **34**, 5 Septembre (6 II).
Aglietta, M., 1979, 'A Theory of Capitalist Regulation', New Left Books, 1st edn 1976, rev. 1982, Paris, Calmann Lévy (2 n. 16; 5 III).
——, 1984, 'Évolution et perspectives de la consommation des ménages', roneo., Paris, CEPII, April (5 III).
—— and Brender, A., 1984, *Les métamorphoses de la société salariale*, Paris, Calmann Levy, (6 I).
——, Ewenczyk, P., Oudiz, G. and Pisani-Ferry, J., 1982, 'Contrainte extérieure, change et dualité dans cinq économies dominantes', Paris, CEPII, January (2 n. 18).
Alter, N., 1985, 'Bureautique, un bilan socio-économique inattendu', Paris, *Futuribles*, April (6 n. 18).
Archambault, E., 1985, 'Travail domestique et emploi tertiaire: substitution ou complémentarité' in M. Vernières, *L'emploi du tertiaire*, Paris, Economica, (6 I).
—— and Greffe, X., 1984, 'Les économies non officielles', *La Découverte*, Paris (6 n. 10).
Armstrong, P., Glyn, A. and Harrison, J., 1984, *Capitalism since World War II*, London, Fontana (3 VI).
Bacon, R. and Eltis, W., 1976, *Britain's Economic Problem: Two Few Producers*, London, Macmillan (3 II).
Baily, M. N., 1981, 'Productivity and the Services of Capital and Labor', *Brookings Papers on Economic Activity* vol. 1 (3 IV).
——, 1982, 'The Productivity Growth Slowdown by Industry', *Brookings Papers on Economic Activity*, vol. 2 (1; 3 II).
Balassa, B., 1967, 'The Impact of the Industrial Countries' Tariff Structure on their Imports of Manufactures from less Developed Areas', *Economica* **34**, November, pp. 372–83 (4 n. 16).
—— and Balassa, C., 1984, 'Protectionism and Trade', *OECD Economic Review* (4 IV).
de Bandt, J., 1983, 'La politique industrielle: réponse de l'État-Nation à la crise?', *Revue d'Économie Industrielle* **23**, Spring (3 n. 7).

de Bandt, J., 1985, 'La productivité dans les activités de service: sens et non sens', Programme mobilisateur, Technologie, Emploi, Travail, Cahier **1**, June, Paris (6 I).
—— (ed.), 1985, *Les services dans les sociétés industrielles avancées*, Paris, Economica (2 III).
Baran, P. A. (ed.), 1959, *The Allocation of Economic Resources*, Stanford, Stanford University Press (2 II).
—— and Sweezy, P., 1966, *Monopoly Capital*, New York, Monthly Review Press (5 n. 9).
Barcet, A. and Bonamy, J., 1983, 'La demande de services industriels', in Commissariat Général du Plan, *Services consommés par le systeme productif*, Paris (5 II).
Barras, R., 1983, *The adoption and impact of information Technology in the UK insurance industry*, London, The Technical Change Centre (6 II).
Baumol, W., 1967, 'Macroeconomics of Unbalanced Growth: The Anatomy of Urban Crises', *American Economic Review* **57**, June, pp. 415–26 (2 I).
Beckermann, W. (ed.), 1979, *Slow Growth in Britain*, Oxford, Clarendon Press (5 III).
—— *et al*., 1965, *The British Economy in 1975*, NIESR, Cambridge University Press (2 II).
Bell, D., 1973, *The Coming of Post Industrial Society*, London, Heinemann (2 I).
Bellon, B., 1984, 'Conditions de la politique industrielle aux États-Unis', *Revue d'Économie Industrielle*, winter (3 VI).
Berle, A. A., and Means, G. C., 1983, *The Modern Corporation and Private Property*, New York, Macmillan (5 I).
Bertrand, O. and Noyelle, T., 1985, *L'évolution des emplois tertiaires*, CEREQ, Paris (6 n. 20).
Blackaby, T. (ed.), 1978, *De-Industrialisation*, NIESR, London, Heinemann (3 II).
Blades, D., 1982, 'The Hidden Economy and the National Accounts', *Occasional Studies—OECD*, June, pp. 28–45 (5 I; 6 I).
Blitch, C. P., 1983, 'Allyn Young on Increasing Returns', *Journal of Post Keynesian Economics* **5**, 3 spring (2 II).
Bluestone, B. and Harrison, B., 1982, *The Deindustrialization of America*, New York, Basic Books (3 V; 6 I).
Boisson, P., 1984, 'Informatique et Emploi', *Rapport au Conseil Économique et Social*, February, Paris (6 II).
Boyer, R., 1979a, 'La crise actuelle: une mise en perspective historique', *Critique de l'Économie Politique* **7/8**, May, pp. 5–113 (2 n. 16).
——, 1979b, 'Wage Formation in Historical Perspective: The French Experience', *Cambridge Journal of Economics* **3**, pp. 98–118 (2 n. 16).
——, 1983, 'Wage Labor, Capital Accumulation and the Crisis: 1968–1982', *The Tocqueville Review* **V**, 1, spring–summer (2 n. 16).
—— and Mistral, J., 1983, *Accumulation, inflation, crises*, Presses Universitaires de France, 2nd edn (2 n. 16).
——,——, 1984, 'The Present Crisis: From an historical Interpretation to a Prospective outlook', Roneo., CEPREMAP-FERE (2 n. 16).
Braibant, M., 1982, 'Le tertiaire insaisissable?', *Économie et Statistique*, June (App. I).
Braverman, H., 1974, *Labour and Monopoly Capital*, New York Monthly Review Press (2 III; 6 II).

Brender, A. and Oliveira-Martins, J., 1984, 'Les échanges mondiaux d'invisibles: une mise en perspective statistique', *Économie Prospective Internationale*, Paris, Documentation Française, 3rd term (4 II).

——, Chevallier, A. and Pisani-Ferry, J., 1980, 'États Unis: croissance, crise et changement technique dans une économie tertiaire', *Économie Prospective Internationale*, Paris, CEPII, Documentation Française (n. 5).

Browning, H. C., and Singlemann, J., 1978, 'The Transformation of the US Labour Force: The Interaction of Industry and Occupation', *Policies and Society* **8** (7–4), pp. 481, 509 (5 I).

Bruno, M., 1982, 'World Shocks, Macroeconomic Response and the Productivity Puzzle', NBER Working Paper, no. 942, July (3 IV).

——, 1984, 'Raw Materials, Profits and the Productivity Slowdown', *The Quarterly Journal of Economics* **49** , 1.29 (3 II).

—— and Sachs, J., 1982, 'Input Price Shocks and the Slowdown in Economic Growth: Estimates for U.K. Manufacturing', *Review of Economic Studies* **49** (3 II).

Buttner, O. and Mouriaux, M. F., 1983, 'Le développement des services marchands aux enterprises: mouvement d'extériorisation ou croissance autonome?' Centre d'Études de l'Emploi, Paris (5 n. 13).

Carson, C. S., 1984, 'The Underground Economy: An Introduction', *Survey of Current Business*, May, pp. 21–37 (6 n. 7).

Caty, G. F. and Ungerer, H., 1984, 'Les Télécommunications, nouvelle frontière de l'Europe', *Futuribles*, December (6 II).

Caves, R. E., 1980, 'Industrial Organisation, Corporate Strategy and Structure', *Journal of Economic Literature* **18**, March (5 II).

Cella, G., 1984, 'The Input-Output Measurement of Inter-industry Linkages', *Oxford Bulletin of Economics and Statistics* **46** , 1 (2 II).

CEPII, 1983, 'Économie mondiale: la montée des tensions', Paris, *Economica* (6 I).

Chandler, A., 1977, *The Visible Hand: The Managerial Revolution in American Business*, Harvard University Press (2 III; 5 II).

—— (ed.), 1981, *Managerial Hierarchies*, Harvard University Press (5 II).

Chenery, H. B., 1960, 'Patterns of Industrial Growth', *American Economic Review* (2 I).

—— and Taylor, L., 1968, 'Development Patterns: Among Countries and Overtime', *Review of Economics and Statistics*, November (2 I).

Clark, C., 1940, *The Conditions of Economic Progress*, Macmillan, rev. edn 1957 (2 I).

CNUCED, 1984, 'Quelques sociétés transnationales dominent le secteur des services', quoted in *Le Monde*, 19 October (4 II).

Cohen, R., 1979, *The Internationalisation of Capital and U.S. Cities*, New York, Ph.D., New School for Social Research (5 II).

Cohen, S. C., 1983, 'Industrial Policy and East Coast Myopia', *The New York Times*, 28 August (3 n. 12).

Commissariat Général du Plan, 1983, *Services consommés par le secteur productif*, Paris, La Documentation Française, November (5 n. 8).

Coriat, B., 1979, *L'atelier et le chronomètre*, Christian Bourgeois, Paris (2 n. 16).

Cornwall, J., 1977, *Modern Capitalism, Its Growth and Transformation*, Oxford, Martin Robertson (2 II).

Dahrendorf, R., 1975, *The New Liberty*, London, Routledge & Kegan Paul (2 n. 8).

Darby, M. R., 1984, 'The U.S. Productivity Slowdown: A Case of Statistical Myopia', *American Economic Review*, June (3 n. 4).

Delorme, R., and André, C., 1983, *L'État et l'Économie*, Paris, Le Seuil (5 III).

——, 1983, 'Matériaux pour une comparaison internationale de l'évolution de longue période des dépenses publiques', *Statistiques et Études Financières*, January (3 n. 9).

Denison, E., 1973, 'The Shift to Services and the Rate of Productivity Change', *Survey of Current Business* **53** , 10, October, pp. 20–35 (3; App. V).

Denison, E. F., 1983, 'The Interruption of Productivity Growth in the United States', *Economic Journal*, March (3; App. V).

Donzelot, J., 1984, *L'invention du social: essai sur le déclin des passions politiques*, Paris, Fayard (2 n. 13).

Dunning, J. H., 1979, 'Explaining Changing Patterns of International Production: in defence of the Eclectic Theory', *Oxford Bulletin of Economics and Statistics* **41** , November, 4 (4 IV).

Durkheim, E., 1898, *De la division du Travail social*, Paris, P.U.F., 7th edn, 1960 (2 III).

Eatwell, J., 1983, 'The Long Period Theory of Employment', *Cambridge Journal of Economics* **7** , 3/4, September/December, pp. 269–85 (2 III).

Ehrsam, J., 1984, 'Les investissements directs à l'étranger', *Rapport au Conseil Économique et Social*, 21 August, Paris (4 n. 17).

Ellis, H. D. and Wallich, H. C., 1961, *Economic Development for Latin America*, London, Macmillan (2 II).

Feige, E. L., 1979, 'How Big is the Irregular Economy?', *Challenge*, November/ December, pp. 5–13 (6 I).

——, 1981, 'The UK's Unobserved Economy: a Preliminary Assessment', *Journal of Economic Affairs*, July (6 I).

Fisher, I., 1906, *The Nature of Capital and Income*, New York, Macmillan (5 n. 17).

Fisher, A. G., 1935, *The Clash of Progress and Security*, London, Macmillan (2 I).

——, 1939, 'Primary, Secondary, Tertiary Production', *Economic Record*, June (2 I).

Fossaert, R., 1977, *La Société*, Paris, Seuil. (2 n. 1).

Fourastie, J., 1949, *Le grand espoir du XXe siècle*, Paris, P.U.F., 4th edn, 1958 (2 II).

——, 1952, *La productivité*, Paris, P.U.F. (2 I).

Freeman, R., 1976, *The Over-Educated American*, New York, Academic Press (2 I).

Freeman, C. (ed.), 1982, *Long Waves in The World Economy*, London, Frances Pinter (6 II).

——, Clark, J. and Soete, L., 1982, *Unemployment and Technical Innovation*, London, Frances Pinter (6 II).

Fuchs, V. R., 1965, *The Growing Importance of the Service Industries*, National Bureau of Economic Research, New York (6 I).

——, 1968, *The Service Economy*, National Bureau of Economic Research, New York (6 I).

—— (ed.), 1969, *Production and Productivity in the Services Industries*, National Bureau of Economic Research, New York (6 I).

Galbraith, J. K., 1958, *The Affluent Society*, London, Hamish Hamilton (2 I).

——, 1968, *The New Industrial State*, New York, New American Library (5 n. 9).

——, 1974, *Economics and the Public Purpose*, London, Andre Deutsch (2 n. 8).

Gardes, F., 1983, 'L'évolution de la consommation marchande en Europe et aux USA depuis 1960' *Consommation*, no. 2, April–June (5 n. 20).

Gaudin, J. and Schiray, M., 1984, 'L'économie cachée en France: État du débat et bilan des travaux', *Revue Économique* **4**, July (6 I).

George, K. D., 1966, *Productivity in Distribution*, Department of Applied Economics, Occasional Papers 8, Cambridge University Press (6 I).

Gershuny, J., 1978, *After Industrial Society?*, London, Macmillan (2 I).

—, 1983, *Social Innovation and the Division of Labour*, Oxford, Oxford University Press (5 III).

— and Miles, I., 1983, *The New Service Economy*, London, Frances Pinter (2 II; 5 III).

Giarini, O., and Louberge, H., 1978, *The Diminishing Returns of Technology*, Oxford, Pergamon Press (3 VI).

Ginsberg, A., 1979, *Good Jobs, Bad Jobs, No Jobs*, Cambridge, Mass., Harvard University Press (6 I).

Glowinski, A. *et al.*, 1980, *Telecommunications en l'an 2000*, Paris, Dunod (6 n. 23).

Glyn, A., 1982, 'The Productivity Slow-down: a Marxist View', in R. C. O. Matthews (ed.), *Slower Growth in the Western World*, NIESR/PSI/RIIA Joint Studies in Public Policy, London, Heinemann (3 IV).

Gold, B., 1981, 'Changing Perspectives on Size, Scale and Returns: An Interpretive Survey', *Journal of Economic Literature* **19**, March, pp. 5–33 (3 VI).

Gordon, R. J., 1982, 'Why U.S. Wage and Employment Behaviour Differs from that in Britain and Japan', *Economic Journal*, March (6 n. 5).

Gorz, A. (ed.), 1973, *Critique de la division du travail*, Paris, Seuil (2 III).

Gough, I., 1979, *The Political Economy of the Welfare State*, London, Macmillan (5 III).

Granou, A., Baron, P. and Billaudot, B., 1983, *Croissance et crise*, Paris, Maspéro, 2nd edn (2 n. 16).

Greenfield, H. T., 1966, *Manpower and the Growth of Producer Services*, New York, Columbia University Press (5 I and II).

Griffiths, B., 1975, *Invisible Barriers to Invisible Trade*, London, Macmillan (4 III).

Gutmann, P. M., 1977, 'The Subterranean Economy', *Financial Analysis Journal*, November/December, pp. 26–34 (6 I).

—, 1979, 'Statistical Illusions, Mistaken Policies', *Challenge*, November/December, pp. 14–17 (6 I).

Habakkuk, H. J. and Deane, P., 1963, 'The Take-Off in Britain', in W. W. Rostow (ed.), *The Economics of Take-off into Sustained Growth*, London, Macmillan (3 n. 1).

Haberler, G. (ed.), 1961, 'Equilibrium and Growth in the World Economy', *Economics Essays* by Ragnar Nurkse, Cambridge, Mass., Harvard University Press (2 II).

Harris, R. and Seldon, A., 1979, *Overruled on Welfare*, London Institute of Economic Affairs (5 III).

Hawrylyshyn, O., 1976, 'The Value of Household Services: A Survey of Empirical Estimates', *Review of Income and Wealth* (5 III).

Heertje, A. and Barthélémy, P., 1984, *L'économie souterraine*, Paris, Economica (6 n. 9).

Hesselman, L., 1983, 'Trends in European Industrial Intervention', *Cambridge Journal of Economics* **7**, pp. 197–208 (3 VI).

Hill, T. P., 1971, *The Measurement of Real Product*, Paris, OECD (1).

—, 1977, 'On Goods and Services', *Review of Income and Wealth*, December (1).

Hill, T. P., 1979, 'Do It Yourself and GDP', *Review of Income and Wealth* **1**, March (1; 5 III).

Hirschman, A. O., 1958, *The Strategy of Economic Development*, New Haven, Yale University Press (2 I).

Holtham, G. H., 1984, 'Profit and Rates of Return', Mimeo, OECD, September.

Houssiaux, J., 1967, *Le pouvoir de monopole*, Paris, Siney (5 n. 9).

Hulten, C. R., and Schwab, R. B., 1984, 'Regional Productivity Growth in U.S. Manufacturing: 1951–1978', *American Economic Review*, March (3 V).

Illich, I., 1975, *Medical Nemesis*, London, Calder & Boyars (5 III).

Intersocial, 1981, Paris, January, **67** (6 II).

Jenkins, C. and Sherman, B., 1979, *The Collapse of Work*, London, Department of Employment (6 II).

Jugand, O. and Lemennicier, B., 1982, *Le travail féminin, la consommation marchande et la production domestique*, Paris, CREDOC (5 III).

Julien, P. A., Lamonde, P. and Latouche, D., 1976, *La société post-industrielle: un concept vague et dangereux*, Paris, Futuribles, summer **7** (2 n. 9).

Kaldor, N., 1966, *Causes of the Slow Rate of Growth in the United Kingdom*, Cambridge University Press (2 II).

——, 1975, 'Economic Growth and the Verdoorn Law: A Comment on Mr Rowthorn's article', *Economic Journal*, December, pp. 891–6 (3 II).

——, 1978, 'Comment on A. Cairncross', in Blackaby (ed.), *De-industrialisation*, NIESR, London, Heinemann (3 II).

——, 1980, *Reports on Taxation I, the Economics of the Selective Employment Tax*, London, Duckworth (2 III; 6 I).

Kalecki, M., 1943, 'Political Aspects of Full Employment', *Political Quarterly* **14** (2 III).

——, 1971, *Selected Essays on the Dynamics of the Capitalist Economy*, Cambridge University Press (6 I).

Karon, M. A., 1982, 'Word Processing: When It Doesn't Work', *Computer World, Office Automation* **16**, 31 March (6 n. 18).

Katz, A. J., 1983, 'Valuing the Services of Consumer Durables', *Review of Income and Wealth*, series 29, no. 4, December.

—— and Peskin, J., 1980, 'The Value of Services Provided by the Stock of Consumer Durables 1947–77: An Opportunity Cost Measure', *Survey of Current Business*, July (5 n. 16).

Kendrick, J. W., 1982, *Measurement of Output and Productivity in the Service Sector*, Philadelphia ARA/Wharton Conference, 'The Future of the Service Economy', 19–20 November, 1982 (1).

Kindleberger, C. P., 1958, *Economic Development*, New York, MacGraw Hill (2 I).

——, 1961, 'Foreign Trade and Economic Growth: Lessons from Britain and France, 1850 to 1913', *Economic History Review* (3 n. 1).

——, 1967, *Europe's Post-War Growth: the Role of Labor Supply*, Cambridge, Mass., Harvard University Press (3 I).

—— and Tella, G. (eds), 1982, *Economics in the Long View: Essays in Honour of W. W. Rostow*, London, Macmillan (2 n. 3).

Kutscher, R. E. and Mark, J. A., 1983, 'The Service-Producing Sector: Some Common Perceptions Reviewed', *Monthly Labor Review*, April (1).

Kuttner, Bob, 1983, 'The Declining Middle', *Atlantic Monthly*, July (3 VI; 6 I and II).

Kuznets, S., 1956, 'Quantitative Aspects of the Economic Growth of Nations: II

Industrial Distribution of National Product and Labour Force', *Economic Development and Cultural Change* (2 II).

——, 1971, *Economic Growth of Nations*, Cambridge, Harvard University Press (2 I).

Lafay, G., 1976, 'Compétitivité Spécialisation et demande mondiale', *Économie et Statistique* **80**, July–August (3 V).

Lamfalussy, A., 1963, *The United Kingdom and the Six: An Essay on Economic Growth in Western Europe*, London, Macmillan (2 II; 3 II).

Launois, R. J., Majnoni, B., Rodwin, R. G. and Stephan, J. C., 1985, 'Les réseaux de soins coordonnés (RSC): propositions pour une réforme profonde du système de santé', *Revue Française des Affaires Sociales*, January–March (5 III).

Lawrence, R. Z., 1984, *Can America compete?*, Washington DC, The Brookings Institution (3 VI; 6 n. 6).

Lecomber, R., 1978, 'Economic Growth and Social Welfare', in W. Beckerman, *Slow Growth in Britain* (5 I).

Lengelle, M., 1966a, *The Growing Importance of the Service Sectors in Member Countries*, Paris, OECD (6 I).

——, 1966b, *La Révolution Tertiaire*, Paris, Génin (6 I).

Leontieff, W. and Dutchin, F., 1983, *The Impacts of Automation on Employment 1963–2000*, New York University, September (6 n. 18).

Leveson, J., 1983, *Services in the U.S. Economy*, Philadephia ARA/Wharton Conference, 'The Future of the Service Economy', 19–20 November 1982 (1).

Lévy-Garboua, L., 1983,'Les modes de consommation de quelques pays Paris, occidentaux: comparaison et loi d'évolution, 1969–1980', *Consommation*, January–March, Paris, CREDOC (5 III).

Lewis, W. A., 1954, 'Economic Development with Unlimited Supplies of Labour', *The Manchester School of Economic and Social Studies*, pp. 139–91 (2 II; 6 I).

——, 1957, 'International Competition in Manufactures', *American Economic Review*, May (3 n. 1).

——, 1978, *Growth and Fluctuations, 1870–1913*, London, Allen & Unwin (2 II).

Lindbeck, A., 1983, 'The Recent Slowdown of Productivity Growth', *Economic Journal*, March (3 V).

Lipietz, A., 1979, *Crise et Inflation. Pourquoi?*, Paris, Maspéro (2 n. 16).

——, 1980, 'Le tertiaire, arborescence de l'accumulation capitaliste: prolifération et polarisation', *Critique de l'Économie Politique* **12**, July–September (2 III).

——, 1983, *Le monde enchanté. De la valeur à l'envol inflationniste*, Paris, La Découverte (1).

Lipton, M., 1962, 'Balanced or Unbalanced Growth in Underdeveloped Countries', *Economic Journal* (2 II).

Lorenzi, J. H., Pastre, O. and Toledano, J., 1980, *La crise du 20e siècle*, Paris, Economica (2 n. 16).

Machlup, F., 1962, *The Production and Distribution of Wealth in the United States*, Princeton, Princeton University Press (6 III).

——, 1980, *Knowledge and Knowledge Production*, Princeton, Princeton University Press (6 II).

McKersie, R. B. and Sengenberger, W., 1983, *Les suppressions d'emplois dans l'industrie*, Paris, OCED (3 V).

Maddison, A., 1967, *Economic Growth in the West*, New York, Norton Library (3 VI).

——, 1982, *Phases of Capitalist Development*, Oxford, Oxford University Press (1; 3 IV).

Magaziner, I. C. and Reich, R. B., 1982, *Minding America's Business: the Decline and Rise of the American Economy*, New York, Harcourt Brace Jovanovich (3 £).

Marglin, S., 1973, 'Origines et fonctions de la parcellisation des taches' in A. Gorz (ed.), *Critique de la division du travail*, Paris, Seuil (2 III).

Marris, R., 1964, *The Economic Theory of Managerial Capitalism*, New York, Free Press of Glencoe (5 n. 9).

Mattera, P., 1983, 'Home Computer Sweatshops', *The Nation*, 2 April (6 II).

Matthews, R. C. O. (ed.), 1982, *Slower Growth in the Western World*, NIESR/PSI/RIIA Joint Studies in Public Policy, London, Heinemann.

Meadows, D. H., *et al.*, 1972, *The Limits to Growth*, New York, Earth Island (5 III).

Michalski, W., 1983, 'Les politiques d'ajustements positives: un concept stratégique pour les années 80', *Revue d'Économie Industrielle* **23**, spring (3 n. 8).

Ministère de l'Industrie, 1982, *Une politique industrielle pour la France*, Documentation Française, November, Paris (3 n. 11).

Momigliano, F. and Siniscalco, D., 1982, 'The Growth of Service Employment: A Reappraisal' in *Banca Nazionale del Lavoro Quarterly Review*, September (5 II).

Muldur, U., 1983, 'La rationalisation du travail de bureau: le taylorisme avant la bureautique?', *Revue d'Économie Industrielle* (6 II).

Murphree, M., 1982, *Office Rationalization and the Changing Structure of Secretarial Tasks: A Case Study of Wall Street Legal Secretaries*, New York, NYU Department of Sociology (6 n. 18).

Myrdal, G., 1957, *Economic Theory and Underdeveloped Regions*, London, Duckworth (3 n. 1).

Nelson, R. R., 1981, 'Research on Productivity Growth and Productivity Differences: Dead Ends and New Departures', *Journal of Economic Literature* **19**, September (3 IV).

—— and Winter, S., 1972, 'Evolutionary versus neo-classical theories of growth', *Economic Journal* **89**, March, pp. 866–905 (6 II).

——,——, 1977, 'In Search of a Useful Theory of Innovation', *Research Policy* **6**, pp. 36–76 (6 II).

——,——, 1982, *An Evolutionary Theory of Economic Change*, Cambridge, Mass., Belknap Press of Harvard University Press (6 II).

Nora, S. and Minc, A., 1978, *L'informatisation de la société*, Paris, La Documentation Française (6 II).

Nordhaus, W. D., 1982, 'Economic Policy and Declining Productivity Growth', *European Economic Review* **18**, pp. 131–57 (3 IV).

Nurkse, R., 1953, *Problems of Capital Formation in Underdeveloped Countries*, Oxford, Oxford University Press (2 n. 2).

——, 1959, *Patterns of Trade and Development*, Stockholm, Almquist and Wiksell (3 n. 1).

O'Connor, J., 1973, *The Fiscal Crisis of the State*, New York, St. Martins Press (5 III; 6 I).

OECD, 1975, *The Arms and Instruments of Industrial Policy: A Comparative Study*, Paris (3 VI).

——, 1979, *The Case for Positive Adjustment Policies*, Compendium of OECD Documents, Paris, OECD (3 n. 6).

——, 1981a, *Electronics and Telecommunications Technologies*, ICCP no. 7, Paris, OECD, DSTI (6 III).

——, 1981b, *The Welfare State in Crisis*, Paris (5 III).

OECD, 1983a, *Transparency for Positive Adjustment: Identifying and Evaluating Government Intervention*, Paris (3 VI).
——, 1983b, *Telecommunications*, Paris.
——, 1984a, *International Trade in Services: Tourism*, Paris (4 n. 15).
——, 1984b, *International Trade in Services: Banking*, Paris (4 n. 15).
——, 1984c, *International Trade in Services: Insurance*, Paris (4 n. 15).
——, 1984d, *Employment Outlook*, September, Paris (1).
——, 1984e, *Economic Outlook*, July, Paris.
——, 1985a, 'The Role of the Public Sector', *OECD-Economic Review* **4**, spring (5 II).
——, 1985b, *Public Expenditures 1960–1990*, Paris (5 III).
Ohlin, G., 1959, 'Balanced Economic Growth in History', *American Economic Review Papers and Proceedings*, May (2 II).
Olson, M., 1982, *The Rise and Decline of Nations*, New Haven, Yale University Press (3 V).
Petit, P., 1984, *Automatisation des services: le cas des services bancaires*, Paris, 8431, CEPREMAP (4 III).
——, 1983, 'Les services: des secteurs abrités dans la crise?', in J. de Bandt (ed.), *Les services dans les sociétés industrielles avancées*, Paris, Economica, 1985 (2 III).
——, 1984, 'The Origins of French Planning: a Reappraisal', *Contributions to Political Economy*, March (3 VI).
Piore, M. (ed.), 1979, *Unemployment and Inflation: Institutionalist and Structuralist Views*, New York, M. E. Sharpe (2 III).
Porat, M., 1977, *The Information Economy*, O.T. Special Publication 77–12, Washington US Department of Commerce (6 III).
Postner, H., 1982, 'Problems of Identifying and Measuring Intermediate Services in the Compilation and Use of Input/Output Tables', *Review of Income and Wealth*, June (5 n. 9).
Ray, E. J. and Marvel H. P., 1984, 'The Pattern of Protection in the Industrialized World', *Review of Economics and Statistics*, May, pp. 452–8 (4 n. 16).
Reich, R. B., 1982, 'Why the U.S. Needs Industrial Policy', *Harvard Business Review*, January–February, pp. 74–81 (3 VI).
——, 1983, 'An Industrial Policy of the Right', *The Public Interest* **73** (3 VI).
Revell, J. R. S., 1983, 'Banks and Electronic Fund Transfers', Paris, OECD (4 III).
Reynolds, P. J., 1983, 'Kalecki's Degree of Monopoly', *Journal of Post Keynesian Economics*, pp. 493–503 (6 n. 4).
Richet, X., 1984, 'États-Unis: les paradoxes de la politique industrielle', *Analyses de la Sedeis*, May (3 VI).
Robertson, J. A., Briggs, J. M. and Goodchild, A., 1982, *Structure and Employment Prospects of the Service Industries*, 177, p., London, Department of Employment (1).
Robinson, J., 1937, 'The Long Period Theory of Employment', *Essays in the Theory of Employment*, London, Macmillan (2 n. 17).
—— and Wilkinson, F., 1977, 'What has become of employment policy?', *Cambridge Journal of Economics*.
Rodwin, V., 1984, *The Health Planning Predicament: France, Quebec, England and the United States*, London, University of California Press (5 III).
Rosenstein-Rodan, D. N., 1961, 'Notes on the Theory of the Big Push', in H. D. Ellis and H. C. Wallich, *Economic Development for Latin America*, London (2 I).

236   *Bibliography*

Rosenthal, N. H., 1985, 'The Shrinking Middleclass: Myth or Reality?', *Monthly Labor Review*, March (6 III and IV).

Rostow, W. W., 1953, *The Process of Economic Growth*, Oxford, Oxford University Press (2 I).

——, 1956, 'The Take-off into Self-Sustained Growth', *Economic Journal* **66**, March, pp. 25–48 (2 I).

——, 1960, *The Stages of Economic Growth*, Cambridge University Press (2 I).

—— (ed.), 1963, *The Economics of Take-off into Sustained Growth*, London, Macmillan (2 I).

Sachs, J., 1979, 'Wages, Profits and Macroeconomic Adjustment: A Comparative Study', *Brookings Papers on Economic Activity* vol. 2 (3 IV).

Sapir, A. and Lutz, E., 1980, 'Trade in Non Factors Services: Past Trends and Current Issues', *World Bank Staff Working Paper*, no. 410, Washington DC (4 III).

——,——, 1981, 'Trade in Services: Economic Determinants and Development—Related Issues', *World Bank Staff Working Paper*, no. 480, August, Washington DC (4 n. 12).

Sargent, J. R., 1982, 'Capital Accumulation and Productivity Growth', in R. C. O. Matthews, *Slower Growth in the Western World*, NIESR/PSI/RIIA Joint Studies in Public Policy, London, Heinemann (3 IV).

Sautter, Ch., 1979, 'L'adaptation du Japon au ralentissement de la croissance et à la ponction extérieure', *Revue Économique* **30**, 6, November (3 II).

Saxonhouse, G. R., 1982, 'Services in the Japan Economy', Communication Conference ARA/Wharton 'The Future of the Service Economy', 19–20 November, Philadelphia (4 n. 10).

Schott, J. J., 1983, 'Protectionist Threat to Trade and Investment in Services', *The World Economy*, June (4 III).

Schultze, Ch. L., 1983, 'Industrial Policy: A Dissent', *The Brookings Review*, fall (3 VI).

Scitovsky, T., 1959, 'Growth Balanced or Unbalanced', in P. A. Baran *et al.*, (eds), *The Allocation of Economic Resources*, Palo Alto, Stanford University Press (2 n. 2).

Shelp, R. K., 1981, *Beyond Industrialization: Ascendancy of the Global Service Economy*, New York, Praeger (4 III and n. 9).

——, 1983, 'Trade in Services', in J. de Bandt (ed.), *Les services dans les sociétés industrielles avancées*, Paris, Economica (6 III).

Schumacher, E. F., 1973, *Small is Beautiful*, London, Blond & Briggs (2 n. 8).

Singlemann, J., 1978, 'The Sectoral Transformation of the Labor Force in Seven Industrialized Countries, 1920–1970', *American Journal of Sociology* **83**, 4, January (1).

——, 1979, *From Agriculture to Services*, Beverly Hills, Ca., Sage Publications (5 III).

Singh, A., 1977, 'UK Industry and the World Economy: A Case of de-industrialization', *Cambridge Journal of Economics*.

Smith, A., 1776, *The Wealth of Nations*, Pelican 1979 (1).

Smith, A. D., 1972, *The Measurement and Interpretation of Service Output Changes*, National Economic Development Office (NEDO), London (1).

Spencer, H., 1882, *Sociologie*, Paris, F. Alcan (2 II).

Stalson, H., 1982, *International Service Transactions*, Philadelphia ARA/Wharton, Conference, 'The Future of the Service Economy', November (4 n. 11).

Stanback, T. M., 1980, *Understanding the Service Economy*, Baltimore, John Hopkins University Press (5 II).

—— and Noyelle, T. J., 1982, *Cities in Transition*, New York, Allanheld & Osmun (2 III; 6 IV).

——, Bearse, P. J., Noyelle, T. J. and Karasek, R. A., 1981, *Services: The New Economy*, New York, Allanheld & Osmun (2 III; 5 II; 6 I).

Steinberg, B., 1983, 'The Mass Market is Splitting Apart', *Fortune*, 28 November (6 I).

——, 1985, 'Le reaganisme et l'économie américaine dans les années quatre-vingt', *Critiques de l'Économie Politique*, spring (1).

Stewart, F., 1979, 'International Technology Transfer: Issues and Policy Options', *World Bank Staff Working Paper* **344**, Washington DC (4 II).

Stigler, G. J., 1951, 'The Division of Labor is Limited by the Extent of the Market', *Journal of Political Economy* **59**, June (2 III).

——, 1956, *Trends in Employment in the Service Industries*, NBER, Princeton, Princeton University Press (1).

——, 1965, *Essays in the History of Economics*, Chicago, Chicago University Press (2 I; 5).

——, 1983, 'The Literature of Economics: The Case of Berle and Means', *Journal of Law and Economics* **26**, June.

Stoclet, D., 1983, 'Les transferts entre marchand et domestique—Travail des femmes, loisirs des hommes', *Observations et diagnostics économiques* **31**, February (6 I).

Stout, D., 1979, 'Capacity Adjustment in a Slowly Growing Economy', in W. Beckerman (ed.) (3 VI).

Streeten, P. P., 1961, *Economic Integration*, Leyden, A. W. Sythoff (2 n. 2).

Swamy, D. S., 1967, 'Statistical Evidence of Balanced and Unbalanced Growth', *Review of Economics and Statistics* **49**, 3, August (2 n. 2).

Sylos-Labini, P., 1957, *Oligopoly and Technical Progress*, Cambridge, Harvard University Press (2 III).

Thirlwall, A. P., 1979, 'The Balance of Payments Constraints as an Explanation of International Growth Rate Differences', *Banca Nazionale del Lavoro*, Review, March (3 I and VI).

Thurow, L. C., 1980, *The Zero-sum Society*, New York, Basic Books (5 III).

——, 1983, *The Case for Industrial Policies* (3 VI and n. 7).

——, 1984, 'The Disappearance of the Middle-class', *New York Times*, 5 February (3 VI).

Toffler, A., 1979, *The Third Wave*, New York, Bantam Books (6 III).

——, 1984, 'L'explosion de l'information', *Futuribles*, February, Paris (6 III).

Tosel, A., 1985, 'L'impensé de la sociologie française, ou Labriola lu par Durkheim', *La Pensée* **234**, January–February (2 II).

Touraine, A., 1969, *The Post-Industrial Society*, New York, Random House (2 I).

Trogan, P., 1984, 'L'emploi dans les services: une croissance quelque peu ambiguë', *Économie et Statistique*, November–December (1; 6 I).

Urquhart, M., 1981, 'Are services recession-proof', *Monthly Labor Review*, October (6 I).

Vanoli, A., 1983, 'Les tracés divers de la notion de production', *Économie et Statistique* **158**, September (5 III).

Veil, E., 1982, 'The Statistical Gap of the World Balance of Payments', Paris, OECD, June (6 I).

Verdier, E., 1983, *La bureautique*, Paris, La Découverte (6 II).

238 *Bibliography*

Verdoorn, P. J., 1949, 'Fattori che regolano la sviluppo della produttiva del lavoro', *L'industria*, pp. 3–10 (2 II).

Verger, R., 1982, *Le développement de nouvelles formes d'activités touristiques*, Paris, Rapport au Conseil Économique et Social, 25–26 May (4 n. 13).

Vernières, M., (ed.), 1985, *L'emploi du tertiaire*, Economica, Paris (6 I).

Vernon, R., 1966, 'International Investment and International Trade in the Product Cycle', *Quarterly Journal of Economics* **80**, May, pp. 190–2.

Weinstein, O., 1983, 'Movement de longue periode, mutations productives et crise', *Issues* **16**, summer.

Weisskopf, T., Bowles, S. and Gordon, D., 1983, 'Hearts and Minds: A Social Model of U.S. Productivity Growth', *Brookings Papers on Economic Activity*, Vol. 2 (2 III).

Wilkinson, F., 1983, 'Productive Systems', *Cambridge Journal of Economics* **7**, 3/4, September–December (2 III).

Williamson, O. E., 1975, *Markets and Hierarchies*, New York, The Free Press—Macmillan (5 II).

——, 1980, 'Transaction Costs Economics: The Governance of Contractual Relations', *Journal of Law and Economics*, March.

——, 1981, 'Emergence of the Visible Hand', in A. Chandler, ed., *Managerial Hierarchies*, Harvard University Press (5 II).

——, 1983, 'Organization Form, Residual Claimants, and Corporate Control', in *Journal of Law and Economics* **26**, June (5 II).

Wright Mills, C., 1951, *White Collar, the American Middle Classes*, Oxford, Oxford University Press (6 I).

Young, A. A., 1982, 'Increasing Returns and Technical Progress', *Economic Journal*, December (2 II).

Index